D0961811

How the Electronic Economy
Has Destabilized the
World's Markets and
Created Financial Chaos

SIMON & SCHUSTER

JOEL KURTZMAN

THE DEATH OF MONEY

New York London Toronto Sydney Tokyo Singapore

SIMON & SCHUSTER
Simon & Schuster Building
Rockefeller Center
1230 Avenue of the Americas
New York, New York 10020

Designed by Nina D'Amario/Levavi & Levavi
Manufactured in the United States of America

1   3   5   7   9   10   8   6   4   2

Library of Congress Cataloging-in-Publication Data

Kurtzman, Joel.
The death of money : how the electronic economy has destabilized
the world's markets and created financial chaos / Joel Kurtzman.
p.   cm.
Includes index.
1. Money—History—20th century. 2. Financial services industry—
Technological innovations—History—20th century. 3. Electronic
funds transfers. 4. Program trading (Securities) 5. Finance—
History—20th century. 6. Economic history—20th century.
I. Title. II. Title: Electronic economy.
HG220.A2K87   1993
332.4—dc20   92-37530
CIP

ISBN: 0-671-68799-9

To my father, Samuel Kurtzman, who taught me discipline
and showed me love

TABLE OF CONTENTS

PREFACE

Money was invented in the temples of Sumer about five thousand years ago. From that time until its death about two decades ago, it remained essentially unchanged. It was a store of value and a unit of account.

But money now is different. No longer is it a discrete object, such as a lump of bronze equal in value to a Sumerian *shay* or a bushel of barley (hence the name of the first coin, the shekel). Nor is it completely symbolic: the great seal of the United States stamped on a piece of otherwise ordinary paper.

Money has been transmogrified. It is no longer a *thing,* an object you can dig up at the beach or search for behind the cushions of a sofa; it is a *system.* Money is a network that comprises hundreds of thousands of computers of every type, wired together in places as lofty as the Federal Reserve—which settles accounts between banks every night that are worth trillions of dollars—and as mundane as the thousands of gas pumps around the world outfitted to take credit and debit cards. The network of money includes all the world's markets—stock, bond, futures, currency, interest rate, options, and so on. It is connected to the huge number-crunching supercomputers at Morgan Stanley & Company and to the PCs of individual investors using the Equalizer program to buy stocks through Charles Schwab & Company. The network is juxtaposed by computers that chart investment risk using the Nobel Prize–winning formulas developed by Harry Markowitz and Merton Miller of the University of Chicago, on the one hand, and the quasi-mystical "technical" formulas developed by Robert Prector, of the *Elliot Wave Theorist,* on the other.

In the new world of money, even the largest banks no longer need vaults. Instead, they store their money on disk drives and computer tapes, and they protect those funds not by hiring brawny guards but by employing brainy Ph.D. mathematicians and software specialists to write secret codes.

The new network of money is much more volatile than the five-thousand-year-old monetary system it replaced. Interest rates, stock prices, currency prices, bond prices—all fluctuate as never before. In the last decade alone, the dollar has lost more than half its value against the world's other major currencies; American interest rates have fallen by 50 percent; world stock prices have more than doubled (they have collapsed then risen in Japan); world real estate prices rose to all-time highs before deflating; and oil went from almost $40 a barrel to $12 a barrel before settling in at the current rate. In each of these cases, changes in supply and demand—the two bedrock tenants of economics—had little to do with the price changes.

For people in business, the ups and downs of the global markets are the economic equivalent of Yugoslavia. And in that kind of economy, where conditions mutate moment to moment, the time frames of investors and the planning horizons of executives have—of necessity—been compressed.

The death of money has also splintered the world into two economies. The smaller of the two economies I call the "real economy." That is where products are made, trade is conducted, research is carried out, and services are rendered. The real economy is where factory workers toil, doctors tend the sick, and teachers teach, and where roads, bridges, harbors, airports, and railway systems are built. Tragically, in the United States, it is also the impoverished part of the economy, starved for investment, backward and in disrepair.

The other economy, the "financial economy," is somewhere between twenty and fifty times larger than the real economy. It is not the economy of trade but of speculation. Its commerce is in financial instruments. Mostly, it is concerned with the exchange of equities, such as stocks, and securities, such as bonds and other forms of debt. The latest and largest type of debt that the financial economy trades, from a technical standpoint, is money.

Unlike the real economy, the financial economy has been undergoing something of an investment boom for more than two decades. And while its ultra-high-tech infrastructure straddles the globe and moves several trillion dollars a day between the major and minor "nodes" on the network, it is largely unregulated.

.   .   .

Few people realize that money, in the traditional sense, has met its demise. Fewer still have paused to reflect on the implications of that fact.

This book deals with the consequences of a world in which markets are linked electronically while countries continue to exist independently. It is about a world in which mathematicians, physicists, and computer designers have become fixtures on Wall Street. And it is about how to bring a measure of stability to what is now a highly volatile world.

Over the course of two and a half years I interviewed more than one hundred people in an effort to better understand the way the new global electronic economy works. Not all of the economists, executives, mathematicians, computer programmers, and investors will agree with my conclusions. But I am indebted to them for taking time to discuss the world situation with me and for putting up with my incessant questioning.

I am particularly grateful to Hyman Minsky, who explained that money is obsolete; R. David Ranson and Mark Miles, who explained the importance of interest rates; Allen Sinai, Edward Yardeni, and Gary Shilling, for showing me the way their forecasts work; Graciella Chilchiniski, for explaining the importance of commodities in the new world order; Charles Schwab, Daniel Siegel, Richard Van Slyke, Peter Schwartz, and Jib Fowles for talking about the impact of new technology on the markets. I am also grateful to Mike Levitas and Leonard Silk of *The New York Times* for their tough and insightful questions.

I would like to thank my editor, Fred Hills, for giving structure to the manuscript, for helping shape my ideas, and for having patience. I am also indebted to Lisa Betty for spending hours in the library digging up articles and looking up facts. I am grateful to my wife, Susan Kurtzman, for reading and rereading the manuscript and for helping me with both the sytle and the substance.

ONE

MEGABYTE MONEY:

How Vast Networks of Computers Linked Together Have Created a New Global Form of Highly Volatile Money and Displaced Governments in Importance

For the last twenty years or so, the world and its economy have been in the midst of a wrenching change. This transformation has been so vast that it has altered nearly every aspect of our lives. It has changed our notion of what is public and what is private, has changed the way we value what we produce, and has radically redefined the concept of ownership and wealth. In just twenty years this little-noticed yet monumental change has caused new countries to rise and once-great ones to fall.

What has changed? Money. Not the dollars in our pockets or the coins in our hands. That money—tangible money, old-fashioned money—now accounts for only the tiniest fraction of all the money that is in circulation around the world today. That money deserves only a cursory nod. It is a phantom from the past, an anachronism. In its place, traveling the world incessantly without rest and nearly at the speed of light, is an entirely new form of money based not on metal or paper but on technology, mathematics, and science. And like Einstein's assumption that a photon of light creates the universe wherever it goes, this new "megabyte" money is creating a new and different world wherever it proceeds.

Money has been changing from a standard unit of value—a

fixed and limited asset, a substantial and absolute "truth"—into something ethereal, volatile, and electronic. Over the last twenty-plus years it has been moving from a government-mandated equivalency—$35 equals one ounce of gold, a concept first developed five thousand years ago—to a new electronic form. It has become nothing more than an assemblage of ones and zeros, the fundamental units of computing. It is these ones and zeros, representing money, that are piped through miles of wire, pumped over fiber-optic highways, bounced off satellites, and beamed from one microwave relay station to another. This new money is like a shadow. Its cool-gray shape can be seen but not touched. It has no tactile dimension, no heft or weight. No other money matters.

As a result of money's transformation, nothing in the world will ever be quite the same. New opportunities will abound and new disasters will loom. It will take decades to assimilate the change.

Money is now an image. Simultaneously, it can be displayed on millions of computer screens on millions of desks around the world. But in reality it is located nowhere and needs no vault for safekeeping. Yet, while money has no real location, it has created an environment that is paradoxically everywhere while taking up no physical space. An environment peopled by millions of investors, traders, bankers, money managers, stockbrokers, arbitrageurs, analysts, policymakers, and government officials—all observing and manipulating money from different video terminals around the world. A community where neighbors, colleagues, and competitors are accessible only through electronics.

THE NEURAL NETWORK OF MONEY

In this new environment, millions of computers are linked in a vast twenty-four-hour, global-trading and information exchange of unimaginable complexity. This immense network has in some ways begun to resemble the network of neurons grouped together inside the brain. Millions of "smart" terminals of one kind or another are all interacting in a syncopated electronic dance, producing an overall rhythm of market ups and downs not unlike the rhythms pulsing through the brain. Money, in its new electrical form, jumps from computer to computer the way nerve impulses jump across synapses. But in the case of money, each time an electron makes its leap, units of buying power—big and small—are exchanged. Goods, wealth, dreams, and power change hands.

Every day, through the "lobe" in the neural network that is New York, more than $1.9 trillion electronically changes hands at nearly the speed of light. These dollars—and the cares, hopes, and fears they represent—appear as momentary flashes on a screen.

Every three days a sum of money passes through the fiber-optic network underneath the pitted streets of New York equal to the total output for one year of all of America's companies and all of its workforce. And every two weeks the annual product of the world passes through the network of New York—trillions and trillions of ones and zeros representing all the toil, sweat, and guile from all of humanity's good-faith efforts and all of its terrible follies.

Sums of similar magnitude pass through the streets of Tokyo, London, Frankfurt, Chicago, and Hong Kong. They shuttle under the sea and bounce off the ionosphere. The financial system, using money that has been liberated from gold, each day conducts transactions hundreds of times larger than those in the so-called real economy—the part of humanity's endeavors where goods are produced and services sold.

Computers have made these neural networks of money possible. They have made it so that distances do not matter, and time and time zones are irrelevant. They have moved us from a gold to a megabyte standard—a standard based on microchips, computer memory, and ultra-high-speed technology. And in the process, by enabling money to jettison its finite mass, they have allowed money to evolve into something entirely new, filled with fresh possibilities.

Although money is the principal means we have for storing wealth and purchasing power, economists have consistently failed to appreciate the significance of its change. Old-guard thinkers are engaged in debates about a world that disappeared long ago. They whisper the conventional wisdom into the ears of business leaders and presidents but are no longer able to produce a working forecast of interest rates, growth, or trade. They can no longer assess the growth of the money supply, predict a recession, or determine how much or how little Americans save or spend. They are like scholars educated only in the Bible who do not realize we have moved to a secular world.

These economists view money the way a fish views water—as something vital, supportive, full of life-giving oxygen but largely invisible. Ask a fish about the water in which it swims, and it won't give much of an answer. Ask an economist about money—someone from the President's Council of Economic Advisers, say—and he will probably just shrug. Money just doesn't matter very much, these wizened old economists will probably tell you. The same rules still apply, they will tell you, whether the medium of exchange is gold, silver, or video images. But they are wrong. Finance and its odd logic have replaced economics.

But if these old-guard economists were to accept the premise that a new evolution in money will give rise to a new economics, if they were to remove their ties decorated with images of Adam Smith and replace them with ties sporting a microchip, then they would have to face the fact that many of their most cherished concepts are out of date. They would have to put themselves out of business—or worse, force themselves to reconceptualize their craft. All but a few of these thinkers, as we shall see, have refused to undertake this daunting task.

NATION STATES LOSE ECONOMIC CLOUT

Along with the change in money have come other underappreciated changes in the world. Rather than functioning as discrete nation-states, each isolated and buffered from the ups and downs of its neighbors, countries have now become increasingly irrelevant, economically speaking. Central banks, such as the Federal Reserve Board, while still powerful, have been downgraded. They are players, yes, but not as independent as before. Borders have been breached. Signals bounced off satellites or hurled through undersea cables do not wait at a customs house to clear. In fact, it is now far easier and faster to move $1 billion from New York to Tokyo than to move a truckload of lettuce or grapes across the California-Arizona line.

In his report to Congress on the stock market crash of October 19, 1987, Treasury Secretary Nicholas F. Brady, who was then head of Dillon Read & Company, said that all markets—stocks, bond, futures, money markets—are now one. They are connected, he said. But after he made that statement, Brady hedged. He explained that he meant all American markets are now connected. He was wrong. In reality, markets everywhere are now linked. We are all on the megabyte standard.

With a modem, personal computer, telephone, and in some cases a two-foot satellite dish on the roof, traders can swap dollars, bonds, or stocks, or they can trade what are called "derivative products" simply by sending electronic pulses down a line.

A derivative product, a concept out of *Alice in Wonderland*, is not really a "product" at all, the way a stock is a product, a unit of ownership in a company. A derivative product, instead, is more akin to an abstract notion. For instance, one derivative product is a contract on future interest rates. These contracts are made on the percentage points that will be charged for a future loan, and they trade separately from the money itself. Interest rates are bought and kept—if the trade is good—for two weeks to a month. If the trade is bad, they are sold within hours. Sold to whom? Bought where? Anywhere the electron travels.

By sending a pulse down the line, traders sitting anywhere can trade the future exchange rates of any of the world's currencies. They can take out options on blocks of stocks, trade warrants on bonds owned by someone else, sell futures contracts, and trade home mortgages. In this strange and eerie electronic world, Japanese pension funds can buy American bonds backed not by gold or corporate assets but by stacks of car loans made by Detroit. They can automate transactions and hedge purchases by buying on one exchange and simultaneously selling on another exchange in another city or country, in another currency. The possibilities for developing new derivative products are endless.

The world in which the new economy functions is more akin to an electronic "commons" than it is to an economy. And like any commons—a grazing commons in an ancient English town, for example—this new electronic space is owned not by governments but by the people who use it.

While President Ronald Reagan and his advisers were fighting against big government, it turned out that government was being swept away. After all, aside from a few of these electronic networks run by institutions like the Federal Reserve Board, the rest are privately held. It is American Telephone and Telegraph, MCI, Sprint, Citibank, International Business Machines, Swift, Cirrus, Plus, Visa, MasterCard, and others that own the fiber-optic commons. Governments just regulate it, if they even do that.

Two hundred years ago John Locke, John Stuart Mill, and Adam Smith wrote at length about money and debt and banking, and even derived theories of ethics and government from their musings. They knew that economics altered the way we live, do business, and carry on our affairs. They also knew that our economic system is a reflection of who we are as a people. They knew that economics and the economic system cannot be divorced from humanity's other pursuits, from its dreams and dreaded nightmares. They knew that economics, far from being just a science, also reflects our values and sensitivities. It is one of the ways in which we, as a society, organize and define ourselves.

Today's debate about the nature and evolution of money and our economy is no less encompassing. Half a dozen schools of thought are at odds with one another about what constitutes money's precise identity and what its impact will be. Half a dozen schools vie for the truth.

Who are these new-school thinkers? They are mathematicians such as Fischer Black and Myron Scholes, who developed ways to trade and value options; James Forrester, a professor of electrical engineering at MIT who invented the core memory for computers in the 1950s, who helped found the Digital Equipment Corporation (DEC), and who subsequently has been trying to build a model of the way the world economy works; Hyman Minsky, an iconoclastic economist from St. Louis who correctly foresaw globalization and its implications as early as 1955 and who believes finance has overtaken economics in importance; Hayne Leland, a former business school professor at Berkeley who was one of the inventors of program trading. And there are others, people who conceive of stocks and bonds not as the units of corporate ownership and corporate and governmental debt but as abstract, electronic "accumulators" of the nation's purchasing power—as symbolic collection points for labor and ideas. These new-school economists will help us understand the new world we are living in and the direction in which we are going.

It is the nature, shape, and contour of the new economy— the electronic commons—that this book will explore. It will examine the ideas and insights of the new guard of economic thinkers. It will show how the world economy is likely to unfold when bankers, investors, traders, policy analysts, government officials, economists, financial experts, and corporate leaders are all linked together like dendrites in the brain. It will explore the new world that advances in telecommunications, computing, and finance are currently in the process of creating. And it will show how major investors in this new world will make their money grow.

Had Ronald Reagan, George Bush, or any of their predecessors chosen advisers whose ties were decorated with the microchip instead of Adam Smith, a decade's worth of turbulence and decline for the United States might have been avoided. Had they paid attention to a generation's worth of changes, they might have been able to contain some of the markets' volatility and kept our nation's wealth growing. Had they paid attention to a subtle yet fundamental shift, they might have put policies in place that would have kept America at the head of the world's economic train. Unfortunately, they did not do that.

THE QUANT FACTOR:

How Mathematicians and Rocket Scientists Have Replaced Stock Pickers and Traders in the World's Money Markets and Shortened the Time Frame for Investing

In the old days—the late 1960s, say—if you were a street-smart hustler with a nose for stocks and bonds, you could probably have worked your way up on Wall Street. All that you needed was street savvy, a feel for which way the economy was headed. A fistful of contacts and some family money didn't hurt.

Back then, a degree in accounting from Brooklyn College or even a reputable night school carried some weight. True, a master's degree in business or a law degree from Harvard, Columbia, or Yale was an even quicker ticket to the top, but not because of the financial or investment techniques taught at those Ivy League schools. Finance was pretty simple fare back then, no matter where you studied it—it wasn't global and it wasn't electronic. What you got from Harvard or Wharton, as opposed to the smaller schools, was contacts—lots of them—especially among the white-shoe leaders at the top.

You still make contacts when you go to Harvard, Yale, or Columbia, and they certainly help. But what is even more important now is knowing computers. Writing software programs, understanding equations, and knowing numbers are what count. Having a familiarity with supercomputers and "expert

systems"—knowing how to build computer models and understanding probability—also helps.

No one can truly enter the world's new electronic economy
without a thorough knowledge of advanced technology. As a
result, Wall Street firms—the ones that trade money as well as
stocks, bonds, and other products around the world—have been
spending big to acquire the technological wherewithal.

They have also been spending big to hire what the Street calls
"quants"—mathematicians, economists, and engineers (former
academics, many of them) who design the quantitative strategies the firms use to make their money. In 1990 at Jefferies &
Company, an investment house headquartered in Los Angeles
but with offices in New York and London, only two out of fifty
people working on its automated trading systems project had
prior brokerage experience. The rest of the team was composed
of mathematicians, economists, physicists, and computer designers. One of Jefferies' quants wrote the computer programs
that NASA used to aim the Galileo spacecraft at Jupiter. Another
specialized in designing "expert systems," sophisticated computer programs that mimic human judgment.

Quants may write software programs for the firm's big computer systems, or they may create what the Japanese call "zai-
tech," elaborately engineered financial concepts and techniques
that allow traders, for example, to buy dollars on one exchange
while simultaneously selling them on another, all with the touch
of a button, Increasingly, this is where the value is.

In the electronic economy, quants are rewarded handsomely
for their Ph.D.s and brain power. A typical quant on Wall Street
can earn $400,000 for doing the calculations and writing the
computer programs necessary to build an advanced trading
system.

In 1983, Fischer Black, a mathematician with a Ph.D. from
Harvard who developed the Black-Scholes model for determining the value of options, was earning $43,000 a year as a pro-
fessor of mathematics at the Massachusetts Institute of
Technology. In 1984 he was hired by Goldman Sachs & Company. In 1986 he became a partner. As one of Goldman's top
quants, Black—a soft-spoken man who is the antithesis of the
Wall Street hustler—is paid a salary and a bonus of more than
$1 million a year.

PH.D.S IN THE TRADING PITS

Quants who actually trade make more, a lot more. A salary plus bonus of $1.5 million to $3 million for a mathematician-turned-trader is not unusual.

Then there are some superstars: Lawrence E. Hilibrand, a thirty-one-year-old mathematical whiz also from MIT, uses computers to trade bonds on the world's electronic exchanges for Salomon Brothers from its headquarters in New York. In 1990, not a particularly good year either, Hilibrand earned $23 million for turning his insights into dollars.

Secrecy surrounds the quants. The software programs they come up with are at the heart of how firms make money on the megabyte standard. Computer programs that can signal when to buy and sell and can also instantly calculate the value of what to buy and sell are closely guarded. And to keep their quants—along with their secrets—from being lured away by other firms, a number of companies refuse to disclose the identities of their best analytical minds.

Bear Stearns & Company, one of the biggest and most prestigious firms on Wall Street, does not even let its quants talk about the money they earn. The rule at the big firm is simple: If you disclose how much you earn, you're fired.

But elevating quants into Wall Street's top income brackets is part of a much larger trend gripping the world's financial community in general as it struggles to apprehend megabyte money. The trend is that electronic trading in general is replacing advice as the major service the financial community sells. Investment bankers who know how to structure a merger or acquisition are being replaced in the hierarchy by traders who know how to shift money from market to market. Merrill Lynch & Company, the nation's biggest investment firm, now has traders heading two of its six divisions, while its merchant bankers have been demoted.

Shearson Lehman Brothers, another big Wall Street firm, has elevated its traders into the upper reaches of its hierarchy, also displacing the more traditional investment banker. CS First Boston, a Wall Street firm owned by Credit Suisse, the large Zurich-based bank, is betting that trading products will replace investment banking as its major business.

The ascendancy of trading, broadly defined as the ability to conduct rapid electronic transactions in a wide variety of financial markets and on exchanges around the world, accounts for a growing share of revenue for the big Wall Street firms. It also accounts for a growing share of the world's overall economic activity.

At Salomon Brothers, trading in stocks, bonds, interest rates, currencies, mortgages, and other products now brings in over 80 percent of its $5 billion or so in annual revenue, up from 70 percent in 1987, according to an article in *The New York Times*. At Morgan Stanley Group Inc., trading brings in half the company's revenue, up from 38 percent in 1987. And it is growing at other firms around the world as well.

THE RISE OF THE "TRANSACTING" ECONOMY

The ascendancy of trading means that finance has shifted its orientation from one of "investing" to one of "transacting," a consequence of the ability of computers and telecommunications networks to effortlessly manipulate vast quantities of information and send it around the world.

The information era has moved finance from its age-old static—even passive—framework, of buying assets or making investments and then holding them, into something new: making money by harvesting minute shifts in value across various exchanges.

But the new transaction mentality does not just apply to stocks. All financial transactions, from the purchase of a certificate of deposit to the placement of funds in a money market account, have been affected by the new transaction mentality. Even the old standbys such as mutual funds are no longer bought and held but are traded like stocks. Dozens of fax letters, online computer newsletters, and "switching" services alert investors around the world when it is time to move in and out of a fund.

Traders are no longer expected to know about a company's history or even its management. If a stock fits a desired mathematical formula for price, volatility, and dividends, it is bought no matter what the underlying company makes or who manages it.

Certainly there are investors who still analyze balance sheets, read annual reports, and visit factories to see firsthand how a company is managed. But rapidly such stock pickers are finding themselves in the minority as the capabilities of the world's financial technology expands.

SPENDING BIG ON TECHNOLOGY

Every year for more than a decade the three hundred or so major firms of Wall Street have invested between them about $3.4 billion to build up their high-tech arsenals of computers, software, telecommunications equipment, and information-gathering capabilities. Their technology budgets rose by 19 percent a year during the 1980s.

In 1991 they planned to spend even more—$7.5 billion among them, according to a survey in the *Economist* magazine of February 2, 1991. That huge figure accounts for 20 percent of their total outlays. On a percentage basis it is roughly four times the technology expenditures of Detroit. These huge sums put Wall Street right up there with the research-intensive pharmaceutical industry.

Research conducted at colleges and universities also adds to the technological arsenal these firms require to stay competitive within the electronic economy. New York State, with the largest concentration of financial firms in the country, has even established a technology research center exclusively for the financial industry at Brooklyn Polytechnic College. At the Massachusetts Institute of Technology, at Berkeley, and at the Wharton School, similar programs also exist. And at the Kellogg School at Northwestern University, at Harvard Business School, and at the labs of many of the big computer companies, scholars are devising ways to accelerate the pace and level of interaction within the electronic economy.

The big Wall Street firms, according to William H. Gates, founder and chairman of Microsoft Inc., the world's largest publisher of computer software, are among the most technologically advanced companies in the world. Gates says they are advanced not just because they have the best hardware and software "but also because they use them in the most sophisticated ways."

But sometimes all that technology can backfire. On March 25, 1992, at 4:00 P.M., a clerk at Salomon Brothers misread a memo and pressed a "sell" button on one of the firm's computers. But rather than selling $11 million worth of a stock for a client, as the memo said, the button the clerk pressed sold 11 million shares from a client's portfolio—more than $100 million worth of stocks. That sale was enough to cause the Dow Jones Industrial Average to tumble sixteen points for the day.

THE BIG BOARD'S RIVALS: PRIVATE EXCHANGES

The firms along the Street and their affiliates around the country have also been spending big to create private twenty-four-hour electronic markets. They have been creating flexible, fast alternatives to the big established markets like the New York Stock Exchange and the American Stock Exchange. They have also been setting up systems to connect traders around the world directly. With these systems a click of the computer "mouse" and a deal is made between parties located anywhere in electronic space.

Some of these new systems are simply computer billboards. A trader sends out a message that he wants to buy 1 billion yen—about $7,575,757—for example. Someone else on the system who has that many yen responds with a price. If it's acceptable, the trade is made. If not, the prospective buyer and seller can haggle electronically for a few seconds until a deal is completed. If no deal is made, they can just sign off, no hard feelings. In fact, no feelings at all, just a series of neat calculations made on their computers.

Other systems have far more intricate software programs than the billboards do. They can help make deals when there are several interested buyers and several ready sellers or when a purchase order is so big—10 billion yen—that it will take several sellers to supply it.

The more intricate systems have programs that electronically weigh all the bids and offers against one another. They are then able to calculate what is called the "auction price" based on how many unites of yen, say, are offered for sale and how many buyers there are that want them. These more complicated systems work by duplicating the rules of supply and demand. By doing so they simulate the activities carried out on the noisy floors of markets such as the Chicago Mercantile Exchange.

Some of these electronic networks, such as the twenty-four-hour electronic futures exchange called Globex, for Global Futures Exchange (which was set up by the Chicago Mercantile Exchange and Reuters Holdings Plc.), allows trading between the parties to be carried out anonymously. The philosophy here is that the best price will result if none of the parties involved knows with whom he is dealing. Globex, which opened on June 25, 1992, cost $70 million to design and test. Currently it trades mostly money—currency futures and options on futures contracts of pounds, marks, yen, Swiss francs, Canadian dollars, Treasury bills, and Eurodollar time deposits. And it does this when the regular exchanges are closed. But Globex is positioned to trade money and other products day and night from any location around the world. And the number of people who can participate on Globex is virtually without limit. Volume on Reuters' trading networks—not counting Globex which is still in its infancy—is increasing at the rate of 45 percent a year.

Other new systems, such as Aurora, the electronic system developed by the rival Chicago Board of Trade, operate under another philosophy: Keep everything out in the open. These systems track each transaction and subject them all to public scrutiny. If you log on to Aurora, you know with whom you are dealing. These systems and others make it possible to conduct millions more transactions each day than before technology invaded Wall Street. They also lengthen the trading day to twenty-four hours.

In the electronic economy, each participant is free to choose whether he wants to trade anonymously or not. The flexibility gives traders of money, stocks, bonds, and other products more choices about where to do a deal. Click the keyboard and move into the region of electronic space where Globex is located and life moves in the shadows. Click yourself into Aurora's network and everybody knows your name.

THOSE POOR, OUTMODED BANKS

Banks, which are increasingly subject to intense competition from Wall Street firms and from the non-banking side of financial economy, have been spending even more, perhaps three times as much as the Wall Street firms, to automate their labor-intensive, globe-spanning businesses.

The banks have to spend more, much more, to compete. Because of technology and the nature of their charters, banks are rapidly becoming outmoded institutions, as the rise in banking failures and forced mergers attest.

According to estimates made by Paul F. Glaser, chairman of Citicorp's Technology Committee, with about $3 trillion in deposits, America's ten thousand largest banking companies have only a tad more money under management than the nation's three hundred largest money management firms—the ones that manage the nation's pensions, mutual funds, and money market funds. And banks are far less efficient.

Today, with a computer, twenty people can easily manage a $10 billion portfolio of investments in a group of mutual funds, such as those run by Fidelity, Dreyfus, and Merrill Lynch. They can offer almost all the services the banks do—check writing, direct payroll deposit, and others—which they simply purchase from the banks and sell to their customers. And they can pay themselves fees of 1.5 percent or more for doing this while also charging investors as much as 5 percent each time they add or subtract from their holdings. These funds have no federally mandated reserve requirements and no insurance requirements. They operate very lean, with close to 100 percent of their money invested at all times. If they buy futures contracts through a margin account, they can have *more than* 100 percent of their money invested during certain periods of time.

But banks, with their huge infrastructures and established ways of doing things, need five thousand people to manage $10 billion.Banks have to have tellers, loan officers, regional supervisors, property managers, appraisers, mortgage committees, loan committees, and a myriad of vice presidents. All the funds need is a few advanced PCs or workstations, some communication equipment, and a lot of software.

As a result, banks are spending heavily on automation. Automatic teller machines and the networks that support them are now ubiquitous. In Manhattan, several banks have full-size branches with no one working in them other than a doorman. All the tellers are electronic.

And the banks are trying to link their payments systems, too. With 2 billion checks written each day, they have a lot to keep track of. The faster they can move money, the better they will do. They are automating their credit reporting systems and their bank card operations.They are devising ways to use computers to take mortgages, auto loans, and leases, and bundle them together into interest-yielding parcels that can be sold to investors around the world. But banks have an uphill fight.

A WINDFALL TO THE MANUFACTURERS

For the companies that manufacture the technology of finance—primarily IBM, Unisys, and DEC—this has meant big growth. Big enough to propel old-guard companies such as AT&T—which supplies many of the fiber-optic networks used by the financial community—into spending $7.4 billion to buy the NCR Corporation, which supplies teller machines, cash registers, and computers, in the hopes that together they can move into the burgeoning financial technology market and dominate it. It has also fueled the growth of new companies such as Stratus Inc., of Boston, which makes computers and terminals designed exclusively for the trader's desk.

Expenditures for technology can really pay off by increasing the volume of transactions the exchanges can process and limiting the risk. (Fifty percent of all trades on the Big Board are for blocks of ten thousand or more shares). Using the latest technology, the New York Stock Exchange has continually increased the number of transactions it can accommodate.

In 1964, when computers first began entering the trading room, the Big Board—with its "tickers" located at staid brokerage firms around the country—had barely enough capacity to trade 10 million shares in a single day. Beginning in 1991 the Big Board can trade a billion shares a day from buyers located anywhere in the world. That is a one-hundred-fold increase in a single generation. And during the week ending March 15, 1991, about 190 million shares were traded automatically by computer—something no one dreamed of a generation ago. And soon the Big Board will be trading twenty-four hours a day.

Salomon Brothers, because of its heavy investment in technology, can now trade as much as $2 trillion (more than a third of the nation's annual gross national product) worth of stocks, bonds, money, mortgages, and other products in a year. Salomon routinely buys 35 percent of all the bonds the government sells and has illegally bought as much as 85 percent of the Treasury bonds offered, which cost its former chairman, John H. Gutfreund, his job. For Solly (Salomon's nickname), putting up $4 billion or more a month to buy the government bonds is simply the cost of doing business.

Each year, for its clients, Salomon Brothers runs nearly the equivalent of the nation's total bank holdings through its computers, a huge undertaking considering the myriad of different accounts its clients have. Salomon can trade products for clients located on exchanges as diverse as those in Tokyo, Hungary, Warsaw, New York, and London.

In Chicago, at the Mercantile Exchange, as much as $50 billion worth of futures contracts on government bonds changes hands each day. In New York, $150 billion changes hands each day as investors buy and sell Treasury bonds.

A NETWORK OF GROWING COMPLEXITY

These expenditures have begun to put into place an incredibly complex network that connects nearly everyone in this world to everyone else whenever money is involved. For example, if you get a subscription to Prodigy, the home-information service available on your PC, you can write checks, apply for mortgages and loans, buy or sell stock, get stock and money fund analyses, compute interest rates, and have your credit analyzed, all electronically. Prodigy, which is a simple, easy-to-use service, enables the least sophisticated computer user to tap into the electronic system.

Have one of Citicorp's new "enhanced telephones" installed (debuting in 1993), and you can do all your banking, bill paying, investing, and even catalog shopping without leaving home. You can even send money overseas.

Install Charles Schwab & Company's Equalizer program in your PC, attach a modem, and you are ready to move your money from one mutual fund to another and in and out of stocks, currencies, and commodities, and you can even pay your bills. But aside from these more sophisticated applications, we are all connected every day to the network in one way or another.

Go to an automatic teller machine today, press a button, and you are in the middle of a global network of incredible complexity and even—the designers would say—elegance.

Buy gas at an automated service station by inserting a card, and you are in communication with the world of megabyte money.

Have your credit card credit limit raised, apply for a loan, pay off a mortgage, use your credit card, write a check—and you are connected to the network.

Make a purchase at a supermarket, and you are not only sending your money into the electronic void but are also delivering information into the store's computer so that food will be processed, trucks loaded, and shelves stocked automatically to replace what you bought. Each time you enter the infinity of electronic megabyte space, your footprints are recorded, tracked, and stored. And all your transactions in the world of money, big and small, are logged in the network's vast database.

MOVING MONEY ANYWHERE

For professional money managers, the megabyte standard has made life different. The network has made their jobs more akin to those of a mathematician than a stock picker or dollar trader.

The billions spent so far have also paid for highly automated trading rooms where, with the flick of a switch, men and women can move billions of dollars' worth of buying power. They can move this buying power anywhere in the world and convert it into what traders call "instruments" and "products." They can package it and lend it to financiers like Martin Sorrel in London, who used it to buy J. Walter Thompson and dozens of smaller advertising agencies around the world, or to "investors," questionable characters like General Manuel Noriega, the imprisoned leader of Panama.

The network has also helped create full-scale information "environments" where traders, analysts, bankers, brokers, money managers, and strategists can gain immediate access to breaking news events anywhere in the world. Clients can also "enter" the environment electronically to watch how their portfolios are doing and to assess their investment strategies. These environments are designed to greatly enhance the speed at which transactions are executed and, perhaps even more important, to deepen the judgment of traders, investors, and money managers about the way the electronic economy is moving on a second-by-second basis.

According to Maurice Estabrooks, a senior economist with the federal government of Canada and author of *Programmed Capitalism*, even the architecture is different in the electronic economy: "A new electronic computer-mediated brokerage house is likely to resemble a video game arcade, an air traffic control center, the control room of a NASA space center, or the war room of a modern military center."

THE NEW TRADING ENVIRONMENTS

One of the new trading environments is at Morgan Stanley Group Inc. in New York, and it includes a trading processing system.

Morgan Stanley's Taps, which cost $25 million for the prototype system alone, executes trades almost instantly and with enhanced accuracy. It also does all the paperwork and tracks each trade so that analysts, traders, investors, and managers can later reconstruct events to learn how to do better.

By accelerating the speed and accuracy of each transaction, it allows the firm's quants to make more trades in a day, increasing their chances for gain (but also loss) and contributing to the overall growth in volume. It also takes the world a step closer to a system of continuous automatic trading and optimally efficient markets—a world-changing concept Adam Smith could never have contemplated even in his wildest imaginings.

What is interesting about Taps is not just cost size or speed but how it is constructed. The system uses two IBM 390 computers that are connected so that problems can be divided between the two machines to simulate the way parallel-processing supercomputers work.

Parallel processing is at the forefront of computer design. These systems can make billions of computations a second, and the aim is to make these machines faster. Today, designers of parallel-processing machines are trying to make machines that function at what they call "teraflop" speeds—a trillion computations a second. A machine this big could read, digest, and process the entire contents of the Library of Congress in just a few seconds.

Unlike conventional supercomputers, with one quick and complicated microprocessor at its heart, parallel-processing computers are composed of dozens, sometimes thousands, of microprocessors. Each of these microprocessors is a powerful computer in itself.

Significantly, in November 1991, when Thinking Machines Inc. unveiled its powerful CM-5 supercomputer, a generation beyond Taps computers that can have as many as sixteen thousand microprocessors, each connected to four math-processor chips, its initial orders went to the nation's top science centers: Los Alamos, Berkeley, and the University of Pittsburgh Supercomputer Center. There was one exception, however: American Express Inc. ordered two CM-5's for its financial businesses.

But it is more difficult to write software for parallel-processing computers than for conventional ones. In a parallel-processing environment, like the one at Morgan Stanley, the software must take a problem—for example, determining the average difference in the price of IBM stock on the Big Board, in London, and in Tokyo, on a minute-by-minute basis for the last week— and divide that problem into its constituent parts. The "disassembly" must be done in a few billionths of a second. Those components are then sent to different microprocessors where they are "crunched" individually. Once crunched, the components must then be reassembled into an overall answer that makes sense—all within a few billionths of a second. A tremendous challenge for the software developers.

With the present-generation Taps system, each trader has an IBM 3270 smart terminal on his desk connected to the mainframe. The Taps system—used exclusively for trading stocks, bonds, and money—has enough computer power to support a large-scale university research laboratory. It is enough computing power to design an airplane and put it through its paces in an elaborate series of computerized simulations.

But Taps is just the beginning. Morgan Stanley, which is often thought to be at the forefront in developing new financial technologies, also has what it calls the Analytical Unit. This high-tech trading system supports and integrates the work of twenty-six people—traders, brokers, analysts, and computer specialists. But unlike Taps, which just executes, checks, and does the paperwork the government requires for a trade, the Analytical Unit also gives advice.

Built into the Analytical Unit is an "expert system," a complicated computer program that sifts through several lifetimes' worth of trading judgments in a fraction of a second. Expert systems are painstakingly constructed by interviewing real experts and converting their decision-making processes into a hierarchical set of rules that computers can follow when they sift and sort through tons of "real-time" data. Real-time processing means that the rules of the expert system are applied to each situation as it is happening, without delay. The expert system at Morgan has applications for trading currencies, commodities such as gold, silver, and oil, futures contracts, and lowly stocks and bonds.

Each trader in the Analytical Unit has terminals that are connected directly into the New York Stock Exchange's "super dot" system (which stands for designated order turnaround), bypassing the company's brokers on the floor of the exchange who ordinarily shout out orders and make their bids.

Super dot electronically routes orders directly between the customer at his computer and the specialists on the floor of the exchange, who buy and sell the actual stock. Traders who use the super dot system can be located anywhere in the world. The system can process a trade of up to 30,099 shares at a time. Soon it will be equipped to trade 100,000 shares at a time. And it can process thousands of these transactions each minute for millions of shares of stock. What's more, super dot operates with almost total accuracy.

By going directly into the super dot system, the Analytical Unit can make a trade without having to wait for a broker. But it still requires the services of a specialist, an outmoded (and potentially dangerous) part of the New York Stock Exchange, as we shall see.

Dialing directly into the super dot system is a little like calling an airline for a reservation, bypassing the reservations clerk and looking into the carrier's computer yourself to book a flight, select a seat, and pay the price. With computers, the transactions take hardly any time at all, but they do require judgment.

The Analytical Unit's computers also contain a program called Pac-Man that constantly weighs the factors that affect each stock's price and signals the trader when the time is right to buy or sell. The Analytical Unit also generates intricate three-

dimensional charts that refer to stock, bond, and exchange rate
prices and give indications of what actions a trader should follow.
To read these 3-D color charts, traders put on special glasses,
like audiences wore at 3-D movies years ago, one of the more
bizarre accouterments of the information age.

As part of the information environment in the new electronic
economy, new systems allow stock trading to continue after the
markets have closed. They also allow trading to occur between
participants located around the world. One system, called Instinet, which is owned by Reuters, gives traders the opportunity
to make deals after the New York Stock Exchange has shut
down for the night. Instinet, which costs just $1,000 to join,
charges a moderate fee for each transaction, from three to seven
cents, but it expands the trading day to twenty-four hours. It
now trades about 8 million shares a day.

With Globex, the Reuters and Chicago Mercantile Exchange
joint venture, a trader can also trade futures contracts on yen,
Japanese or American Treasury notes, dollars, marks, or gold
futures, and future contracts on stocks twenty-four hours a day
with participants located anywhere.

Not only does Globex allow for these trades to be executed
instantly, it also automatically records the entire transaction and
does the paperwork.

Instinet and Globex are only two of many global electronic
exchanges for trading stocks, bonds, futures contracts, and
money from a PC or terminal anywhere in the world at any time.
There is also Soffex, the Swiss Options and Financial Futures
Exchange.There is Fox, the automated system at the London
Futures and Options Exchange, and the New Zealand Futures
Exchange. Cores is the Computer Assisted Order Routing and
Execution System at the Tokyo Stock Exchange. Tiffe is the
Tokyo International Financial Futures Exchange. Tse is the
automated system at the Toronto Stock Exchange. Cats is the
Computer Assisted Trading System, also in Toronto. Auto-Ex is
an automated system for executing orders on the American
Stock Exchange. And there is old Nasdaq, with roots going back
twenty years; it is the National Association of Securities Dealers
Automated Quotation system in New York. Nasdaq can be en-
tered from computers anywhere, and soon it will be connected

to London's Seaq system. Seaq stands for Britain's Securities Exchange Automation Quotation system.

A number of smaller, private exchanges are also operating. With the right software, these exchanges can be logged onto from PCs or terminals located anywhere in world. One such exchange—Posit, which is run by Jefferies & Company—allows traders to thin their inventories or build up their portfolios after the larger exchanges close. More than 3 million shares a day changes hands on the Posit system. Posit is designed for the big investor—pension funds and insurance companies primarily—that have big inventories of stock they want to exchange anonymously at the lowest possible cost. Jefferies owns other private trading systems as well.

Another system, started by Steven Wunsch, a renowned rock climber as well as trader, is simply called Was, Wunsch Auction System. Not everything can be traded on Was, only the shares of companies that sign up. So far, several dozen companies have done just that. Another private exchange called Spaworks lets traders make deals for stocks a few hours before the New York Stock Exchange opens to take advantage of overnight developments.

A NETWORK OF FINANCIAL NETWORKS

Every year more of these systems are added to the world's financial infrastructure. But perhaps even more important, all these systems are linked together.

With the right passwords, codes, and exchange membership, a trader or money manager can access tremendous accumulations of buying power around the world. He or she can let that buying power sit ever so briefly, then use it to buy into a myriad of different products—stocks, money, options, bonds, and so on—hoping to see it increase in size with every transaction. Moving money in this way, with the right programs and the right judgment, has made many traders rich beyond belief.

Through electronics and automation the new megabyte economy, if managed correctly, could ideally help to rush capital to wherever it is needed. And it could get that capital to wherever there are opportunities. No would-be entrepreneur with his or her better mousetrap, computer chip, or potato chip would want for start-up money. A nearly perfect market, one in which money flows with the speed of light, would mean that every seller would be able to find a buyer, and prices and values would fall into line. If markets were as efficient as the technology promises, growth would almost certainly accelerate. It is a mighty big if, however.

Efficient markets do not necessarily mean smooth markets. Wall Street's new-technology expenditures have created an exquisitely sensitive system for moving large and small units of buying power around the world. But it has also created a system, however intricate, that dumps information onto the desks of the world's money managers in quantities far too vast to assimilate.

Perhaps it will be different tomorrow, but today's expert systems are still not sufficient to clear the traders' desks of this excessive and often confusing information. They are still not sufficient to keep up with the number of deals speeding through the lines or with news events or changes in the economy.

As a consequence, traders are still playing catch-up. They are still lurching from one transaction to the next. And they are still fighting their way through an ever-growing number of "average" daily transactions with progressively taller spikes and deeper valleys.

A system that is so responsive to the world's mood swings is one that can also get afflicted by the jitters. The megabyte standard to a large degree has institutionalized rather than smoothed volatility. It has done so not just here but in Europe and Japan as well.

Prices have been gyrating since the onset of the megabyte economy on just about everything. Over the last decade the dollar rose to twice its 1970s value and then declined to less than half that value against other major currencies. During that same period, stock markets around the world climbed to new highs, held steady, and then tumbled by magnitudes previously unheard of. At the same time, interest rates, which had stayed steady for decades, rose and fell like the tides at the Bay of Fundy. Real estate values, too, which have always been the economy's safe haven, rose and fell like at no other time. And the same is true for commodities. In the first half of 1991 alone, the dollar increased its value against the German mark by 50 percent.

Then, in July of that year, the dollar lost 29 percent of its value against the mark.

This volatile system has also done away with the notion of "patient capital." With the aid of its vast and increasingly expensive arsenal of technology, Wall Street has changed its mindset. No more do institutions buy stocks to hold because they believe in the underlying value of the company. Instead, with the touch of a button and the aid of a few mathematical formulas, institutions such as staid pension funds, insurance companies, and mutual funds increasingly trade in and out of stocks, keeping their holdings for decreasing periods of time.

Rules governing mutual funds and pension funds require that these big accumulators of buying power keep their money invested exclusively in one type of product, such as foreign currencies or stocks. Because of these rules, money managers are also forced to trade more often than they would otherwise. This shortens Wall Street's time horizon further and, because the system is so sensitive, increases the potential for volatility. To paraphrase Lawrence H. Summers, formerly of Harvard and now chief economist of the World Bank, the markets just work too well; because they are linked electronically, they have no mechanism to dampen trading activity.

The new megabyte standard has been built to take advantage of minuscule changes in prices—not just the price of stocks and bonds but the price of anything that can be charted, bundled, and traded. It was created to make profits from shifts that in the past would simply have been ignored.

The new system is different from anything that preceded it. The rules governing the world's vast capital markets are very different from the rules governing industry. As a consequence, the megabyte standard has contributed to the bitter divorce between the concrete "real" economy, where products are made and goods and services traded, and the highly abstract "financial" economy, where financial products are bought and sold purely for financial gain.

The extent to which these two economies are separate is increasing, and technology is contributing to the estrangement. In practical terms, the financial economy worldwide is now many times larger than the real economy—between thirty and fifty times bigger, according to estimates by Citicorp's Paul F.

Glaser. That means that for every dollar spent on something "real," a hammer, scissors, screwdriver, car, or bottle of wine, $30 to $50 is spent on a stock, bond, futures contract, or insurance policy.

With a disparity that has grown so big, the high-tech financial economy, with its boom-and-bust cyclicality and its daily volatility, has taken nearly complete charge of the real economy. For humanity as a whole, that is a new and highly uncertain condition.

THREE

THE ROOTS OF MEGABYTE MONEY:

How Reuters Holdings Invented the New Electronic Economy a Century Ago—and Continues to Exploit It

F ew people have been as prescient when it comes to the electronic economy as Marshall McLuhan. During the 1960s and 1970s, McLuhan, the eccentric Canadian philosopher, wrote a series of densely packed, disorganized little books about the emergence of the information age. Those books, with their tangled sentence structure, hundreds of footnotes, and weird illustrations, had to be deciphered rather than read. But each book contained dozens of gleaming insights.

Perhaps the most important of McLuhan's ideas was expressed in *War and Peace in the Global Village,* which was written in 1968. (The book was "produced" rather than published, McLuhan said, since he believed books were a thing of the past, an artifact of a bygone age.)

In *War and Peace in the Global Village,* McLuhan said that since the new electronic information environments "are direct extensions of our own nervous system, they have a much more profound relation to our human condition than the old 'natural' environment." For finance, especially, the thought is profound.

The currency of the nervous system is information. The brain does not deal directly with events. It participates in neither a kiss nor a pinch. It only deals with information about the event supplied to it through the senses. The brain, remote and yet aware, learns about a burned finger or a fragrant rose through coded information sent to it by the nerves. And then it causes the body to act.

Similarly, oil traders learn about an explosion at an oil refinery or dollar traders learn about a change in interest rates indirectly. Their stomachs may burn, their palms may sweat, but almost all the time they are miles away—sometimes continents away— from the event itself. Traders do not experience events directly, only vicariously. They learn about events, and then they act.

The nervous system is our sole means of perceiving the world. If it is altered—biologically in the individual or electronically in the collective—our notions of reality and its borders change as well. Yet, though our beliefs about reality have been affected through our information-gathering and -disseminating technologies, there is no way to tell whether what we regard as the "real" or "natural" really deserves that name. In economics, finance, and even investing, that means the old rules may no longer apply. Even the way we describe the world may be out of date.

In addition, because it is our nervous system that has been extended outward through technology, the new electronic economy is by definition nervous, changeable, reactive, and, from time to time, overloaded.

Though these changes may be dramatic, profound, and encompassing in the way they have changed our economic and social reality, they are also, according to McLuhan, invisible: "Man-made environments are always unperceived by men during their period of innovation. When they have been superseded by other environments, they tend to become visible."

THE INFORMATION BAZAAR

A number of major companies contribute to the stream of information flowing through the electro-economic network of computers and software. McGraw-Hill Inc., publisher of *Business Week,* and Dow Jones Inc., publisher of *The Wall Street Journal* and *Barrons,* are two of the most venerable companies that provide online information directly to the world's trading desks. Through Dow Jones/Retrieval you can dial up stock quotations, news releases, and even airline schedules. You can dial into a vast database on companies and access every article in *The Wall Street Journal* and in other newspapers as well. You can also dive deeply into a given company's finances, read its annual reports, and study its filings with the various regulatory bodies such as the Securities and Exchange Commission. But you cannot buy or sell stocks or any other financial product.

Dozens of smaller companies, such as I.D.E.A., which is based in London, send financial data and analyses via computer to subscribers around the world. Some of the services are quite sophisticated. For instance, through the BBN—for Bloomberg Business News (Michael Bloomberg is a former trader at Salomon Brothers)—traders can dial up the insights of dozens of stock, bond, and commodities analysts who comment on breaking news developments. If IBM, for instance, announced it planned to lay off workers, within minutes BBN would have its stable of analysts put their assessments of IBM onto its network. These analysts give traders new earnings forecasts for the company for the short and long term. Bloomberg has analysts online specializing in hundreds of different companies and markets. The service sends information and even rumors out at the speed of light to participants in the world's financial communities. Though you can't actually trade products through BBN, you can get the information you need to understand what you ought to pay for a product.

Similarly, I.D.E.A. constantly collects the forecasts of dozens of economists here and abroad on interest rates around the world, trade balances, and production figures. Through I.D.E.A. you can get a look at individual forecasts, or you can get a consensus forecast that averages the various pronouncements.

IT'S EXPENSIVE TO BE INFORMED

Many of the ratings agencies, such as Standard & Poors and Moody's, also put their information onto the world's financial computer network for easy access to anyone with a PC and the right passwords. For participants in the megabyte economy, whether they are located in an office on Wall Street, a ski lodge in Aspen, Colorado, or a hut in the jungles of Sri Lanka, there is equal access to analytical talent—if they can pay for it. It is all part of what Maurice Estabrooks, author of *Programmed Capitalism,* calls the "computer-based information infrastructure."

And then there are small "boutique" services such as High Frequency Economics in New York, with specialists in daily assessments of international economic events. High Frequency, so-named because it releases a new report each day, specializes in forecasting interest rates; its customers are mostly bond traders who pay $15,000 a year or more for this service. Carl Weinberg, the firm's chief economist, travels the world with a laptop computer crammed with formulas. Wherever he is, he writes his overnight assessments, dumps them into the company's computer in New York, and then has the information faxed or sent via modem to the firm's customers around the world.

IT STARTED WITH REUTERS

While there are dozens of large and small companies selling financial information or offering private electronic trading "floors," the company that started it all is Reuters Holdings Plc., based in London.

Reuters, which started as a service that sent carrier pigeons from Aachen to Brussels in 1849, set up the first truly electronic money-trading system in 1973, two years after exchange rates were set free and megabyte money was invented. By doing this Reuters seized the opportunity to begin the transformation of the trading-room floor. Rather than go at each other elbow to elbow, traders—thanks to Reuters—now have the chance to make money just by sitting in front of a cool-green (or blue) computer screen. With the press of a button they can make deals for dollars (yen, pounds, marks, or whatever else they want) anywhere in the world. Reuters was the first service to electronically link buyers and sellers of financial products, especially currencies, and offer them the opportunity to make a trade.

Reuters realized that once exchange rates were free to float, traders needed information fast. They needed to know, for instance, how much a dollar is worth today, right now, in Milan, Beijing, and Tokyo. And they had to know how much to pay today for a Swiss franc that they did not want delivered until next year.

Reuters' chief Glen Renfrew, the sixty-five-year-old Australian who began as a news reporter for the company, saw the need to get information to traders instantly and for a way to give those traders a mechanism by which they could make their deals.

Reuters was positioned well for that task. The company had a unique history as a purveyor of financial information. Its capabilities as a news-gathering organization with more than a century's worth of experience covering the world's financial markets gave it a strong global infrastructure. And it also did not hurt that it owned a small company called Stockmaster.

Stockmaster, though primitive by today's standards, was an early computerized system that gave share quotes to European investors and traders. Although Stockmaster was small, it served as a platform from which Reuters could launch the information age.

Reuters was founded in the mid-1840s by Israel Beer Josaphat, a German Jew living in Paris who changed his name to Paul Julius Reuter and his religion to Christianity. Based in Paris originally, Reuter had reporters covering the Continent. They filed their stories on that new invention, the telegraph, and Reuter sold the stories to newspapers throughout Europe and then the world. Reuter was one of the first people to see the potential of electronics (such as it was 150 years ago) for changing the way business was conducted.

But Reuter also saw a need to cover financial news. By the mid-1850s the service had set up an office in London that sold news and financial reports—primarily about the activities on the Continent—to England's traders and London's press. It also sold reports on the Continent's stock exchanges to London's big investors.

One hundred and twenty years later Reuters was everywhere. The company that broke the news to Europe of Abraham Lincoln's assassination had terminals and tickers in newspapers around the world and had Stockmaster machines at brokerage houses throughout Europe.

In the early 1970s, Glen Renfrew decided that the company should use its global electronic network to get into the business of trading money. In 1973 he launched the Monitor service, which listed currency prices on small computer terminals that could fit on traders' desks. Back then, that was something of a novelty. The PC was still a decade away, and when people thought of computers, they thought of monster machines that were big, slow, and dumb.

These terminals could be installed anywhere since the news they carried was transmitted over telephone wires. Soon these machines were in thousands of brokerage houses around the world. Not only did the Monitor terminals carry currency prices, but they also brought the news wire into the trading room. Dispatches from Reuters' correspondents around the world could be called up on Monitor.

For the first time traders not only had access to the same financial information at the same moment but they also had access to the same news. The electronic financial network was now linking minds as well as wallets. Political and economic events could be added in real time to the complicated mix by which traders made their decisions.

The Monitor service was a success. It grew steadily through the 1970s, but it had one limitation. Although it transferred information throughout the world, it was a one-way service. You could buy information but not trade money through Monitor. Trading still had to be done over the telephone or through telex because it required sophisticated software that could link one person on the network with anyone else directly. It also needed computational power.

The sophisticated software to turn the Monitor service into a two-way trading network was not available until the late 1970s, and it was not until 1981 that Reuters launched a new system called Dealing. With a Dealing terminal or a PC, subscribers could communicate with one another and actually execute trades. An updated version of Dealing, called Dealing 2000, which made its debut in 1990, allows traders to communicate and even haggle with as many as four parties at once.

To supply the system with news in addition to price quotes, Reuters has about fourteen hundred correspondents around the world. Compare this to the three hundred or so business reporters, editors, and copy editors at *The Wall Street Journal* or the seventy-five business and financial editors and reporters at *The New York Times*, and it is immediately clear that Reuters, though not an in-depth service, is certainly a powerhouse.

There are now more than two hundred thousand Reuters financial terminals in use at more than thirty thousand locations in 120 countries. The company also has more than ten thousand new pocket terminals in use. These tiny terminals receive data over special frequencies of the FM radio band and display that information on a tiny screen. Reuters terminals, which are equipped with several different kinds of programs, from simple ones that just give price quotes and news to the more complicated ones that allow traders to make deals for currencies, stock, and even futures contracts, earn the company a great deal of money.

The Dealing 2000 terminal, for example, leases for $5,400 a month. The simpler Monitor terminal leases for $1,800 a month. According to *Forbes* magazine's October 30, 1989 issue, as much as 40 percent of the world's money now trades through Reuters' machines. Since about $800 billion is exchanged each day in those markets, that gives Reuters, which gets a commission of a few cents on every trade, a hefty share of its income. In 1991 the company had revenues of about $2.3 billion.

Soon a new terminal and product called Money 2000 will be replacing the old Monitor system. Money 2000 will be equipped with a sophisticated analysis program and will be able to display charts and graphs—and give advice.

The Reuters Dealing and Monitor systems run on two Digital Equipment Corporation Vax computers. These big mainframes work in tandem: One makes the trades, and the other is a backup that follows each move. In Hauppauge, New York, where the computers are located, a forest of satellite dishes beams around the world the strings of zeros and ones that all computers use. The machines process about 1 million transactions between terminals each day, and the average trade takes less than twenty-five seconds from start to finish.

A LESS-THAN-PERFECT MARKET

Reuters was the pioneer, but others have followed. While these services have grown, they have not replaced the noisy exchange floors. Rather, they have augmented them. Trading goes wherever it can be done fastest and cheapest. It also goes wherever the rules and regulations are most favorable. Traders who bend or break the law go where there is the least watchfulness. Traders who are scrupulous stay where their business is subjected to the toughest regulator's gaze.

On the one hand, the megabyte standard offers nearly unlimited choices from moving money from market to market. But on the other, it bombards the participants with information that they often have difficulty assimilating.

In an ideal world, economists say, everyone would have equal access to information. With smoothly functioning markets, such equal access would make decisions rational. Money would flow to where it is needed, and prices would accurately reflect the value of a company, commodity, bond, or currency.

But this is not a perfect world. As a result, some traders are more favored than others. Sanford Grossman, Trustee Professor of Finance at the Wharton School, wrote in *Innovation and the Markets*, that market "participation and information retrieval and evaluation is neither effortless nor costless. If one party wants to sell, this information is not costlessly disseminated to, and processed by, all buyers." That means that the traders who can pay more for obtaining and processing information have an advantage in the market since knowledge—at least the kind that counts financially (and probably most other types as well)—is costly. If, for example, you want to invest in bonds and can pay Carl Weinberg at High Frequency Economics $15,000 a year, you are probably at an advantage over someone who can pay only $15 a month for a daily newspaper. If you can spare $5,400 a month for a Dealing terminal, you most likely have an advantage over someone who can afford only a PC. One consequence of that logic is that wealthier firms have an advantage when it comes to trading. The ability to pay for expensive information does, in turn, make them wealthier still.

That is one of the contradictions of the information age. While relatively cheap technology has made information accessible, the cost of obtaining that information is usually rather steep. As a result, though information is produced plentifully, its effect has so far been to concentrate wealth and power even more.

For these reasons individuals have largely left the markets as direct participants. The only way they can compete with wealthy firms—the ones that invest hundreds of millions of dollars a year in technology, software, and information—is by joining funds such as mutual funds. As a consequence, most markets are now dominated by professionals.

Professionally dominated markets are different in character from markets where the individual was an important participant. Time frames are shorter, decision-making is concentrated, and the investment process is much more automated than ever before. The high price of information has added to the trend that favors quick trading over long-term investment.

These changes cannot be reversed unless information becomes cheaper so that individual investors will return to the markets as direct participants.

FOUR

A WEIGHTLESS DOLLAR:
How President Nixon, Choosing Expediency over Good Judgment, Inadvertently Created Megabyte Money

The new neural network of money made its debut rather abruptly on Sunday, August 15, 1971, although most people did not recognize its appearance for at least a decade. It came into being more out of expedience than careful planning when Richard M. Nixon, then president, was saddled with a forecast of a recession occurring just months before the presidential election of November 1972. Nixon was also faced with a trade balance that had suddenly climbed to a negative $4 billion, an inflation rate of nearly 5 percent, an unemployment figure of just under 5 percent, and billions of dollars in expenditures to support the war in Vietnam—very alarming circumstances for the time. Nixon's critics—and they were legion among both Republicans and Democrats—charged that he was mismanaging the economy, and they demanded action.

Action is what they got. To fix the "sick" economy (it was sick with a sniffle by today's standards), Dr. Nixon, as he was called in a subsequent headline in *The New York Times,* tried shock therapy. In a televised speech Nixon—upper lip wet with sweat, voice resonant—announced that he had signed a presidential order freezing wages and prices for ninety days. He said he would try to persuade Congress to make it illegal for unions to strike during that time, that he had imposed a 10 percent surtax on imported automobiles and other products, and that he would propose a cut in income taxes to Congress. He also said, to quote the day's vernacular, that he had closed the "gold window."

The last item, closing the gold window, although buried in a long laundry list of essentially useless economic policy changes, represented the biggest challenge to the world economy since the Great Depression; it meant the value of the dollar was no longer linked to the amount of gold in Fort Knox. It was a change of monumental proportions that not only redefined money but created the opportunity to dramatically speed up the rate at which transactions between companies and countries took place. It created enormous arbitrage possibilities and set the stage for the invention of a myriad of new financial products. It also initiated the process of decoupling the "money" economy from the "real" economy. As a result, two-plus decades later, the money economy, where transactions take place purely for financial or speculative gain, and the real economy, where the world's raw materials, goods, and services are produced and traded, are badly out of balance. That was Nixon's economic legacy.

NEW WORLD, OLD INSTITUTIONS

So dramatic were the changes brought about by shutting the gold window that within a decade and a half much of the pre-1971 financial system—banks, savings and loan institutions, and even the stock market, to name just three—had either failed, were shrinking, or were simply obsolete. The damage—$500 billion lost by the savings and loan institutions and another $100 billion or so lost by the banks—was due at least in part to the fact that these obsolete institutions were competing in a world that had changed remarkably. Bailouts, sweeping legislative changes, and restrictions on new competition could not save them.

By closing the gold window Nixon destroyed the carefully crafted post–World War II economic system and replaced it with what former German Chancellor Helmut Schmidt, an economist and an architect of the German economic miracle, called a "floating non-system." Nixon's actions also precipitated a monetary crisis around the world and threw the world's credit markets into chaos. Within a week the value of the dollar decreased by more than 17 percent against the world's other major currencies. At the same time, prices on the world's stocks and bonds markets gyrated up and down as the world's money managers tried to assess the consequences of the new floating non-system.

For the world's finance ministers the new uncertainty and financial volatility was too much. Within one day of Nixon's announcement they temporarily shut the world's largest foreign-exchange markets. At the same time governments around the world that owned dollars or U.S. Treasury bonds or notes were forced to hoard those investments or risk watching them lose their value. Critics contended that by unilaterally abandoning gold, the United States was committing a form of economic extortion. Normally it is the responsibility of the country issuing a currency to ensure the value of its money internationally. But in the new non-system, for the first time ever, it was up to the creditors of the United States to work to keep the dollar strong. Since they owned so many dollar-denominated investments, any loss of the dollar's value meant their holdings would be diminished, and, ultimately, the value of their currencies would have to fall as well.

According to Michael Hudson, a balance of payments economist who worked at Chase Manhattan Bank when gold was abandoned, putting the burden of sustaining the dollar's value on America's creditors was not an accident. "It was a consciously undertaken policy decision," he said in an interview. Hudson has since abandoned corporate finance to study the history of economics.

THE POST–WORLD WAR II ERA ENDS

Before Mr. Nixon worked his magic, the world economy was governed by what were called the Bretton Woods Agreements, named after the town of Bretton Woods, New Hampshire, where the agreements were negotiated and signed on July 22, 1944. The main feature of the Bretton Woods system was that all of the world's major trading currencies were rigidly linked to the dollar in a system of fixed-exchange rates. The dollar, at the center of the system, had its value anchored firmly to gold. The Treasury Department was obligated by law to redeem foreign-held dollars for gold at the official rate of $35 an ounce. The gold window was where those dollars were redeemed.

Because the dollar was convertible to gold and all other currencies were convertible to dollars at fixed rates, the world was effectively on the gold standard, even though no one publicly said so. Countries could expand their money supplies only if they could maintain the value of their currencies against the gold-based dollar. Effectively, that meant the world's money supply expanded at about the same rate as its real rate of growth. Dollars, francs, pounds, and lire were produced, roughly, as they were needed for the orderly expansion of growth and trade. The real economy and the money economy expanded and contracted together. They were balanced on a fulcrum of gold.

A money supply that expands at the same pace as the supply of labor, goods, and services will keep prices stable. That is because a simple but fundamental rule of economics says that when there is too much money around, prices rise to absorb it; when there is too little money available, prices shrink to compensate. This rule says that money, like almost everything else in this world, is valued more highly when it is scarce than when it is abundant. And it also says what most people know intuitively: Inflation, in large part, is simply the consequence of printing too much money. Deflation is the opposite. When these insights were combined with some historical data, a few sets of equations, and a fancy title, they earned Milton Friedman, a monetarist economist from Chicago, the 1976 Nobel Prize for Economic Science.

This idea was also at the heart of the Bretton Woods Agreements. Memories of Germany's hyperinflation before the onset of World War II were still fresh in the minds of the economists who negotiated the agreements. The gold anchor and fixed-exchange rates were supposed to prevent that from happening again. They were supposed to keep the system honest by limiting the amount of dollars that could be created, thereby imposing a certain measure of economic restraint. Money was supposed to come into being as the real economy expanded and, to a much lesser extent, as more gold was discovered. Money was not supposed to be created by fiat or when the economy needed a little boost. Its creation was intentionally limited in order to keep prices stable.

.   .   .

But there was also a measure of flexibility in the Bretton Woods system, which was part of its elegance. In the Bretton Woods system, not every dollar needed to have $1/35$ of an ounce of gold behind it before it could be printed or otherwise produced. If the real economy produced the goods and services and investment opportunities that people really wanted and if confidence in the system was high, then there would not be much of an incentive for people to redeem their dollars for gold. Gold was an anchor, it was not a vehicle for investment. Nor was it supposed to be a medium of exchange. As a result, the world economy needed, perhaps, one foreign-held dollar in eight or ten (maybe even less) to be backed by gold, although no one ever arrived at a precise calculation.

For nearly thirty years the Bretton Woods system provided an environment of stability. The world economy grew by about 7.47 percent a year during its heyday in the 1950s. Oil and commodity prices were stable for more than twenty years. Interest rates were usually between 3 percent and 4.5 percent, inflation was practically nil, mortgages and other loans were at low fixed rates, and the dollar's value was set by law. It was the perfect environment for investing in long-term productivity-enhancing technology and for adding capacity. And with productivity growing but other costs more or less fixed, wages could increase without harming a company's bottom line. With decades of stability under the Bretton Woods system, billions of people around the world climbed out of abject poverty and into the middle class.

WHEN AMERICANS WERE LONG-TERM PLANNERS

During the Bretton Woods era, American companies were considered masters of the long view. But it was not because their leaders were smarter than their counterparts today or because their mentalities were so remarkably different. The stability of the Bretton Woods system, unlike the volatility of the "floating non-system" of today, rewarded business leaders handsomely for thinking ahead. It rewarded them for investing in the future. It was a tightly managed system that held oil prices, interest rates, exchange rates, and commodities prices constant from the first days of 1950 until the middle of 1971. Knowing prices would be stable, business leaders knew precisely how much they would benefit from investing in the future. No wonder the 1950s and

1960s were decades of optimism and hope. No wonder they were decades of rapid growth.

But there was a problem with the Bretton Wood postwar system that ultimately led to its ruin and to Nixon's abandonment of its rules. The problem was this: The Bretton Woods system demanded too much from its leader, the United States. It demanded not only that the United States assume the role of the world's financial manager but also that it be the world's policeman. The role of global policeman was simply too much for one nation to bear, even one as wealthy, productive, and powerful as post–World War II America. It was also expensive beyond belief.

American taxpayers might send their sons to war, but they resented sending their money to Washington to pay for those wars. As a consequence, American politicians maintained the world order not through taxation but by borrowing or simply printing money. Presidents Kennedy and Nixon (like Ronald Reagan two decades later) cut taxes sharply while spending more on defense.

During most of the Bretton Woods era, the United States had troops stationed on five continents. At its height, in Vietnam alone there were 589,000 American soldiers engaged in fighting an unwinnable war with heavy casualties and large material losses. Another 600,000 to 800,000 soldiers, depending on the year, were stationed in other parts of Asia and in Europe, with thousands more sailing the world's oceans on the Navy's six hundred ships. Hundreds of Air Force airplanes and tens of thousands of support personnel were also stationed overseas. Thousands more were stationed at electronic listening posts in Iran, Ethiopia, Turkey, and Australia. Another half-million troops in the United States were regularly rotated abroad. And then there were the reserves.

These troops had to be provisioned, supported, and cared for, and they had to be paid. Supplies had to be sent overseas, bases had to be built, and contractors had to be paid—with dollars.

To support the troops and America's commitments abroad, harbors had to be widened and runways had to be maintained. Roads had to be paved, wells had to be dug, sewer lines had to be laid and electricity had to be generated. Food and fuel had to be purchased, and supplies had to be loaded and stored securely in warehouses located around the world. Defending the world's post–World War II system was a phenomenal undertaking.

American soldiers also had to have dollars to spend when they went on shore leave and on rest-and-recreation leave in Asia and in Europe. They had to have dollars to pay for the postcards, food, cameras, radios, televisions, and stereos they bought, to pay for the entertainment, liquor, gifts, and parties, and to pay for their binges. Every place these dollars were spent they accumulated as slowly growing pools of capital. Every pool fed our competitors' investments in factories, schools, and services. Korea, Singapore, Taiwan, Hong Kong, and even Japan used this capital to fuel their growth. It is no accident that today the United States runs huge annual trade deficits with each one of these countries.

Most of the dollars that went to pay for these expenditures were borrowed or simply manufactured. And if they were manufactured, it was at a rate far faster than the pace of growth in the real economy. With too many dollars being printed, inflationary pressures were starting to appear, and the money economy grew.

By 1971 the cost of the Vietnam War coupled with the continued cost of defending and maintaining the post–World War II economic system had not only strained the American economy but had also transferred billions of gold-backed dollars abroad. So many dollars were printed that by 1965, $100 billion were in foreign hands. European leaders, most notably French President Charles de Gaulle, were beginning to express their concern. By 1965 de Gaulle was arguing that the United States could no longer support the dollar's value with gold. It had became clear to him and a few others that the United States was no longer the prudent, self-disciplined manager the Bretton Woods system demanded. It became clear that it was just a matter of time before the gold dollar collapsed.

THE SEARCH FOR CHEAP LABOR

As the United States pursued its military responsibilities during the 1960s, American business was changing in a way that also undermined the system. Increasingly, companies shifted their production overseas by investing in Europe, Latin America, and Asia to take advantage of cheap labor. While American companies continued to produce about 25 percent of the world's manufactured goods, the share of it produced at home decreased. This meant that when foreigners bought an American product, fewer dollars returned to our shores. Many dollars stayed overseas to pay America's foreign workers. And when an American bought a TV set made by an American company in Taiwan, some money stayed here, but more gold-linked dollars also fled our shores.

According to Seymour Melman, a professor emeritus of industrial engineering at Columbia University and an expert on America's civilian and military economies, during the 1960s "entire industries were exported."

Melman, a soft-spoken man, can also be a fiery debater. Armed with an encyclopedic knowledge of what makes a country industrially competitive, he is also an expert, in particular, on machine tools. Though machine tools—those rather prosaic machines that cut, shape, and form metal—are not the sexiest element in a nation's economy, they are certainly one of the most important. Without machine tools no industrial activity can take place. In a way, the health of a nation's machine tool industry is a gauge of its overall health.

In the 1960s, Melman studied the Soviet Union's machine tool industry. He came away from that encounter thinking that perhaps Nikita Khrushchev, a former premier, was right: Russia would bury the United States. Its machine tool industry was perhaps the most advanced in the world. A report Melman wrote about Russia's industrial might made it to page one of *The New York Times* just prior to Khrushchev's visit to the United States in 1962.

When Melman returned to the Soviet Union, during the days of Mikhail Gorbachev, he found its machine tool industry in ruins. By restricting computers, in an effort to control the country and keep information in the hands of the few, Russia's bureaucrats missed a great leap forward in industrial technology. They missed out on automation and robotics, and doomed their economy. Whereas they had led the world in these bedrock industrial tools in the 1960s, they trailed the rest of the world badly in the 1980s. For Melman the collapse of the Soviet economy came as no surprise. It could be easily discerned in the erosion of its real economy.

But for Melman the damage was not confined to the Soviet Union. The other leader of the post–World War II world, the United States, had also erred badly. In his book, *Profits Without Production,* Melman showed how the American machine tool industry also lost competitiveness. But in our case it was not for lack of computers. Instead, it was because military orders made it much more profitable for American machine tool companies to produce specialized machines for defense work rather than mass-produce them for broader industrial applications. As a consequence, few American companies make robots or truly world-class metal cutting and forming tools. General Motors, Ford, and Chrysler, among the largest consumers of machine tools, have increasingly used products from overseas. Cheaper, more versatile imports have stolen business from American firms. And now, without huge defense budgets to draw on, it is questionable how many American machine tool companies will survive.

Machine tools, along with dozens of other industries, barely exist in America. According to Melman, "The consumer electronics industry, the machine tool business, subway and rail transportation equipment manufacturing, shipbuilding, textiles, and steel-making are all gone." Most of these industries ceased to exist by the mid-1970s as imports became a way of life.

In addition, much of the industry that was left inside the United States shifted its production from civilian goods—products that could be exported to bring back dollars languishing overseas—to the production of more profitable war materials. Ethical questions aside, most weapons were either given away, sold at preferential prices, or limited to NATO or American troops. As a result, even though defense expenditures were huge and exports considerable, these goods rarely earned back much in the way of dollars held overseas. But America continued to build tremendous reserves of capital abroad—money that could be borrowed, often at incredibly low rates of interest.

What were the costs of being the world's policeman? Almost $7 trillion during the Bretton Woods period, according to Melman. Much of that $7 trillion was paid for simply by running the printing presses. (Two trillion dollars of this debt remains outstanding.) What is this immense expenditure equal to in human terms? From the end of World War II until Nixon's resignation in 1973, the "military consumed sufficient resources to more than rebuild everything in the United States that is man-made," said Melman. "That means that the entire industrial infrastructure of the United States could have been rebuilt from the ground up. All the factories, roads, airports, ports, bridges, everything existing today could have been made anew. Imagine the effect this would have had on our nation's competitiveness."

DOLLARS EXPAND OVERSEAS

Foreign holdings of dollars grew remarkably fast. In 1968 foreigners held about $150 billion, although the exact number is difficult to arrive at. And while a good portion of these dollars were simply borrowed or printed, there was still the obligation to redeem them for gold. At that time, $150 billion was equal to about 10 percent of America's total annual income.

These dollars were not the lightweight megabyte dollars of today, either. Thirty-five Bretton Woods dollars bought an ounce of gold: $1,000 bought a Toyota; $5,000 bought the top Mercedes-Benz automobile; and $6,000, the top-of-the-line Cadillac, the world's luxury standard at the time. In most parts of the country you could still buy a nice middle-class home for about $20,000 with a 4 percent or 5 percent mortgage. The typical American earned between $7,000 and $9,000 a year, and each family of four needed only one wage earner to live comfortably.

While foreigners held a huge reserve of cash, the American economy was vaster still and could offer the kinds of products and investments to keep these foreigners buying our products instead of our gold.

But by 1971 foreign holdings of dollars had reached and then exceeded $300 billion. This was enough money to pay the salaries of about half the American workforce for a year, and it was more than the entire nations of Germany and France earned in a year. The trouble was, while foreigners held $300 billion, the United States government had just $14 billion worth of gold buried in its vaults at Fort Knox. For every dollar's worth of gold we had (at $35 to the ounce), they had $22 to redeem. And with the Vietnam War dragging on and confidence in America flag-

ging, foreigners wanted too many of these dollars turned into
gold.

With so many dollars printed to pay for America's commitments abroad as top cop and with so much of industry shifted
abroad, the Bretton Woods system had to come to an end.

Dr. Nixon conceived of his medicine to treat the ailing economy—and convulse the world—entirely in secrecy. Only after
the changes were announced did he even bother to send one of
his top economic advisers, Paul A. Volcker, then a mere under-
secretary of the Treasury, to Europe to explain what he had
done.

Decades of stability were replaced with nanosecond volatility.
Fixed exchange rates were replaced with wildly gyrating rates.
Interest rates rose and fell in seesaw fashion. The prices of most
commodities soared, pulling other prices with them. And a generation later, with no glimmer of discipline remaining, Ronald
Reagan let the remnants of our financial system collapse and
crumble under a mountain of debt.

Many people wonder if Bretton Woods could have been maintained if the war in Vietnam and some other programs had been
paid for by raising taxes instead of by borrowing or just printing
money. The answer to that is most probably yes. The old, stable
Bretton Woods system was designed to last for generations. All
it needed was prudent management to keep rices stable and real
growth high. All it needed was for Presidents Kennedy, Johnson,
and Nixon to be more responsible and to be willing to ask the
American people to pay for the services they were offering the
world. But instead, while spending increased, taxes were low-
ered and the value of the dollar was undermined. The Bretton
Woods system did not collapse of its own deficiencies.

What caused it to collapse? "America had ruined the position
of the dollar as the foundation of the Bretton Woods system,"
said former Chancellor Helmut Schmidt in *The Way It Was: An
Oral History of Finance, 1967–1987*. It did so by "financing the
Vietnam War."

THE END OF MONEY

On August 15, 1971, money—in the old sense, the traditional
sense—was repealed. Dr. Nixon transformed it into something

totally new, a currency without any underlying value whatsoever and without any limitations on the government's (or private sector's) ability to create it. Nixon turned money—traditionally a symbol of real, tangible wealth—into a twisted abstraction.

"The dollar has become a circular argument," said R. David Ranson, Oxford and University of Chicago–trained chief economist of Wainwright Economics in Boston. "It is still a promise to pay. But to pay what to whom?"

That remains a vexing question to this day.

FIVE

STORING VALUE:
Why Megabyte Money Behaves Differently from Gold-backed Money, and Why Economists Fail to Recognize That Fact

Ask those who are familiar with megabyte money what it does best, and they will probably recite a long litany of things: It is an excellent vehicle for making transactions, despite—or perhaps because of—its lack of intrinsic value. It is a superb accounting unit, despite its detachment from the real economy. It can be moved easily and quickly. It can be imprinted magnetically on a computer tape and can be converted from one nation's currency to another's in the slimmest margin of time. It can be traded swiftly on the world's markets and transformed nearly instantly from bonds to stock and even options and futures contracts. It takes up virtually no space, can be counted automatically, and never wears out, rusts, or tarnishes.

But ask them where megabyte money falls short, and they will probably tell you this: Electronic money is a poor storage mechanism for your buying power. To preserve each measure of buying power takes more money each year.

The old gold-backed currencies, with their links to the real economy, were excellent at storing value. That was the function of gold. In boom times or in busts, an ounce of gold could always be counted on to buy a fine man's suit, or so the legend goes.

Not so with these new electronic dollars. Over time, megabyte money always loses buying power.

WHAT IS INFLATION, ANYWAY?

Most economists admit that prices have lost a measure of stability since the new currency came into being. But they blame it on inflation: Too much money chasing too few goods equals rising prices, they say. An old definition of an old bugaboo.

Inflation is certainly part of the problem, but it is not all of it. In fact, most old-guard economists fail to see the link between rising prices—as high as 500 percent since 1971—and our new electronic currencies. Policies suggested by them and undertaken at all levels of government short of bringing on a recession have been unable to break these price increases.

One exception: Richard D. Bartel, a former staff economist of the Joint Economic Committee of Congress, went out on a limb in the spring of 1988 by saying that within this new world order, economists no longer really understand all the causes of inflation. Bartel, who is editor of *Challenge,* the most influential magazine for economists, went so far as to tell a group assembled at the prestigious Levy Economics Institute at Bard College that it is now time to begin studying the causes of inflation anew.

Bartel is a careful, precise, and original thinker with a doctorate from Princeton, a tour in Army intelligence, and a career on Capitol Hill. He told the group, which numbered Wall Street and academic economists including Nobel Laureate James Tobin of Yale (a former economic adviser to John F. Kennedy), that there is currently no theory of inflation adequate to describe its causes and no set of policies sufficient to cure it when it occurs. The old remedies no longer work in this new global economy, he said.

A few economists in academia and on Wall Street are beginning to agree with Bartel. Edward Yardeni, the influential chief economist at C. J. Lawrence in New York, is trying to put together a conceptual model for what he calls the "New Economics."

Yardeni, who studied at Cornell University and received a Ph.D. from Yale University under the guidance of Nobel Laureate Tobin, is trying to reformulate economics to take into account the global nature of markets, currencies, and commerce. His concoction takes as its most basic premise the unity of the world's markets—that is, that a world in which capital can flow freely across borders and between companies is somehow different from the world that went before it. In such a world, where an investor can invest in more than ten thousand companies listed on the exchanges of the twenty largest countries, all with equal ease, and can buy thousands of different international currencies, futures, bond and options products through any large investment firm, the rules have got to be different. In Yardeni's view, inflation, growth, money, and recession must all be rethought.

A GLOBAL SPECULATIVE EXPLOSION

Part of the reason megabyte economy is so different is that so much money changes hands in the world's huge speculative markets each day. The speculative markets now dwarf the "real" markets. For example, Kenichi Ohmae, the economist who heads McKinsey & Company's Tokyo consulting practice, estimates that $20 billion to $25 billion is exchanged every day in the world's foreign currency markets to cover global trade in goods and services.

That huge figure is more than enough to account for all the Toyotas shipped from Japan to the United States and Europe, all the disk drives shipped from San Diego to Tokyo, *and* all the airline seats sold between countries in 1991. It is enough to cover all the grains shipped internationally and all the oil, coal, and ore that is sold in the global markets each day during the same year.

But big as it is, $25 billion is still a small fraction of the $800 billion that changes hands every day in the world's currency markets. Most of the $800 billion in currency that is traded, Ohmae and others think, goes for very short-term speculative investments—from a few hours to a few days to a maximum of a few weeks. It goes for options trading, stock speculation, and trade in interest rates. It also goes for short-term financial arbitrage transactions where an investor buys a product such as bonds or currencies on one exchange in the hopes of selling it at a profit on another exchange, sometimes simultaneously by using electronics.

Against this bulging $800 billion backdrop, the world's real transactions are small indeed. The financial economy, which used to be the tail, is now the dog. And it does a lot of wagging.

Compared to these purely financial transactions, the daily sale of one or two Boeing 747s, a few million barrels of oil, or one or two Cray Supercomputers is peanuts. The sale of these items barely gets a nod from the investors who preside over the world's speculative pools of capital. And though real exports from America have picked up recently, they still total less in a year than what is traded before lunchtime on the world's speculative markets.

DECIDING WHAT'S IMPORTANT

Currency managers who trade dollars for marks and yen each day are looking for return on investment. They want to guard the overall buying power of their portfolios. So the cues they look at first are the purely financial ones: interest rates, the level of the stock, bond, and futures markets, as well as the level of overall debt—government and private.

From their point of view the economy really can be summarized by these numbers. Joblessness, the trade balance, retail sales, sales of machine tools and durable goods—the indicators most old-guard economists use—are important only in the way they affect the markets.

This means, for starters, that the major actors in the global electronic economy are reacting to radically different cues from the rest of us. And since they are by far the nation's (and the world's) biggest economic players, with $20 to $50 (no one knows for sure) in the financial economy for every $1 in the real economy, what they say goes. As a consequence, speculation holds far more sway over each nation's economic livelihood than we generally give it credit for.

Speculation means abrupt change. Money flows quickly into a rising market and just as quickly departs when the market begins to fall. Technology exacerbates the speed of these movements. So do the complicated financial equations most big financial managers now use. Volatility on all of the world's major money, stock, bond, and futures markets is up, and so is skittishness.

These fluctuations add a lot of uncertainty to the world, which is what, after all, speculators trade on. Without volatile markets there could be no speculation. For there to be winners in the speculative markets there have to be losers. For there to be big winners there have to be sharp highs and lows. No investor anymore is content simply with the interest paid on a bond. Investors want to add to that profits from trading. And no investor is content just with stock dividends and a gentle appreciation of an asset. They want (and need) more because, for one, their money buys less. They hope to get greater returns by trading in and out of each product more frequently. And they hope to get more by using newer, more innovative trading strategies. Almost all markets are now driven not so much by investment opportunities—the way they were in the past—as by transaction opportunities.

But the skittishness and uncertainty that comes with playing in these volatile markets is now a way of life even in the real economy. The reason is that the real economy and the speculative economy intersect at several important points. They meet, for example, over interest rates. Interest rate futures, mortgage-backed securities, and Treasury bonds and notes are important speculative products that are traded electronically. But the way these products perform in the speculative markets also affects the real economy's ability to borrow, expand, and adapt to change. The real economy is choked off from growth when interest rates are too high. Volatile interest rates cause real-economy investors such as home and car buyers to think in shorter time frames or to put off purchases entirely. But for the speculator, interest rate volatility represents an opportunity to cash in.

Both economies also meet over exchange rates. Most tangible products are not really made in any one place anymore. Instead, they are assemblages of parts made all over the world. Cars, computers, jet planes—no matter what company produces them—are made with a substantial percentage of imported parts due to the exodus of American factories and capital two decades ago. Rising and falling currency values, driven by the $800-billion-a-day currency market, affect how much these parts cost. Their value fluctuates on a daily basis, and that affects profit margins in the real economy.

And, of course, the two economies meet over stock prices,

bond prices, futures contract prices for financial products and commodities, and sometimes even over options, warrants, and other derivative products. Because the two economies have so many junction points, the uncertainty that goes with speculation has crossed over into the real economy and addled it. Its presence has brought added costs and a general feeling of uneasiness.

PUTTING SPECULATORS ON THE PAYROLL

Large international companies all have speculators on staff, although they don't call them that. General Electric, IBM, General Motors, and other big American and international companies as well, have economists working for them to forecast interest rates. Most of them also have currency traders or contracts with investment firms and banks to act as their currency traders. And some of these companies have traders, who are also strategists, setting up programs to hedge the risks that result from dealing with rapidly fluctuating exchange rates.

To protect themselves, these real-economy companies—manufacturers especially—are forced to deal in the risky world of futures products. They are forced to buy and sell contracts for foreign currencies, for example. And they buy interest rates in the form of futures contracts on government bonds, notes, and mortgages. To prevent sharp dips in their stock prices, some even speculate in options and warrants. As a result, to be a manufacturer you also must be a financial engineer. And you must use the whole menu of new products.

No more can companies leave their money in a bank account to accumulate interest. Each afternoon computers "sweep" those accounts and move that money to where it will earn the best rates.

And no longer do companies simply hold stocks to earn dividends and appreciate. Increasingly, companies from the real economy employ computers to buy and sell portfolios across many markets. As a consequence, they are forced to move with both feet into the finance economy using such techniques as:

Black box, trading that uses mathematical formulas to make investment decisions;

Matrix trading, which continually compares bond yields to stock yields;

Pairs trading, which uses computers to buy one stock and sell another in the same industry short;

Cross trading, where programs analyze the different relationships between different sets of securities;

Straddles, where stocks are simultaneously bought on one exchange and sold on another;

Swaps, where there is a constant switching between short- and long-term bonds. And there are others.

No longer do companies simply keep their outstanding loans. Now they trade them for their interest rates.

No longer do companies simply buy foreign exchange. They trade currencies on the world's money markets and hedge those with contracts for currencies bought on the futures markets.

And no longer do companies simply take out mortgages on land or property or borrow money from big money center banks. Now, increasingly, they go into the credit markets themselves to issue commercial paper—a form of unsecured bond—which is bought by investors who trade that paper with one another.

All these techniques and others have transformed business by making real-economy companies perform more like financial-economy companies. As the line blurs, companies even forget what they are, as when American Can Corporation, the nation's largest maker of containers, transformed itself under the leadership of Jerry Tsai into Primerica, a financial products and insurance company. Or when Ford Motor Company's profits are sustained not by its manufacturing prowess but by the health of its Ford Credit Corporation, which is a big player in the speculative financial markets. Or when General Electric Corporation, one of the nation's leading manufacturers, sells off its consumer electronics subsidiary to concentrate more heavily on building General Electric Credit Corporation into a major financial player. These machinations must make managers wistful for the 1950s and '60s when money, prices, and interest rates were stable.

For a major corporation to concentrate on finance is not necessarily a liability. A lot of money can be made from finance, which in turn can provide resources to the rest of the corporation. But if wages, which have been stagnant for years, are to grow and the United States is to continue as a prosperous country able to compete with the rest of the world, we will have to make certain our real-economy companies also do well. Those companies must do well because that is where the nation's wages are highest, and high wages mean a higher standard of living. It is also where the bulk of America's exports lie.

THE COST OF VOLATILITY

No one really knows how much all this speculative uncertainty costs the real economy, but uncertainty always has a price. Individuals and companies tend to protect themselves against the vagaries of the future by raising prices to cover expected or potential losses. They do not lower prices in the face of uncertainty.

At minimum, the volatility of the electronic economy probably adds a couple of percentage points to the cost of doing business each year. More likely, it has added several percentage points. No one knows for sure. These added costs cycle through the entire economy.

The costs are not static. They increase as volatility increases, and it has been increasing. As a consequence, protecting against global financial uncertainty may be no less expensive than buying insurance to protect against flood, fire, theft, and liability. Just as physical insurance costs continue to escalate, so do the costs of financial insurance in the information age.

This tug-of-war between the real and the speculative economy, while adding costs to the real, garners profits for the speculative. The two are, in a way, in conflict with each other; not always, but usually. And they interact in ways we still do not fully understand.

Are the costs of uncertainty and the costs of international market volatility enough to account for a stubborn underlying inflation rate of 4 percent a year? A rate that will not go away, no matter what policies Congress, the Administration, and the Federal Reserve pursue? Possibly they are. But we still do not know for sure.

PRICE INSTABILITY BECOMES NORMAL

Inflation was built into the new system from its very start. As soon as Dr. Nixon performed his shock therapy, prices began to move and uncertainty began to mount. In many ways the world, two decades later, is still recovering from that blow.

For example, after 1971, the era of stable growth simply came to an end for the United States. Eighteen months after the gold window was shut, American wages, adjusted for inflation, reached their all-time peak. America went from being number two in pay then to number eight now. Productivity increases began to taper off. And since then the average American worker has been losing ground. Family income has gone up, which is the statistic most politicians point to, but it now takes two workers in each family to make that income, whereas in 1971 it took just one. The percentage of families that own their own homes, a crucial indicator of a nation's "real" wealth, has been declining in the United States. The housing affordability index has also taken a tumble.

Prices around the world were affected immediately by the decision to cut the link between gold and money. With $300 billion on deposit in foreign banks suddenly losing a large share of its buying power, prices began to rise to compensate. For governments and individuals alike, the safest way to protect dollar holdings was to invest them in U.S. Treasury bills, bonds, and notes. This made it easier for Congress and the Administration to run big federal deficits. Since these debt instruments were already denominated in dollars, buying them could be done without having to sell dollars for other currencies on the world's exchange markets. Thousands of investors suddenly switching out of dollars, when the link to gold was cut, would have caused the dollar to fall further.

So many dollars were suddenly pursuing Treasury instruments that an entirely new speculative market for them was created in London, New York, and Chicago. Within three years currency futures and futures contracts on Treasury bonds were traded around the world in an effort to absorb those dollars. Overnight, tens of thousands of long-term investors—the kind that invests in dollar-denominated bonds, bills, and notes and holds them for years for safety—were converted into speculators. Today, $150 billion in Treasury bonds is traded every day.

Many of these investors were dumbfounded. In many countries, after all, dollars were held in secrecy and were even illegal; they were used for financial emergencies and were saved in an effort to flee when political repression built up. To these investors the dollar had always been as "good as gold."

But while the world's financial investors were able to preserve a good measure of their buying power, at least initially, by taking advantage of the growing new speculative markets in London and then in Chicago, New York, and elsewhere, real-economy investors saw the value of their holdings plundered. The world's oil producers were probably hurt most by the dollar's drop.

Oil in the early 1970s was traded as a commodity to be used, not speculated in. Oil companies, airlines, shipping companies, chemical manufacturers, and truckers all entered into long-term supply agreements with the producers. Oil traded for about $4 a barrel in 1952, and it traded for about $4 barrel in 1971. You might be able to pick up a deal on the spot market in Rotterdam if a company bought too much oil, but generally, spot prices were not that much different from long-term supply arrangements.

For decades oil was priced in dollars. And when OPEC suddenly saw the value of the dollar fall by 17 percent in a single day, as it did in 1971, it watched its future slip away. For OPEC, shutting the gold window was more than a disaster; it represented the grim possibility that their struggling countries would slip back into poverty. The OPEC countries, which since the organization's founding in 1952 had behaved as rivals, for the first time began acting as a cartel.

In 1973, OPEC voted to continue pricing its product in dollars because the dollar was by far the most plentiful currency and because everyone still believed in the United States. But it quadrupled its prices to $16 a barrel, a significant increase due to the cartel's lost buying power.

With its newfound unity and strength, the cartel continued raising its prices throughout the 1970s. In 1982 oil reached $39 a barrel. And OPEC's unity and success inspired other commodity producers to do the same. The price of bauxite, tin, rubber, coffee, grains, iron, copper, lumber, jute, manganese, gold, platinum, palladium, tungsten, uranium, and every other commodity followed oil's example.

With the cost of all these goods up, the price of manufactured goods and even the price of services also increased. The price of real estate—commercial, private, industrial, farmland, and even mines and timberland—also rose. By the late 1970s the world had seen an overall price increase of roughly 400 percent.

These tremendous price increases altered markets everywhere. Suddenly OPEC was awash in dollars. Suddenly, too, oil was traded as a speculative commodity. The other commodities also began to be traded more speculatively. Tin, tea, coffee, rubber, and bauxite producers established cartels and based them in London. These cartels, which set prices, skewed production. Cash-starved producers sold their commodities outside the markets, and speculation thrived alongside the cartels. Futures markets around the world expanded vigorously. Foreign exchange markets grew as well, and the financial economy began to take off.

All these commodities were (and continue to be) priced in dollars. Dollars were what these producers accumulated. They deposited billions of them in the world's banking system and lent billions more to the U.S. Treasury to finance the debt. Billions more were invested in stocks, bonds, and real estate. These investments contributed to the rapid growth and instability of the financial economy.

By the mid-1970s the $300 billion deposited by the United States overseas had grown to perhaps twice that size. Banks everywhere, flush with petrodollars, had to struggle to find enough big customers to whom they could make big loans. Brazil, Mexico, Argentina, Nigeria, and others were wonderful customers, borrowing hundreds of billions' worth of these "recycled petrodollars," as they were called.

And the banks were only too happy to move the money out the door. If they could not pawn off these loans on someone, they would have to pay interest on all that money, yet get nothing in return.

According to H. Robert Heller—an international economist at Bank of America in San Francisco during the 1970s who went on to become a governor of the Federal Reserve Board and then head of Visa International—just moving that money out the door was an achievement since the sums were so vast. Bankers had to struggle to find clients. Never mind that at least $500 billion of those loans turned sour. Never mind that for a decade the biggest borrowers did not make a single principal payment. Nor, in all likelihood, will they ever.

THE DOLLAR'S GLOBAL ROLE

Dollar lending in the early 1970s became a huge business and the market grew steadily, but not just to countries such as Mexico, Argentina, and Brazil. Soon German and British companies began to borrow dollars and settle their accounts with one another in dollars. Foreign-produced products were even priced in dollars. Intermediate goods—the chips, disk drives, and engines, but not the cars or computers—were priced in dollars.

The dollar market soon became a huge global market. But so many dollars were in circulation that their purchasing power began to fall. As the purchasing price fell, prices continued to rise, and interest rates accompanied them. Rising rates coupled with growing dollar debts began to constrain growth in the real economy.

The Third World fell into recession first and has yet to recover. The advanced countries slipped in and out of recession during the petrodollar years. Recessions in 1974 and 1979, and then again in 1981 and 1982, hurt the real economy, but the financial economy, flush with electronic funds, continued to grow. Wages in the United States may have peaked in 1971, but the stock market continued rising. It was not until about 1990 that the financial economy ran into a wall, and then only in the United States where bankrupt savings and loans, banks, businesses, companies, and individuals caused a curtailment of lending.

Few leaders in the late 1970s and early 1980s realized how much Dr. Nixon's shock treatment affected the world's way of doing business. They were particularly unprepared for the run-up in the price of commodities such as oil and for the inflation and instability that ensued. "What I did not foresee back then was the first oil price explosion," said Germany's former Chancellor Helmut Schmidt. "Oil would never have attained such enormous economic importance if the dollar had not been depreciated."

The world was indeed different following Nixon's action. And as the financial economy grew so much larger than the real economy, volatility was baked into it. Interest rates, overall prices, stock and bond prices, and commodity prices all gyrated terribly along with exchange rates. This provided wonderful opportunities for speculators.

Take the prime rate, the interest rate that banks charge their best corporate customers. It was about 4 percent from the end of the war in 1945 through the end of the 1960s. It was stable and contributed to certainty and a long-term commitment to growth. But after closing the gold window, it began to move as never before:

In 1971 the prime had climbed to about 5 percent; in 1976 it was at 7 percent; at the beginning of 1978 it was up to 8 percent.

Then, by the end of 1978, it was at a 11.75 percent. A year later, in December 1979, it was at 15.25 percent. By December 1980 the prime had climbed to 21 percent before it began to fall to 15.75 in December 1981.

In May 1984 the prime was down to 12.5 percent; in August 1986 it was at 7.5 percent; in February 1989 it was at 11 percent; and in July 1991, 9 percent.

For those speculating in interest rate futures and bonds, there was money to be made on these changes. But for the real investor, it was burned-fingers time. Twice in the 1980s the housing and commercial real estate market collapsed; it is still struggling to recover.

What do these rapidly changing rates represent? Simply that the new electronic dollar retains its value poorly. The institutions that support it and look after the new dollar are having a terrible time keeping it stable. Inflation and instability are both endemic to the new electronic economy. The tremendous disparity between the size and the interests of the real and financial economies suggests that uncertainty, upheaval, and volatility will not soon disappear.

AN UNSTABLE SYSTEM

Hyman Minsky, a senior fellow at the Levy Economics Institute, has been watching the way the electronic economy has been unfolding for years. He was one of the first to write about the new instability.

Minsky, a brilliant thinker with a warm sense of humor, says that the electronic economy has a higher degree of instability built into it than what went before it. That instability is largely the result of the growth of finance. And finance is changing daily, he said. "When I was teaching finance at Washington University," he said in an interview in New York, "I had to revise the course every time I taught it because of all the innovations and new products."

But while the economy may have become unstable, we have

yet to devise policy tools to correctly manage it. And though the government plays a far larger role in the economy than ever before—as a participant in the credit markets, for example—it has very meager resources with which to manage the economy's ups and downs.

In a report to the Twentieth Century Fund, a non-profit research organization in New York, Minsky wrote that "the dynamics of a capitalist economy which has complex, sophisticated, and evolving financial structures leads to the development of conditions conducive to incoherence—to runaway inflation or deep depressions."

Minsky is optimistic that governments will learn how to temper the instability, but so far, he believes, they have not learned how.

CREATING MONEY:
How the Fed Was Set Up to Avoid Banking Failures and Issue Money but Ended Up Losing Power and Influence to the Private Sector

Despite its bluster as the world's most important financial institution, and despite its chairman's monthly appearances before Congress, the Federal Reserve has lost much of its power. Though by no means insignificant, the Fed is an anachronism, an institution better suited to the era of Queen Victoria or Teddy Roosevelt than the world of Cray XMP Supercomputers and global markets. The Fed, whose job it is to control the money supply and, by inference, prices and the economy, was conceptualized during the industrial age, long before the advent of the electronic economy. These days the Fed is hard-pressed to do its job in a world without true borders, where currencies are exchanged on a monumental basis, and where megabyte currencies have been substituted for the old-style brand of lucre.

Megabyte money, which is volatile, no more weighty than a glowing electron, and almost as fast as the speed of light, is a curious invention. It cannot exist without a tremendous array of global institutions to support it. It needs technology, government, and the private banking sector, and it needs commerce. It also needs markets where it can be exchanged from one currency type to another and from one product—stocks, bonds, futures contracts, and so on—to another. It needs an entirely new mathematical lexicon to use when manipulating it and measuring its risk. It needs complicated equations that constantly compare today's buying power with tomorrow's projected costs.

This money comes in only one denomination: vast. Eight hundred billion dollars of it is exchanged each day in the world's currency markets. Fifty billion dollars of it is traded each day in a single futures pit at the Chicago Mercantile Exchange; $150 billion is traded in the bond market each day in New York. Trillions pass through the nation's brokerage houses and bond houses each year.

In New York, CS First Boston, one of the world's leading bond traders, trades more money each year than the entire gross national product of the United States. Salomon Brothers, CRT Government Securities, Goldman Sachs, and Citicorp are not far behind CS First Boston with trillions of dollars passing through their trading rooms as megabyte money is endlessly exchanged.

By coupling global economic models with high-technology communications systems, Japanese and European investment firms buy, on occasion, as much as 40 percent of the long-term debt of the United States government sold at the monthly Treasury auction. Using the same technology and models, American investment firms buy nearly a third of Europe's corporate debt. While government and corporate bonds were once valued investments that were kept until they reached maturity—usually somewhere between ten and thirty years—now investors buy and then resell these bonds after an average of only twenty days.

And yet, in spite of all its fervid activity, money remains a naked symbol with no intrinsic value of its own and no direct linkage to anything specific. It is, as the French economists like to say, merely a "token," a simple game-board piece moved from one file to another in the world's vast computerized database. As a symbol, says R. David Ranson, the British economist who heads Wainwright Economics in Boston, money must maintain its value largely by trading on what people think of it and on how much confidence they have in it. A nation's currency is a lightning rod, so to speak, for all the assumptions people have about the country and how it is managed.

By its very nature this new money is global. It was created

out of the vast ocean of dollars left overseas by the United States
when its biggest exports were its currency, its troops, and its
factories. Its origins were in those $300 billion in foreign-held
funds that were suddenly set free of Washington's control in
1971.

INVENTING THE FED

Money comes into being through a number of different mechanisms. In its crudest form it can simply be printed. In the
United States the printing presses are run under the auspices
of the Federal Reserve Board.

Although it may seem as though the Federal Reserve has been
around since the beginning, it is really a relative newcomer to
government. It was created by Woodrow Wilson in 1913, in the
aftermath of the panic of 1907 when a number of big New York
banks were on the verge of collapse. As word spread about the
precarious position of these banks, depositors rushed to withdraw their funds. Soon there were runs on other banks around
the country that were affiliated with the big New York banking
houses, and then there were runs on all the nation's banks.
Panic engulfed the country.

In those days, long before the Glass-Steagall Banking Act of
1933, when federal deposit insurance first came into being, financial panics were regular occurrences in America, happening
about every twenty years. After each panic new rules governing
banks and money were written, but politics always seemed to
get in the way of effective legislation.

During the panic of 1907 there was actually a shortage of
currency. To get dollars the nation's smaller institutions in the
Midwest, South, and West had to pay a premium price. They
paid that price with gold and silver. In effect that meant the
United States, which was then on the gold standard, had several
different regional currencies, each with a different exchange
rate for gold.

This was not a situation the lawmakers liked very much. The
banking failures were one thing; they could deal with that. The
lawmakers could always patch together some compromise. But
why should some regions of the country fare better than others
when it came to the nation's currency? Why should Kentucky's
tobacco farmers do worse than New York's investment banks

because of unequal exchange rates? Congress decided it needed a better system. So it did what lawmakers in the United States always seem to do when they are faced with a thorny issue: established a commission.

The commission, called fittingly enough the National Monetary Commission, in 1908 recommended the creation of a central bank, and it outlined the ways that bank might work. For the United States of 1908 it was really quite a revolutionary move. The United States was the only advanced country that did not have a central bank. And even when the commission finished its work, most people were still against the idea, fearing a central bank would encumber Congress's ability to act. It took five years of political dickering, but on December 23, 1913, the Federal Reserve System came into being.

The Federal Reserve is a creature of compromise that has been modified over the years by Congress. It is a quasi-private, quasi-public institution with a central board of governors and twelve regional reserve banks, each with a president and a separate charter and each issuing money in concert. Each of these twelve regional banks must see to it that its dollars are worth the same amount as their counterparts' dollars. Seven governors, one of whom is chairman, oversee the entire Federal Reserve System, including the regional banks and their printing presses.

In theory the Federal Reserve is "owned" by the nation's banks. In reality the Fed is the banking system's chief regulator, and it is in charge of everything from check-clearing operations to how much money a bank must keep in its vaults. The president appoints the chairman and the other governors, and Congress must approve the president's choice. A governor is limited to one fourteen-year term, and the chairman assumes office for a renewable four-year term.

That is the quasi-public part.

The quasi-private part is that, once appointed, the Federal Reserve Board chairman acts pretty much on his own. With the governors, the research staff in Washington, and researchers at the twelve regional banks, the Fed determines how much money to print and what to do about interest rates. The Fed may print too much money or too little, it may raise rates too high or bring them down too low, but there is nothing that the president or Congress can do about it. They cannot even audit the Fed.

And that is precisely the way the National Monetary Com-

mission wanted it. The commission wanted to keep politics out
of the decision-making process. The Fed, the commission
thought, is supposed to have enough independence to stand up
to the Administration and to Congress. The tougher the Fed,
the more independent it is, the less likely the possibility of future
panics and bank runs.

THE FED'S FOREMOST JOB

When Andrew Brimmer, a former Federal Reserve governor,
was asked whether the Federal Reserve should lower interest
rates in order to prevent a recession in early 1990, he replied
that the job of the Fed was to maintain stable prices. When
asked if the Federal Reserve did not feel any responsibility for
stopping an economic slowdown by lowering interest rates, he
replied again that the job of the Federal Reserve was to keep
prices stable. His view is echoed by most of the current governors, who really do see themselves as independent of the government. The chairman, however, with a much shorter term
than the other governors, is much more likely to be swayed by
pressure from the White House. This makes for a give and take
at the governors' monthly meeting. Most of the time the chairman wins, but sometimes the governors prevail.

Though the Federal Reserve could probably stop a recession
in its tracks if it moved quickly enough, it has no obligation to
do so. And lately the Fed has occupied itself with other matters
such as trying—but largely failing—to keep prices stable and
to manage the value of the dollar against other currencies.

Previous to the creation of the Federal Reserve, the Treasury
and Congress had some of the powers the Federal Reserve has
now. The system then was not unlike what exists in Britain
where the Bank of England is weak and subject to oversight by
Parliament. If Parliament pressures the Bank of England to
lower interest rates or increase the money supply to stimulate
growth, the bank will in the end be forced to comply.

The independence of the Federal Reserve has infuriated many
in government and in business. In the 1940s and 1950s Wright
Patman, the powerful Texas congressman who was chairman
of the House Banking Committee, was so incensed by the independence of the Fed and its lack of enthusiasm for acting as
a prod to growth that he tried to have the institution abolished.

Having failed at that, he tried to charge the Fed rent since it resides in a building in Washington provided by the federal government. Patman failed at that, too.

More recently, Congress and the Bush Administration publicly pressured Federal Reserve Chairman Alan Greenspan to lower interest rates in 1990 and 1991 so that growth would pick up. There were well-publicized statements by Treasury Secretary Nicholas F. Brady and Michael Boskin, Bush's chairman of Economic Advisers.

Fed Chairman Greenspan hemmed and hawed, but in the end he complied, but only just so, letting interest rates slip ever so slightly after the recession had started in the summer of 1990 and then easing rates down a quarter percentage point at a time over the next year. But Greenspan's tardy response to pressure from the White House was repaid by the Administration when it waited until there was less than a month left to the chairman's term before it announced that he would be reappointed. The Fed's sluggish action was not sufficient to reignite the stumbling economy.

HOW TO CREATE MONEY

For the Fed, creating money is easy enough. Basically, all it has to do is buy Treasury bonds through the New York Federal Reserve Bank, one of its twelve regional banks. When it buys these outstanding bonds, the Fed is putting money into circulation. It can do this by using the cash it has on hand or by issuing credits that are called Federal Reserve Notes, which we call "money." These notes, which are issued in dollar denominations, are technically a form of debt, which is to say obligations to pay. But they are a very odd kind of debt. They have no redemption date.

If the Federal Reserve wants to contract the money supply, it simply runs its machinery backwards. To do that, it sells the bonds it owns in the open market. When investors buy these bonds, they pay for them with money that is then taken out of circulation. As a result, the money supply contracts.

In all its activities the only bonds the Federal Reserve is allowed to deal in are those issued by the Treasury. When the Fed buys or sells securities, it is conducting what are called

Open Market Operations. These operations are overseen by the Federal Open Market Committee, which is composed of the chairman and the board of governors.

The Fed can alter the money supply in other ways, too. It can do this by changing some of its regulations. Most of the time the Federal Reserve requires its member banks to hold an average of just under 12 percent of their deposits in reserve so they will have cash in the event that their depositors need it. The money the banks held in reserve is money that is kept out of circulation. This money must be deposited in a reserve account at the Federal Reserve Board, which pays no interest. Some of the banks' money, however, can be held in the form of certain marketable high-grade securities such as Treasury bonds that pay interest. Either way, the reserve requirements take money out of circulation.

But the Federal Reserve can also decide to change its reserve requirements, if Congress agrees, which will either increase or decrease the supply of money in circulation.

Finally, the Federal Reserve has control over the money supply by controlling various interest rates. The Federal Reserve controls the discount rate, which is the rate of interest charged to the member banks when they borrow money from the Fed. It also indirectly controls the federal funds rate, which is the rate at which banks and the Federal Reserve's own district banks borrow from one another. When the discount rate is lower, banks tend to borrow more money from the Federal Reserve. That indirectly puts more money into circulation since that money is usually lent to consumers.

With the Fed there are really just two levers for creating money: the big lever and the small lever. The big lever is the Federal Reserve's Open Market Operations with its bond buying and selling activities. The little lever is everything else the Fed does, such as altering interest rates.

But the Federal Reserve is no longer the only game in town. Private banks also create money and what is called "near" money. Near money is easy to create: Issue a credit card with, say, a $2,000 credit limit, and you have created $2,000. According to Duncan McDonald, Citibank's chief counsel for its credit card operations, the average credit card Citibank issues has a $2,000 credit line. With 25 million credit cards outstanding, Citibank alone has created $50 billion in so-called near money.

And then there are the 75 million or so credit card holders who do business with smaller banks and credit unions The average credit card holder of one of these cards also has been issued about $2,000 in credit. That equals another $150 billion in near money. Add to this near money the very short-term near money issued by American Express—18 million card holders who can charge an unlimited amount for up to thirty days but then must pay it back in full. That grants billions more in spending power to the nation. There are many types of near money, all of which are private and virtually unregulated except by the forces of the market.

The more traditional way that banks create money is by lending their deposits. For instance, if Bank A receives a $100 deposit, it puts that money in an account. The Fed says that about 12 percent of that money must be kept in a reserve account, although the actual reserve requirement varies depending on the type of account and the size of the bank.

But if the bank must hold 12 percent of its deposits in reserve, it can lend $88 out of every $100 it takes in as deposits. When it does this, the original $100 remains in Bank A's books even though $88 of it now goes to a customer who deposits it in Bank B.

Bank B now has new cash to lend. Because of the 12 percent rule, Bank B can lend only $77, which it usually does. That $77 now goes to Bank C.

After just three transactions the original $100 has grown to $265. Bank A lists $100 on its balance sheet; Bank B lists $88; and Bank C lists $77. If three more of these transactions are completed, the original $100 will grow to a total of $443, and its growth is far from over.

The banking system, which multiplies the number of dollars in circulation as they are lent, does the same to salary checks, payroll checks, mortgage income, and all other forms of money as well. This works because the banking system functions as a whole and because most people need access to just a fraction of their funds each day.

For banks, having money in their vaults is a liability—they have to pay interest on it. For banks, having a loan outstanding is an asset because they receive interest payments on it. As a consequence, it is in the bank's interest to lend money—your money—to someone else as swiftly as possible. And that makes the money supply grow.

SEVEN

THE GLOBAL MONEY-MAKING MACHINE:

When Money-creating Goes International Outside the Control of Governments

There is something quite magical about the way money is created. No other commodity works quite the same way. The money supply grows through use; it expands through debt. The more we lend, the more we have. The more debt there is, the more money there is. And, the argument goes, as long as money expands roughly at the rate it is used, prices remain relatively stable and interest rates can remain low.

Even the Federal Reserve's reserve requirement, which is supposed to serve as an insurance policy against a run on the banks, slows but does not stop the growth of the money supply. As long as money is borrowed from banks, credit unions, savings and loan institutions, or similar institutions, and then lent again, the money supply continues to expand.

In fact, the only way to really shrink the money supply is for the Federal Reserve to sell bonds in the open market, which it can do but only in limited quantities, or for the nation's borrowers to pay off their loans—but not their credit cards. Pay off your credit cards, and you are dealing with near money that is subject to a different set of rules.

Just consider the original $100 that was created by the Federal Reserve and deposited in Bank A, then B, and so on. If all these borrowers suddenly paid back their loans, it would create havoc. All the new money that was created by the banking system— $343 after just six transactions plus the original $100 deposit— would suddenly be extinguished; that money would cease to exist as assets on the banks' books. All that would remain would be the original $100. And if the people who sold bonds to the Fed bought them back, the original $100 would vanish, too. No one would have any money left to purchase anything. If all debts were suddenly repaid, public and private, all commerce would stop for society as a whole. Money, therefore, arises as a consequence of debt. Without a gold or commodity link, money is not a form of equity. It is not even a real asset, like real estate or stock. It is an abstraction.

CREATING MONEY INTERNATIONALLY

There is an international component to this money creation business as well. Remember 1971? Back then, $300 billion was deposited in the international banking system away from America's shores. Most of that money was moved offshore to pay for America's cold war commitments abroad.

That money—$300 billion of it—became the supersaturated solution out of which megabyte money was created. It was the seed capital, if you will, that led to the creation of an autonomous money supply largely outside the Federal Reserve's control. Those expatriate dollars were named Eurodollars because most of them were deposited in European banks or in the European branches of American and Japanese banks. Though Eurodollars were related to their domestic cousins, they generally preferred living overseas. And while these dollars could purchase American products without having to undergo any type of change— unlike German marks which must be converted into dollars before they can purchase a New York apartment or a Cadillac Seville—most Eurodollars have been employed solely as a means of funding international purchases. Trade between big international companies, even when the companies are not American, is most often conducted in Eurodollars. So is trade in commodities such as oil, coffee, gold, tin, silver, and the like.

For more than two decades these $300 billion in Eurodollars have been dancing from bank to bank. They have been lent and relent and lent yet again. Ford of Europe often borrows these stateless dollars when it issues its corporate bonds. So does Volkswagen, IBM, General Motors, Daimler-Benz, Phillips, Unilever, Exxon, Royal Dutch Shell, and almost every other global company in need of cash.

Governments of various countries have been borrowing these funds as well. The Netherlands and France have each issued bonds denominated in Eurodollars. So has Spain, Portugal, and even the Soviet Union. The World Bank borrows in the Eurodollar market, and so do the developing countries it lends to, such as Argentina, Mexico, and Brazil. Eurolending—a misnomer since Eurodollars have long ago ceased to reside just in Europe—has been growing rapidly for two decades. Eurodollars, which have never been a physical paper or metal currency but an electronic one, have been growing as well.

Although this money conforms to the same rules of money creation and growth that governs Bank A, Bank B, and Bank C, there is a difference. Until 1987 these stateless dollars represented an autonomous form of money that was completely controlled by the private sector. No single government regulated them in international transactions. As a result, these dollars were far less fettered than their domestic cousins. For example, there were no reserve requirements for Eurodollars. (In some countries this is still the case.) Until 1987, in almost every country, a bank dealing in Eurodollars could lend 100 percent of the dollars it had on deposit. Without a reserve requirement, these funds could grow faster than their domestic rivals. Because they grew in such easy conditions for so long, the original $300 billion is now believed to be worth about $1.5 trillion or perhaps even as much as $2 trillion. In addition, two decades' worth of big American trade deficits—especially huge during the Reagan years—sent tons of new dollars overseas.

LOSING TRACK OF THE DOLLAR

According to Robert Brittan, an international economist at Salomon Brothers in New York who specializes in the dollar markets, there is no longer any way to measure how much money there is in the world. Nor is there really any way to define it. The old definitions of money such as M1 (all currency and all transaction deposits, like checking and NOW accounts), M2 (which is M1 plus savings accounts, overnight repurchase agreements, and overnight Eurodollar deposits held by American residents), and M3 (which is M2 plus large time deposits and certain money market accounts) have become meaningless, he says. Add to this meaningless mire the near monies, the very short-term near monies, and the new near-money products such as home equity lines of credit. Then add to the mix quasi-banking actions of the so-called non-banking financial institutions such as General Electric Credit Corporation which lends to individuals and businesses by borrowing money domestically and internationally in the world's credit markets. Then add the effect of taking domestic credit products, such as home mortgages, and selling them overseas. And then add to all this the effect on the money supply of the world's financial markets. It soon becomes clear that calculating how much money exists is nearly impossible.

Not only can't we define and measure the size of the money supply, we also can't measure the number of times each dollar turns over each year. This figure, which is called velocity, is part of what Brittan calls the overall measurement problem.

Measurement problem or not, the Eurodollar market is huge. But it is not the only Euromarket out there. Since 1971, billions of yen, marks, and pounds have also become stateless Euro-currencies. So vast is this money market that companies can now borrow freely in any currency they want from locations anywhere in the world.

FITTING THE FED INTO THE MIX

The Federal Reserve still figures into this global mix of international monies. But the Fed's power is much diminished, not just over the size of the money supply—the big lever—but over the small levers as well. Consider, for example, how many bonds the Fed would have to sell to lop off $500 billion from the domestic and Eurodollar money supply. But if the remaining money is lent and relent, that $500 billion that the Fed siphoned off would soon be replaced as the world's banks conduct their lending operations. And even if the Fed did attempt to bring those bonds to market in an earnest effort to shrink the size of the money supply, could it really sell so many bonds? And what interest rate would the Fed have to offer in order to clear that much money out of the world's financial system? Rates would have to be high enough to draw money away from banks and from other investments. Terms would have to be attractive enough to entice investors away from other investments such as mortgages. If the Fed attempted to clear the system of its excess money, it would have a very considerable task ahead of it, one that is probably far beyond its capacities.

Of course, the Federal Reserve along with its counterparts around the world could impose tough regulations on the world's banking system. It could require tougher reserve requirements and stiffer capital requirements for banks. The world's central bankers could together attempt to exercise control. But it took sixteen years, until December 1987, for the Fed and its counterparts to impose any reserve and capital requirements on the Eurodollar market. That is when the world's central bankers met at the Bank for International Settlements in Basel and agreed on global reserve standards. It is unlikely that without some major financial disaster these bankers would assemble once again in an effort to tighten the reins. But if they did, it is unlikely that the world's central bankers even together have enough power to go against the wishes of this vast private market.

After all, how much can the Fed and its counterparts around the world do now to control the value of the dollar against other currencies? Not very much. The bankers can meet, they can be photographed together, and they can talk tough, but even together they no longer have the wherewithal to go against the wishes of a foreign exchange market that trades $800 billion a day. Nor can their bond sales make much of a dent when the world trades $150 billion a day in Treasury bonds in New York alone.

Allen Meltzer probably knows more about the Fed than any other economist. Meltzer, a professor of economics at the University of Pittsburgh, is a monetarist's monetarist. He believes that the quality of money determines prices—period. Meltzer is also chairman of the Shadow Fed, a quirky group if ever there was one. The Shadow Fed is made up of economists from academia and from banking. Jerry Jordan, who is now a governor of the real Fed, was a member of the shadow group when he was chief economist at First Interstate Bankcorp of California.

Mickey Levy, chief economist at CRT Government Securities, is also a member of the Shadow Fed, along with a number of academics.

Around the time that the real Fed's Open Market Committee meets to determine whether to raise or lower interest rates and whether to increase or decrease the amount of money in circulation, the Shadow Fed meets to discuss these same questions. Both meetings usually take place in Washington, D.C. The real Fed meets in secret and does not release its notes for a month. That keeps Wall Street, the banks, and the world's financial markets guessing as to what will happen next in the economy. The theory behind the Fed's secrecy is that if the minutes were distributed immediately, business and investment activity would slow down prior to the release of those notes, especially if word leaked out that the Fed was discussing a shift in interest rates. For a number of reasons, that theory is flawed.

The Shadow Fed, which has no power, releases its notes immediately.

Like Civil War reenactors, the Shadow Fed's committee fights the same battles as the Fed, and it does so by interpreting the same data that the real Fed interprets. It looks at interest rates, money in circulation, the velocity with which that money turns over, the behavior of the markets, price stability, and a wide array of related information such as unemployment, factory orders, consumer debt, automobile sales, housing starts, and so on. And, perhaps most important, the Shadow Fed looks at these indicators from a politically neutral perspective, a luxury stemming from its utter lack of power.

For more than twenty years the shadow group has been meeting and conducting its exercise. Those meetings have given it an enormous amount of experience.

Meltzer, who has been with the Shadow Fed since its founding, also knows about the world's other central banks. In his view, even if all the world's central bankers joined in, they could only muster a fraction of the $800 billion the private markets trade each day—hardly enough to change the direction of the flow. And coordinating actions among banks would be tough since each bank has its own agenda and is working for its own nation's ends. For example, in the first quarter of 1992, Germany's Bundesbank raised its interest rates despite pleadings from Treasury Secretary Nicholas F. Brady, Secretary of State

James A. Baker III, and the finance ministers of France, Britain, and Sweden. Germany was worried about inflation, whereas the other countries were worried about recession.

But if the world's central bankers were able to pull together, they could trade only about $14 billion a day, Meltzer says. And they would have to risk losing that money, just as the private traders do. If they rushed to create new money to pay for their losses, they would run the risk of pushing up prices.

Central bankers are politicians. They are appointed by parliaments and congresses. They answer to presidents and prime ministers. If they lost the $14 billion they were capable of trading, they would have to justify that loss to their masters. And while they explained their losses, the market would continue trading, just as it does every day. As a result, central banks, though not as powerless as the Shadow Fed, certainly have their limitations. The greatest of these limitations, according to Meltzer, is that they are not nearly powerful enough to go against the will of the market.

But what if the Fed joined with not just the world's other central bankers but also with the mighty U.S. Treasury Department? That would still not give the Fed enough clout to move the markets, Meltzer says. Money moves the markets—$800 billion a day. The Treasury, though full of puff and policy, just does not have enough of the stuff. The government's resources are just too meager to move the gigantic global money markets. Meltzer estimates the Treasury has on hand a mere $100 million to $300 million, a couple of drops compared to the ocean of funds controlled by the electronic traders.

DIMINISHED GOVERNMENTS

Although the Federal Reserve can still raise or lower short-term interest rates, it is increasingly powerless to affect longer-term rates that are set by the markets. It can alter the rules of banking and stiffen or relax some regulations, but only providing Congress agrees and the banks do not simply take their business offshore to a location where the rules are more hospitable. The Fed can still force ailing banks to merge, and it can make emergency loans to keep weak banks afloat. And of course it continues to have moral authority. But as an institution, as a central bank,

the Fed is not the powerhouse it once was. Money has long ago
lurched away from its control.

But not all the world's central bankers really understand this
message, at least that is what former German Chancellor Helmut
Schmidt thinks. "All central banks in the world have underes-
timated a number of new developments," Schmidt said. "Number one, they did not see that they were losing their grip over
the markets when they allowed commercial banks to establish
offshore affiliates. Second, they did not detect that the so-called
recycling of petrodollars, only to roll over the credits every three
months, was building up what nowadays is called the debt crisis.
Third, they did not observe and prevent all these new financial
instruments from coming about which nowadays have made the
international financial markets almost uncontrollable. In the
fourth place, despite what they think of one another, they are
not really cooperating closely enough to prevent the internation-
alization of financial flows without an international controlling
agency. Nowadays you have one worldwide stock exchange. Nobody is controlling it. You have one worldwide money market.
Nobody is controlling it. The central banks are still living in the
world of the 1970s, some in the 1960s," he said.

THE ELECTRONIC COMMONS

What has replaced the Federal Reserve is a vast electronic banking "commons" that, though seeded by America's initial dollar
"contribution" of $300 billion, is now highly independent and
autonomous. These funds go where they are needed and roam
the world constantly. They move across markets and are transformed from one product to another. This vast electronic commons has "become the world's central bank," said Madis Senner,
a dollar trader at Chase Manhattan Bank in New York.

This is not money as we knew it. Megabyte money, on the
electronic standard, is, as the French say, a token or a marker.
It may start the morning as dollars, travel through the exchange
markets of London to emerge as German marks by midday, and
wind up in the afternoon in Chicago as an option contract on
an index of five hundred stocks. What determines what this
money becomes is the rate of return it can pay to its owner.
Trillions of these tokens are circulating through the world's elec-

tronic commons day and night, and they are undergoing trans-
formations on a grand scale.

In a sense, all that we are really dealing with is an abstract
concept called "buying power." Instruments—dollars, yen,
marks, stocks, bonds, and the like—are methods for accumulating, storing, and manipulating that buying power. Computers,
stuffed with programs that are in turn filled with complex mathematical equations—some of which have won Nobel Prizes for
their creators—tell the traders where to move their tokens to
get the greatest rate of return. The traders follow the computers'
advice by moving their tokens onto squares of buying power that
either expand or contract. Interest rates are one important de-
terminant of where the computers say to move the money. Arbitrage opportunities—which means the profit that can be made
by buying a product on one exchange and then selling it, perhaps
even simultaneously, on another exchange—is another deter-
minant. Other trading opportunities also determine where to
move the token.

According to Robert Brittan of Salomon Brothers, it is the
technology, which includes the software as well as the computers, that drives profits in these markets.

Trillions and trillions of dollars, marks, yen, and pounds travel
through the electronic commons every day in a never-ending
dance of changing forms. All of this money is seeking just one
thing: to increase its buying power, to fight against the entropy
of finance, which is to say, the tendency of megabyte currencies
to lose their purchasing power.

THE NEW INDICATORS

With all these dollars in circulation, what determines their
value? "The key indicators I look at," said Wainwright Economics's R. David Ranson, "are confidence and interest rates. The
price of money, in other words." It is a strange system that
Nixon's action has created, when interest rates determine the
value of the dollar instead of the other way around.

But that is the system that we now have. Indeed, it is the only
system we could have when the size of the finance economy—
and its need for big returns—has grown so much larger than
the real economy. And it is the only system we could have when
the rate of borrowing and the actions of the private banking

system, virtually alone, determine how fast the money supply grows.

If interest rates, along with confidence in America as a whole, are the main valuators of the dollar, what does this imply about, for example, the price of commodities? According to Graciella Chilchiniski, a professor of economics at Columbia University who has built a mathematical model of world oil demand, interest rates—not demand—now determine the price of oil and other commodities as well.

Interest rates determine oil prices "because investors need a rate of return for their oil investments that is comparable to the rate of return they will get from simply putting their money in a financial investment of one kind or another," Chilchiniski said in an interview in New York. "If they get a better rate of return from lending money to companies than from exploring for oil, the oil will just stay in the ground or its price will rise so it becomes as attractive an investment as the ones in the financial sector."

By abandoning gold, Nixon enlarged the size of the finance economy by several orders of magnitude. He also moved the world onto a new standard: the interest rate standard. From that point of view all investment, finance and real, has a single benchmark: interest rates. And all investors have one simple goal: to earn more than the cost of money.

In high interest rate countries—the United States, Canada, and Britain—companies have been forced to abandon long-term, lower-rate-of-return investments, such as manufacturing, in favor of finance to get sufficient returns. In low interest rate countries, such as Germany and Japan, manufacturing and the production of real goods still deliver a sufficient rate of return. And while low interest rate countries have factories that produce goods, high interest rate countries, such as the United States, are left only with debt.

EIGHT

THE ELECTRONIC ECONOMY GOES HAYWIRE:

When an Information Overload Caused the Single World Market to Collapse with Trillions in Losses but Few People Hurt

No one likes to remember October 19, 1987. In fact, according to Amatai Etzioni, a sociologist at American University, people have a predisposition to forgetting unpleasant events, especially when they are also inexplicable. For Etzioni, people will not allow themselves to focus on an event like Black Monday until it is repeated at least once more. No matter that billions of dollars were lost, Etzioni testified before Congress, people cannot face the truth about market instability and risk until the events are reinforced.

That conclusion is as unfortunate as it is sobering. The reason it is unfortunate is that the new electronic economy is not only exceptionally complex and responsive, but it is also prone to volatility. The electronic economy is, if you will, temperamentally high-strung. It is an economy that is "in progress" rather than complete, an economy whose markets—according to Lawrence H. Summers, chief economist at the World Bank in Washington—work too well and cost too much. But it is an economy that in some respects is also surprisingly forgiving.

The world at large caught its first glimpse of the new economy the day the international stock markets crashed together in a chaotic and monumental destruction of wealth. On that day,

October 19, 1987, the New York Stock Exchange's Dow Jones Industrial Average plunged 508 points, from a high of about 2,247. On a percentage basis it fell 22.6 percent, twice as far as the crash of October 1929. The drop occurred when millions of stockholders around the world panicked. With the aid of the latest technology, money managers traded more than 600 million shares on the Big Board alone, seriously taxing the limits of the exchange and its participants.

COMPUTERS AND WALL STREET

The volume of 600 million shares—more than 90 million shares an hour—was sixty times greater than when computers first moved onto Wall Street at the urging of the SEC. The SEC was then investigating what happened on May 28, 1962, when, in a single day, the New York Stock Exchange fell by an astonishing thirty-five points, a loss of 6.68 percent in the value of the nation's most important companies.

The selling took place that day, according to *The New York Times*, because President Kennedy called the leaders of the steel industry to the White House and told them not to raise their prices. Investors were worried that a cap on prices would hurt profits.

The SEC concluded that stocks fell so far in part because the Big Board lacked sufficient technology to match buyers and sellers in a timely enough fashion. Sell orders came in, principally by telephone and telex, but the specialists on the floor of the exchange could not process these orders fast enough by hand. They needed a way to speed up their operations so the SEC instructed the exchanges to buy computers.

Interestingly, the SEC in its report recognized the possibility that computers not only would be able to speed up the paperwork but would someday do the trades. The futurists at the SEC in 1962 envisioned networks of computers linked together sometime in the distant future.

In 1964 the first of the computers arrived at the exchange. They were big, lumbering beasts constructed by the Burroughs Corporation (now part of Unisys Inc.), and they filled a room. Their diets were punch cards. And though they were sitting at the heart of the Big Board, they may as well have been a million miles away from the rest of the earth. Computers in those days could not talk to one another; modems had not been invented yet, nor the codes by which they talk. Most state-of-the-art PCs today have more power and speed than that first stock exchange system did. And, of course, PCs today are thousands of times cheaper than the old electronic beasts.

Aside from the addition of these new number-crunching behemoths, no changes in the stock market were sought by the SEC. It was a little like replacing a two-lane country road with a six-lane freeway. But the freeway was installed while the old rules governing the country road remained in force. And this new freeway was still policed by a single cop on a motorcycle—the SEC. There was no highway patrol.

By the time the October 19, 1987, crash occurred, the Big Board, the American Stock Exchange, the National Association of Securities Dealers, and the futures markets were all highly automated and very efficient. Their basements were filled with a dazzling array of the newest equipment, all of whose components could talk to one another (Unisys still the dominant supplier). The exchanges also had computers at other locations in Manhattan, in Brooklyn, and on Long Island. Backup systems were in place for security reasons at secret locations elsewhere. This equipment could communicate with the world at large. It had a voracious appetite for numbers. It was exceedingly fast.

ADVANCED COMPUTERS AT THE EXCHANGES

But on October 19, 1987, *despite* advanced technology, investors in the New York Stock Exchange lost more than $500 billion, $90 billion an hour of wealth and buying power was extinguished, in part due to the disparity between the capability of the technology and the antiquated rules governing their use.

The next chaotic day, however, while the regulators in Washington and New York dithered over what to do, the markets made back 5.33 percent. Buyers, principally from overseas, rushed in to scoop up values in the quality stocks, *The New York Times* said.

Then, on October 21, the Big Board made back another 9.10 percent. Prices rose because news spread that interest rates around the world were coming down. Falling rates would give the world economy enough bounce, government leaders hoped, to compensate for the losses in the stock market. Falling rates also signaled a possible jump in inflation.

For investors who had temporarily parked their money after the crash in safe money market accounts, lower interest rates and the threat of inflation meant their yields would go down. As a result, investors took their money out of hiding and nervously bought stocks; for the second day in a row prices rose.

But by the end of the week chaos had returned. Prices fell 3.92 percent on Thursday, October 22, and then rose 4.49 percent on Friday. The following Monday, October 26, prices fell by 8.26 percent, the third largest drop since the end of World War II. It was an especially gloomy period with incredible changes in the value of the nation's most important corporate assets. These changes had nothing to do with how the companies actually performed.

If measured from the height of the bull market in August 1987, investors lost a little over $1 trillion on the New York Stock Exchange in a little more than two months. That loss was equal to an eighth of the value of everything that is man-made in the United States, including all homes, factories, office buildings, roads, and improved real estate. It is a loss of such enormous magnitude that it boggles the mind. One trillion dollars could feed the entire world for two years, raise the Third World from abject poverty to the middle class. It could purchase one thousand nuclear aircraft carriers. It is a third of all the money Americans have in the bank.

These big price fluctuations continued through the end of the year. The volatility of the markets drove smaller investors out of stocks and into safer, more reliable investments such as Treasury bonds and certificates of deposits. As a consequence, now more than 60 percent of the shares traded on the Big Board are owned by institutions. These technology-laden institutions, pressed to make profits ever more quickly, will add even more to the global economy's volatility.

INFORMATION OVERLOAD

Never before had the value of stocks fallen so quickly or so deeply. Nor could it have. The events of October 19 required that investors be wired together in a jittery electronic syncopation. The events that day also required the easy flow of information to spread the panic.

The links between the players were nervous. Thirty- and forty-year-old American MBAs were managing billion-dollar portfolios of mutual fund money. They were too young to have experienced any of the previous crashes either before or after World War II. They had no frame of reference when their colleagues began to panic. They had no experience with sudden jumps in volume, either. They had little to look back on but slowly rising markets.

Japanese investors were wired into the chaos as well. And they also had little experience with volatility. Furthermore, they were working for extraordinarily conservative banks and insurance funds in Tokyo. They were the first to panic.

The Europeans who managed big money and pension funds in London and Paris had the most experience with chaos. Some of them had weathered the dollar wars of the 1960s and 1970s, and some of them had technology superior to their colleagues in Japan and the United States, which enabled them to forecast prices better. They were also the most global in their outlook. Nevertheless, they watched the volume of sell orders mount, and they, too, panicked.

Information of all kinds was overloading the system. And the new ease of executing orders from anywhere in the world meant that when the market began to break, it broke from everywhere. No stockholders, wherever they might be located in this world, were exempt from the news that the sky was falling. Information on this event was as plentiful as it was when the space shuttle Challenger exploded in midair with astronauts aboard. Everyone everywhere knew what was happening within minutes.

But the collapse of the Big Board on October 19 was just one of several crashes that happened that day. Aside from Tokyo, where the Nikkei index dipped less than the other stock exchanges—it fell only about 9 percent—the crash was truly a global event. In London the stock market lost almost a third of its value. In Singapore it lost more than half of its value. The Hong Kong market went down by 50 percent. Paris lost a third of its value, as did Amsterdam. And there were other casualties as well. Around the world, trillions of dollars were lost.

1987 DID NOT EQUAL 1929

These losses, big as they were, all occurred in the fluid world of the electronic economy. Yes, trillions of dollars were lost worldwide in a few hours. But in reality this crash was different from 1929. During the 1929 crash, thousands of investors were wiped out. Some of the biggest brokerage firms closed. What followed were suicides, a depression, and finally a world war.

But in the 1987 crash, with a plunge twice as great as the 1929 debacle, relatively few people were hurt. Some were stunned, yes. Some were bruised, perhaps. But really hurt? No. And there was only one suicide, and it was only tangentially related to the drop.

While the traders may have had no experience in dealing with these record volumes, the leaders of the world's central banks were older and wiser. They came to their jobs armed with sharp memories of the Great Depression and the havoc it wrought. Megabyte money was lost, so these men—the world's central bankers—created new megabyte money to fill the void.

Within a year the stock market had regained almost all its lost ground, not just here but abroad as well. Within a year volume in New York had returned, not to the 600-million-share level but to a comfortable 150-million- to 200-million-a-day range. Within two years the markets had sailed above their previous highs, poised—sorry to say—for future falls. Within two years the $1 trillion that had been lost during the crash was once again circulating through the global electronic grid. Within three years—because fresh new money was buying musty old stocks—the book of who owns what in America had to be rewritten.

THE BRADY COMMISSION'S ERROR

The technology in October 1987 was good, and it worked almost flawlessly. More than 90 percent of the trades that were executed were correct. The computers ensured that the paperwork, which by law must track each trade, was complete as well. The right papers were filed, delayed only by the sheer volume.

Just as in 1962, when a special SEC panel investigated the May crash, a panel was set up to investigate what occurred in October 1987. The panel, officially called the Presidential Task

Force on Market Mechanisms, was headed by Nicholas F. Brady, now Treasury secretary, then chairman of Dillon Read & Company, a white-shoe Wall Street investment firm with clients such as AT&T. The panel became known as the Brady Commission.

Like the 1962 report, the Brady Commission advocated more technology. It said that the computers ought to be enhanced. The problem in 1987 was still the same one as before—matching sellers and buyers. Another problem, the report said, was that all the nation's markets were now linked so that there was only one market.

But here the Brady Commission made a fundamental error. It is not just the American markets that are linked, but all markets everywhere. This is even more prevalent today than in 1987. Someone with a PC who has paid the right fees and gotten the right passwords can buy and sell almost anything anywhere. That person, with a satellite dish on his roof the size of a medium pizza, can command the movement of billions of dollars in futures contracts for gold, silver, hog bellies, eggs, or options on interest rates. With that satellite dish the same trader can buy in Chicago and sell in Zurich, Hong Kong, London, or Tokyo.

DANGEROUS ANACHRONISMS

The Brady Commission also uncovered some problems in the market system that have inhibited the development of a truly electronic grid. And they have caused the system to veer toward volatility and chaos.

Two especially dangerous anachronisms were in the system in 1987, and they remain there today. These anachronisms inhibit the smooth functioning of the market and add to the potential for a rapid market break.

One anachronism, which was technological, was referred to only tangentially in the Brady report. The other, which was structural, was faced head-on but without any real recommendations.

The technological anachronism is the telephone. Aside from Charles Schwab & Company and its buy-sell PC program called the Equalizer, which links about twenty thousand users to the company's headquarters in San Francisco by modem, the bulk of America's 51 million individual stockholders still use the telephone.

While it is true that the telephone is the basis of almost all the other telecommunications technologies, voice communication within the global grid is simply outmoded. It is just too slow. Voice transmission can carry only about 16 bits of information a second over the nation's fiber-optic lines. This means that during the frenzy of a trading day, voice communication can send only the amount of information contained in about four medium-sized words each second. Unless those words come from someone of very great importance, they take up too much space in the electromagnetic spectrum and too much of a trader's time. As a consequence, on October 19, those messages were ignored.

By contrast, a computer with a modem can send anywhere from ten to one hundred to one thousand times more information each second, depending on how the technology is configured. In the fast-paced environment of the electronic economy, with relevant information coming from all over the world, it is necessary to have that much capacity.

Not only that, but telephones can create tremendous bottlenecks. Traders at their desks looking at information displayed (and continuously updated) on a screen can monitor dozens of portfolios at once. They can monitor news and information reports from around the world. They can also run expert system programs to help them sort through the information until they get at the relevant facts. And traders can click their mice, tap their terminals, or press keys to get orders moved along.

But a broker on the telephone is tied up with one customer at a time—perhaps two or possibly three if he dares press the hold button. That is the nature of the medium. As a result, a customer who uses the telephone to sell 1 share of stock can occupy almost as much of a broker's time—perhaps even more— as a customer who wants to sell 30,099 shares of stock directly through the Big Board's super dot system. This may not be too crucial on a day when the volume of shares traded is light, but when the world is ending—as it did on October 19—it makes a considerable difference. And, of course, computers don't ask one another about the weather, how their kids are doing, or whether they're free for lunch. They just crunch numbers.

This little anachronism—the one-conversation-at-a-time telephone—made it so that individual investors could not reach their brokers. (Why would a broker want to talk to a small investor

trying to make a deal on three shares of stock?) It also made it
so brokers couldn't reach their own people on the floor of the
exchanges. At Charles Schwab it was nearly impossible to get
someone on the line to place an order on October 19, 1987. As
a result, brokers were sued by clients over their losses that day.

But Schwab's customers who used the Equalizer program got
through to the trading desk in San Francisco without any problems. Their trades were executed even though the law requires
that every computer trade be checked by a human eye to make
sure the investor is who he says he is. But with computers, the
people at Schwab's electronic trading desk could receive an order
electronically on their screen, call up the client's electronic file,
determine whether the order was legitimate from the data in
the file, and send the order to New York—all in seconds, far
less time than it takes by phone. And they could work on more
than one order at a time.

Slow telephones impeded the work on the exchange. Because
of the lags, some small investors who telephoned on the morning
of October 19 did not learn what happened to their orders until
the next day. As a result, most individuals lost track of the value
of their holdings. The worth of their retirement accounts, savings, and investments was unknown. Although they tried to sell
a stock at, say, $10, because of the long delays they had no idea
what the stock actually went for. They were, in effect, selling
blind.

If computers and modems were substituted for the telephone,
at least on heavy-volume days, the market would work much
smoother and with fewer people selling out of panic. More orders
could be processed, more small orders could be batched together
into larger trades, and the buyers and sellers could be matched
more efficiently.

OUTMODED SPECIALISTS

There was another anachronism: the so-called specialist or market maker system. Specialist firms are a remnant from the dim-
mest days of Wall Street's past. They go back to the exchange's
beginning in 1792 and are almost completely out of place in a
high-volume electronic market. Even the 1962 SEC report foresaw that specialists could be replaced.

In fact, these firms often stand in the way of a fully computerized system for buying and selling stocks. Getting around the specialists is one reason entrepreneurs are starting their own all-electronic exchanges. It is also a reason that the Big Board's after-hours trading will be electronic and direct.

Specialist firms are the Big Board's intermediaries. They are licensed middlemen who "make markets," as the terminology goes. They buy stocks that are falling, hold them a few hours or at most a few days, and sell them as prices begin to rise. They are not brokers, nor are they interested in maintaining an inventory of stocks as an investment. They are traders eager to profit on the price disparity between buyers and sellers on any given day. They are traders who, every day, want to sell everything that they bought. In a technical sense they are buffers.

By moving in between buyers and sellers and holding stocks for the very short term, specialists are supposed to keep prices orderly. Having a middleman with cash means that stocks are less likely to collapse—unless the company is folding. Falling stocks, to the specialist, means that an opportunity exists to make a killing later in the day. These firms are licensed to make markets in just one or two companies at a time, and that is all they buy. But every day they buy all or nearly all the shares offered for sale in excess of what ordinary investors demand.

In the old days, before the electronic market, specialists could keep prices from falling too fast or rising too high. But they took on a great deal of risk for themselves in the process (and stood to make big gains as well). But in the potentially more volatile electronic age, when in a single day far more shares can change hands than was possible in the past, specialists take on a greater risk. They need huge lines of credit to make their purchases and cover themselves should volume increase.

On October 19 the specialists quickly became overwhelmed. There were plenty of sellers but no buyers. To hold the market steady the specialist firms had to come up with tremendous reserves of cash to buy all the shares that were for sale. They could not do this because the banks cut off their lines of credit. As a result, for several periods of time on October 19 certain stocks had no buyers. None at all. The buffers collapsed.

Specialists worked fine when volumes were small, but when the system was being upgraded to handle 1 billion shares, there was no way they could do anything but give the market a false sense of security. Even so, during the crash of 1987 some specialists simply refused to buy stocks. They were in business to make money, not commit suicide. If that was the case, why did they deserve their privileged position of licensed intermediary? Why were they authorized to take their seats on the floor of the exchange? Why were they given a position that required almost all trades to go through them?

If electronic markets were allowed to move freely, unfettered by the specialists, the software available could quell volatility. At each moment of the trading day (and night) investors could get the true price for the stocks they wanted to buy or sell without a middleman intervening. Technology has superseded the specialists.

NINE

ADVENTURES IN CYBERSPACE:
Why the Crash of October 19, 1987, Was Different from Anything That Preceded It

L et's look deeper at the October 19 stock market crash. Many people have tried to explain it away by calling it just another example of Wall Street's excesses—a replay of 1929, the old-guard thinkers said. Something that a few new rules from Congress can fix. There was nothing especially significant about the crash, in some people's view, just greed clashing with a weak economy. Thank God the 1980s are over. "It was simply a correction," President Reagan said about the 508-point dip as he walked to his helicopter that day.

But the events of October 1987 hint at something quite different: a change in the way the world is organized. And most of the commentators discussing the significance of Black Monday, as it was later called, missed the point. Black Monday did not happen in the day-to-day, nuts-and-bolts economy we are most familiar with. It happened in electronic space. It was a quiver in the information sphere.

October 19 remains significant for a number of reasons.

First, though deeper than the 1929 crash, it was not followed by a Great Depression. At least not so far.

Second, although there was a tremendous loss of wealth,

greater than had ever occurred before, it is hard to find people who really suffered.

True, individual investors stopped investing in stocks on their own and moved to mutual funds and other, safer instruments. And it is also true that as a result of these changes in investing behavior, several thousand people—as many as fifty thousand—were laid off from their jobs on Wall Street and at firms around the country.

But with $1 trillion lost, one would expect to see layoffs throughout the country numbering into the millions. Fifty thousand jobs lost is a lot, especially if one of them is yours, but it is hardly significant in an economy that employs more than 118 million people. And since most of the fifty thousand financial specialists who lost their jobs found new employment in other areas of the economy—banking, insurance, corporate finance, computers—it hardly seems to have amounted to much.

Third, what happened on October 19 was financial, yes, but oddly, it did not have significant financial repercussions. It did not raise interest rates, cause panics, curtail trade, cut consumer spending, or even dampen by very much the pace of growth. In fact, the year after the crash, 1988, was a fairly strong year for growth despite many economists' predictions of catastrophe. And the recession that finally followed, in late 1990 lasting through mid-1991, was shorter and shallower than most recessions that happened before the megabyte standard was devised.

WHY THE WORLD IS DIFFERENT

Today's electronic world is very different from the world of the past. Economic success in this world—especially in the financial sector but increasingly in other sectors as well—is dependent on assimilating large quantities of information very rapidly. Not only that, but each year the quantity of information that must be digested increases as the time frame shortens. Decision-makers must make their judgments with rapid fire. Yet, strangely, with so many facts and so much analysis popping up ready-made on the computer screen, there is absolutely no time to assess their consequences before decisions are made. Judgments are therefore often made by reflex and intuition. There is no time for reasoned thought.

For traders at their screens operating within such an intense informational environment, life is more than hectic. The tensions are tremendous. Traders, like aircraft controllers at the major airports, must constantly piece together a world view based on tiny fragments of data that are updated continuously. Some investment houses, such as Morgan Stanley and Jefferies, have tried to automate decision-making. But even so, it is easy to overload these systems when a panic is in full sway.

The trading rooms at the big investment houses are graphic symbols of the information age. They are densely packed "nodes" along the world's neural network. They are environments where information jumps from one screen to another across an almost infinite synapse of space. In the human nervous system, charged ions and intricate organic molecules carry packets of information across the biological gaps between nerve cells. That is how thoughts (it is believed) travel through the brain.

Similarly, in the neural network of money, information arrives at one screen—or one window within a screen—and jumps across to another with the aid of the human mind. The trader, manager, or analyst at the console adds enough "charge" to the system from information gleaned from one electronic source to press a button and jump the gap. Human judgment is to the electronic network what charged ions and long chains of molecules are to the brain.

Yet real judgment requires time. It requires thinking, digesting, and musing over the facts. It requires relating those facts to an interconnected world of data. It requires that an assessment of the present be based on some knowledge or experience from the past. It requires years of training—seasoning, if you will.

But in place of judgment, electronic space has only gut feelings and hunches. People in electronic space are increasingly relegated to the job of just saying "no" (or "yes") to the information on the screen. They process information the way computers do, in a simplified, binary form—zeros and ones. The screens only ask for "yes" or "no" judgments. That reduces the human mind to the level of a calculator.

That's how it works in trading rooms such as the one at Salomon Brothers, high up in a tower in the World Financial Center in lower Manhattan. In a good year Salomon Brothers Inc. trades $2 trillion worth of stocks, bonds, and commodities. Sometimes it buys $4 billion worth of bonds at a shot. Sometimes it has traded too much, as the scandal of August 1991 showed when Salomon's longtime chairman John H. Gutfreund was forced to resign.

Solly, as it is called, also trades contracts on such esoteric instruments as "interest rate futures" and buys and sells home and commercial mortgages. All of Salomon's offices—London, Tokyo, Budapest, Sydney, Dallas, New York, and elsewhere— are wired together.

Because the offices are linked (the homes of many of the traders and senior staff members are, too) Salomon Brothers is always open, everywhere. Its circuits (in computer talk) have been initialized; they are on. In fact, Salomon's technology makes it impossible for the firm to close. Activity along Salomon's network is like activity in the brain. Some periods are more active than others, but the network never sleeps.

SOLLY'S TRADING ROOM

The big six-thousand-square-foot trading room is dazzlingly bright. Its walls are white, and its floors are covered in a light carpet. The ceiling is high, and the room is bathed in light— sunlight pouring in through the windows, fluorescent light radiating from the ceiling, and the faint glow of computer screens luminescing from the void in various shades of green, blue, and black and white.

The view from the room is stunning. You can see Jamaica Bay, the Statue of Liberty, Staten Island, Long Island, the planes taking off and landing at John F. Kennedy Airport, and the curvature of the earth. From those windows it seems you can see far into the future.

But the traders never look out the windows. They are too busy moving their cursors from line to line and from window to window on their screens. Their job in the world of money is to jump the gap: They push information across electronic synapses. The people who can do it faster, more nimbly, and more often during the day earn the most. The companies that can process that information—take inferences and turn them into dollars—do the best.

The trading room at Salomon Brothers, and at other houses as well, is arranged very much like the newsroom of a newspaper or television station. And it should be. Trading stocks, bonds, currencies, futures contracts, Treasury notes, home mortgages, oil contracts, and anything else, for that matter, is just another way to manipulate information.

There are no offices in the trading room. It is a single open room without any interior walls. People sit clustered together at hundreds of interconnected desks that are organized along odd angles. Aisles snake between the desks. The bond traders sit in one cluster, the currency traders in another, the oil traders in a third, just as they do at a newspaper or network newsroom where the business reporters and their editors sit together, the city reporters and their editors sit together, and so on. Underneath the desks thousands of copper and fiber-optic cables disappear into the floor in clusters that wind their way into the company's computers.

Bunching people together facilitates the exchange of information. Exchange, of course, is a polite word because in practice the exchange is often very noisy and brusque. People in trading rooms shout out questions, exchange scribbled information, read over each other's shoulders, listen in on conversations, interject opinions, and shout out new developments. Concentrating in the midst of the noise can be difficult, especially when traders with "down time," as they call it, tell jokes or exchange war stories (or have rubber-band fights) next to traders who are busy working. The pitch and intensity can rise and fall like a wave during the day, a perfect mirror of current events.

Most supercomputers, such as the Cray YMP and the Connection Machine—the really fast ones that can process a billion or more operations a second—are also arranged with their microprocessors in small, densely packed clusters. They are organized so that the distance between processors is minimized to speed the flow of information. The consoles in the control rooms of the nation's airports are organized exactly the same way. In the architecture of information exchange, the faster information can be dispersed among the processors and then gathered back in, the faster it can be analyzed. That is why information-intensive environments work best when all the human (and silicon) elements are densely packed together.

At Salomon and at the other big houses the desks of the traders can have as many as a dozen telephone lines. Each desk also has four and sometimes five computer screens, and each of these screens has multiple windows for displaying several different types of information at once. A trader with his systems all up and running might be looking at as many as twenty different screens or partial screens, each displaying information in a different way—charts, graphs, numerical lists, changing price quotes, static displays, buy and sell recommendations, and so on.

Along the ceiling of the trading room there are illuminated signs with real-time pricing information for commodities, stocks, currencies, bonds, and so forth. The computer screens on the traders' desks are programmed to carry this information as well as reports from the news wires such as Reuters, I.D.E.A., Bloomberg Business News, and Dow Jones & Company. These screens also bring up weather forecasts around the world—which are especially important if you trade commodities such as wheat, corn, soy beans, rice, or hogs—and analysts' and economists' reports.

The computer terminals are also filled with long- and short-term economic data. With a touch of a keyboard they can display world interest rates, the estimates of the growth or contraction of the money supply in selected countries, the rate of inflation, supplies of heating oil on hand, and so on.

The screens give you the consensus forecasts of the nation's leading business economists. These forecasts chart the gross national product, future interest rates, housing permits, retail sales, factory expenditures, and so forth.

Whenever something new and significant pops onto the news wire inside the trading room—a fire at a big oil refinery, the explosion of a major grain silo, the death of a world leader—the first person who learns about it shouts it out. Acting on this kind of information can make money. If the oil refinery catches fire, the price of gasoline and other refined products goes up. But watch out if the fire is extinguished in just a minute or two.

The traders' computers are also programmed to give buy and sell signals. Some of this is automatic. If oil rises to a certain level on a certain market, the computer signals the trader. The trader can then press a button or make a call, depending on the commodity, stock, or bond, in order to make a deal.

Some of it is semiautomatic. The changing value of the dollar against the world's other major currencies might be plotted on a chart, minute by minute.

TRADING IN CYBERSPACE

Traders are clustered together physically, but they are also clustered together in what people are beginning to call "cyberspace," a term borrowed from science fiction. Cyberspace occupies no space at all. It is, in fact, the neverland of computers (originally called cybers). People in cyberspace occupy no place geographically. They are simply (in computer talk) addressable points on the network.

Operating in cyberspace means that your world is not limited to the people within your cluster in the trading room. It means that the people you talk with, think about, work with, and react to are all the people on the network. The people you are closest to might be the ones you've never seen or met. They are the people with whom you share your computing power.

Since they operate together in cyberspace, these traders learn what other traders around the world look for in deals. And, of course, they learn how to structure deals to attract the interest of their addressable colleagues who are somewhere else.

This technology carries information the way a hose carries water. It does not matter to the hose whether the water is salty or sweet. It does not matter to the fiber-optic network whether the information it carries is relevant or irrelevant, true or false. It just sends its electronic packages down the line.

Jokes that begin on the floor of a New York firm might be repeated within a fraction of a second in Bahrein. Rumors passing through the corridors of a firm in London might be whispered a few seconds later inside the corridors of firms in Tokyo, Frankfurt, or Los Angeles.

Some traders never leave their "addressable nodes" along these complex neural networks. They may walk out of their office space in lower Manhattan, but as they do, they can be seen punching in their colleagues' numbers on their cellular phones. They might send a fax from their car on the way home. And at a party they might sneak a look at their pocket Quotrek device. Quotreks, which receive special FM-band radio waves, give stock, bond, currency, and commodity prices twenty-four hours a day. They can be programmed to buzz or vibrate when prices reach a certain level. Couple that with twenty-four-hour

CNN and the wire services, and insomnia can become a money-making strategy.

For a certain type of person, cyberspace can be comforting. At any moment of the night or day there are people to talk to, bargain with, and plot with (or against). There are other souls out there to spread rumors to. And if a grown-up goes off to live in cyberspace (the equivalent of a child becoming a video-game junkie), he—and, increasingly, she—need never be lonely again.

But cyberspace, like the earth itself, is becoming polluted. Too much information is filling it. And our brains are just too tiny to sort through it all. Information overload threatens to bring further catastrophes to cyberspace, no matter how well the trading rooms are designed.

BLACK MONDAY: A CYBERSPACE EVENT

The crash of October 19 happened in cyberspace. It was one of cyberspace's first real disasters. But it was not precipitated by information of a strictly financial nature. In fact, while investors grew panicky in the summer of 1987, the world's underlying economic situation had changed very little: America's trade and budget deficits were as wide as ever, the dollar clung to its value, factory orders and output continued without change, labor was making no new demands, Japan and Europe had neither less nor more unemployment, steel production continued at the same rates as the year before, and so on.

But the psychological and informational climate had quickened. With the Dow hitting new highs almost every week of the year, traders began asking themselves, "How long can this go on?"

One trader, the manager of a $220 million mutual fund owned by Chase Manhattan Bank, said in an interview that during the spring of 1987 he had a particularly good week. He said the market was moving up so rapidly that in one day he increased the value of his own personal pension fund by $50,000.

But in the next breath he said, "Don't you think it will all come crashing down? It's too good to last." This fund manager's comment reflected a growing unease—a new jitteriness—with the market that had nothing to do with any of the underlying economic or financial fundamentals. He was getting jumpy simply because the good times were lasting so long. And that jumpiness entered the electronic loop.

Other traders and fund managers were also getting nervous for precisely the same reason. And some were also feeling guilty. They were making astronomical sums of money, and yet they had to wade through a sea of homeless people as they climbed to their towers on Wall Street.

New York's nervousness was transmitted around the world through telephone calls, electronic mail, and face-to-face talk. It also moved through the nation's trading rooms. As it moved from money center to money center, it became steadily amplified, like electricity traveling through a transformer coil.

Suddenly, sales of a book that had been languishing for months in obscurity began to soar. It was called *The Great Depression of 1990,* and it was written by an unknown professor of economics from India, Ravi Batra, who was teaching at a small Texas college. The book was a blend of mysticism, Indian philosophy, and economics. It was the kind of book that all but the fringiest of traders would ordinarily have ignored. It was a book that showed how low a gifted academic mind could sink when left unattended in the hot Texas sun. But copies of the self-published book were quietly being passed around on Wall Street until a major publisher took note and released an edition of its own.

Ravi Batra's book stayed on the top of the best-seller list for months. He was a frequent guest on talk shows. Soon the book's message had entered the psyches of the people who work in the cyberspace corridors of international finance: "The good times will soon be over."

REAL-WORLD ANXIETIES

The summer of 1987 also had its share of real-world anxieties, but they were not really economic. The war between Iran and Iraq was intensifying. As the fighting increased, the United States made a deal with Kuwait to protect its ships by sailing them under the American flag.

A huge armada of American naval vessels was dispatched to the Persian Gulf to patrol its waters. Some ships collided with mines, others collided with each other. These ships were heavily armed and exposed to fire from Iranian and Iraqi naval vessels and planes.

Although the world was awash in oil—and its depressed day-to-day prices confirmed that fact—the threat of a wider war in the gulf, possibly involving the United States, made people nervous. Then, shortly before the stock market crash, a Kuwaiti ship, flying an American flag for protection, was fired on by an Iranian patrol boat. The patrol boat was sunk, and that was that. Realistically, the situation was contained and the war had not widened. Neither Iran nor Iraq, which at the time received aid from America, wanted to fight the United States. But inside cyberspace, knees were quaking. Inside the confines of the trading room, gossip was flowing.

Into this psychological stew the first real economic developments arrived. They had consequence, but no reasonable person had cause to be frightened. The underlying economic conditions were just as sound in 1987 as they were in 1986 or 1988.

In August 1987 a dispute between the United States and Germany erupted over interest rates. The United States, a heavy borrower of foreign funds to finance its deficit, had to keep interest rates substantially higher than its allies did in order to attract new funds. But Germany, fearing a slight rise in inflation, wanted to raise its interest rates to slow down its overheated economy and keep inflation in check. Since Germany is a major supplier of capital to the United States, Germany's decision to raise rates concerned the Treasury Department for two reasons.

First, since the Treasury must borrow from abroad to finance the debt, higher interest rates overseas means that the rates offered by the United States government must also go up. Higher rates would slow the economy and could cause a recession. With a presidential election just a year away, the Republicans feared recession might give the Democrats an edge.

Second, there was the fear that if rates climbed overseas, investors in the United States would sell their American holdings and buy foreign bonds. That could bring down the value of the dollar and the stock market. It was a farfetched fear at the time (and the situation never developed), but it was being whispered through the halls of cyberspace.

The announcement of Germany's rate hike only increased Wall Street's nervous investors' sense of dread. James Baker, who was secretary of the Treasury at the time, told Germany

publicly that it must not raise its rates. He was rebuked by Karl
Otto Pöhl, the chairman of the Bundesbank, Germany's central
bank. German interest rates began to rise, but the dollar stayed
firm.

Next came some bad statistics—America's balance of trade
with the rest of the world continued to deteriorate in August.
Nothing new in and of itself, but within the unstable climate of
the time, it increased in significance.

The Op-Ed pages of *The New York Times* and *The Wall Street
Journal* carried articles written by prominent economists on the
possibility of the dollar's collapse, making investors even more
squeamish. In *The New York Times*, Kenichi Ohmae, the economist who heads McKinsey & Company's Tokyo practice, predicted the collapse of the Japanese real estate market and with
it a sudden implosion of funds that could wreck the overvalued
Japanese stock market and the American stock market, too.
Nothing like that actually happened, but Ohmae raised the spec-
ter of collapse in Japan. The trading rooms and newsrooms were
vibrating with fear.

In August 1987, *Barrons,* the financial weekly, printed a
roundtable discussion with four noted investors who had all
turned deeply pessimistic. One, James Rogers, who had made
a fortune in the early 1970s as a partner in the Odyssey Fund,
went so far as to recommend selling all stock. He was expecting
a depression, he said. The only investment he was buying was
government securities backed not by the Treasury Department
(he expected the federal government to default on its obligations) but by government-owned mortgages. Copies of these
Op-Ed articles and the roundtable discussions were passed
through the trading rooms and faxed around the world.

Then, during the summer, the Japanese, who were buying as
much as a third of the Treasury Department's bond offerings—
thereby lending the government the money it needed to carry
on its operations—pulled out of the market. Instead of buying
Treasuries, they began buying new higher-yield German government bonds. And they also began buying European real estate. Faced with a bond offering but not enough buyers, the
Treasury was forced to raise interest rates on its bonds. Cyberspace was reeling.

The next event to happen was even more devastating. During
the week of October 12, Japanese investors caught New York's

jitters. According to Taggert Murphy, at the time Chase Manhattan's chief of private placements in Tokyo, "the Japanese observed what was happening between the United States and Germany with respect to interest rates. As a result, they began selling their stock and buying bonds in huge quantities." (This was said in a private telephone conversation in March 1988 in Tokyo.)

In Japan, according to Murphy, the financial markets were highly concentrated. There are less than two dozen major banks, versus more than ten thousand in the United States. This tremendous concentration of wealth within Japan's financial community meant that the decisions of just a few dozen senior managers could move tens of billions of dollars in investments in a matter of moments.

So, said Murphy, during the week of October 12, almost all of Japan's fund managers began thinking alike. They began instructing their offices in New York to move money out of the stock market and into bonds. Because the concentrations of resources were so great, these movements began to pull down the value of American stocks sharply. On Friday, October 16, the Dow fell 108.35 points, and investors lost $145 billion as 344 million shares were traded and the collapse began. It was the tenth largest percentage decline since the end of World War II.

While the press speculated on what would happen on Monday after Friday's collapse, traders, individual investors, and money managers from around the world communicated with one another over the weekend through the new technologies of cyberspace. They adjusted their assumptions, set their strategies, and made their investment decisions. They were a very pessimistic lot.

The following Monday, Black Monday, began with more selling by the Japanese and continued as other investors sold their stocks as well. By noon the computer programs that monitor the markets clicked in, dumping millions of shares onto the market, causing the worst single economic catastrophe the investment community has ever known. Markets tumbled everywhere.

WHY BLACK MONDAY WAS "BLACK"

In ordinary times the economic events preceding Black Monday would not have amounted to very much. If the Japanese had pulled out of stocks, they would have done it slowly, and it might have pulled the market down a few points. But everyone was waiting and primed for a collapse. The neural network of money conveyed emotions—mostly fear and guilt—as much as it conveyed thoughts. Every time the stock market fell a point or two in the six months leading up to the crash, pundits speculated whether the "big one" was on its way. To an outsider they might have been talking about earthquakes along the San Andreas Fault in California. But the network of money is a curious beast. Its nervousness has no dampers, nor does its optimism. In fact, the network has no dampers at all.

Two days after the crash British social commentator and historian Paul Johnson said in an interview: "What has happened shows the two distinct time frames under which we now operate. On the one hand, there was the crash. It happened worldwide and was over within a matter of minutes. It was electronic.

"On the other hand, now the governments of the world will have to take a look at events," he said. "Studies will be commissioned, inquiries will be held. It will take months, perhaps years, before the reports are finished and legislative action is taken. And when the governments finally do act, because of the time lag, the situation may have already changed dramatically. Or worse, when the reports are released, no one will any longer be interested in what they say."

Johnson was right, of course. Within days of the crash, Congress, the stock exchanges, futures exchanges, Securities and Exchange Commission, General Accounting Office, Treasury Department, individual brokerage firms, and university professors had all begun to research the crash. Similar studies were being commissioned abroad. The reports were issued over the next three years.

But when those reports came out—including the Brady Commission Report, the most important of them all—little interest was left. The recommendations of the Brady Commission, some of which were quite good, were never fully implemented. As a consequence, the global market and cyberspace remain virtually unregulated.

The world that was revealed on October 19 is one that never existed before. It is a world that responds to whim, worry, and abstract thought. It is a world where the only distinction between relevant and irrelevant information is whether people pay attention to it. It is a world where information feeds upon itself.

In this world the movement of information alone is often enough to determine events. Market busts, investment booms, and the value of the dollar are no longer determined by fundamentals but by how we feel about them. How else can it work? In a world where the flow of information is already enormous and growing daily, how else do we sort out what is relevant from what is irrelevant except by feeling? The volume of information is simply too vast to make a reasoned assessment of each bit of data that hits our screen. As a consequence, the network that has been built to field good judgment rapidly around the world (judgment, that is, that must be translated into either a simple yes or no) from time to time will carry nothing but hysteria. Luckily, the damage done has so far been kept within the walls of the electronic economy.

TEN

ELECTRONIC LOSSES:
Why So Few Investors Were Hurt in the Largest Collapse in History

Black Monday has now receded into history. Yet its strange new form of informational chaos is bound to happen again; it has to. The utter responsiveness of the electronic economy and its ability to move money around the globe instantly make it inevitable. The fact that the global electronic grid lacks dampers will contribute to it. In fact, in a slightly different form, Black Monday already has repeated itself—in Japan.

Between December 1989 and March 1990, and then again in the first quarter of 1992, the Tokyo stock exchange experienced its own brand of chaos. In each of these three-month periods the Nikkei index, Japan's equivalent of the Dow, lost more than 25 percent of its value—something on the order of $250 billion to $300 billion each time. Since its height in early 1989, the Nikkei has lost about half its worth. Since 1989, Japan's biggest companies—Toyota, Sony, Mitsubishi, and others—were suddenly worth that much less. Prior to the collapse Japan had the largest stock market in the world. After the market's tumble, Japan became number two, just after New York.

The Japanese slow crash, so-called because it took three years, was not precipitated by new economic news. Like the October 1987 meltdown, Tokyo's fundamentals had changed very little either before or after the crash. To money managers working in Tokyo's financial district, it was simply a case of nerves. Stocks were simply "overvalued," the analysts said, and so they sold as many of them as they could.

But what does overvalued mean, anyway? And why were Japanese stocks overvalued in January when they were considered undervalued a few months earlier? And if facts be facts, the overall performance of the majority of Japanese companies—the same ones the analysts said were overvalued—actually improved during the period of Tokyo's slow crash.

MEASURING "BREAKUP" VALUE

By one measure, overvalued means that a company's stock is selling for more than the company is worth if the company were broken up and sold off piece by piece in the open market. Mitsubishi Heavy Industries, the reasoning goes, would be overvalued if the value of Canon (its camera-making subsidiary), Mitsubishi Motors (its automobile and truck-manufacturing subsidiary), Mitsubishi Electronics (its computer-making subsidiary), Mitsubishi Estate (its real estate division), and so on, were worth less when sold independently than the total value of all the company's outstanding stock. Companies that are overvalued by this measure languish until their stock comes down.

But that reasoning holds true only in countries where the breakup value of a company is a motivator for buying stock. That reasoning may hold true in the United States or Britain, where a raider like Carl C. Icahn buys shares in USX, formerly United States Steel, and pressures the board of directors to separate the company's oil-producing and steel-making divisions into two separate companies. Or it happens when Trans World Airlines is purchased, again by Carl C. Icahn, and its valuable routes are sold off to different airlines, one by one, to pay off the debt accumulated when the raider borrowed money to buy the company's stock in the first place.

But this does not really happen in Japan. The structure of Japanese boards of directors is somewhat different from the structure of American or British boards. Japanese boards are made up of people who do business with the company they govern, people with a stake in keeping the company whole. A company's bankers, suppliers, and customers often serve on its

board of directors. Getting onto that board is not easy. And sometimes Japanese companies have two boards: an inner board,
where the real power rests, and an outer board, which is largely
for show.

Sony has two boards, and an American, Michael P. Schuloff,
sits on one of them. But Schuloff, head of Sony's software operation (including its film and records division in the United
States), sits on the outer board. He has little real power to determine company events. If Sony's stock were accumulated by
a raider, the decision of what to do would be made by the inner
circle. Sony's creditors and business partners—people with a
big stake in keeping the company whole and its stock price
stable—sit in the inner circle.

T. Boone Pickens, the corporate raider who heads Mesa Limited Partnerships, a natural gas producer in Amarillo, Texas, and
the Boone Company, got his fingers burned finding out how
difficult it is to get a seat on a Japanese board of directors to
prepare taking over a company. Pickens bought 23 percent of
Koito Manufacturing Industries' stock and became its biggest
shareholder. But Koito, which supplies Toyota with lighting and
electronic equipment, refused to give Pickens a seat on the board
because Toyota, which holds less than 10 percent of the company's stock, would not allow Pickens on the board. Toyota,
Koito's biggest customer, needs the company to remain whole
and healthy, not broken up into its constituent parts and then
sold off for quick profits.

Despite a proxy war, attempts to pressure Koito through the
Bush Administration and the media and the retention of a high-
priced Tokyo law firm, Pickens lost his fight. He never was
"invited" onto the board. Nor could he force his way onto it,
either. Pickens had to sell his stock, and Koito remained whole.

With stock but not voice, raiders cannot flourish in Japan. So
the term "overvalued," with respect to a company's breakup
value, makes no financial sense.

MEASURING DIVIDEND VALUE

Another meaning to the term has to do with what the company
pays its investors. This measure, the price/earnings ratio, which
has more credence in the United States than in Japan, is figured
in two steps. First, the earnings of a company are divided by

the number of outstanding shares. This figure is then divided by the price of an individual share. If a company has earnings of $10 million and has 100,000 shares that sell for $5, then its P/E ratio is 20 to 1 ($10 million divided by 100,000 divided by $5 equals 20). In a very rough way these calculations plot the return an investor gets on his money.

Theoretically, the lower the P/E ratio, the more profit there is for an investor, although other factors also intervene.

American companies generally have a P/E ratio of less than 20. Ratios of 10 to 15 are common. In fact, as a rule of thumb, many analysts say that when the stock market in the United States has an overall P/E ratio above 20, the market as a whole is overvalued and will come down. So far this has been a fairly reliable indicator.

In Japan, on the other hand, P/E ratios of about 50, 60, and even 70 are quite common without cause for alarm. Even though a P/E ratio of 50 means Japanese investors have lower returns than American investors, it really matters very little. In Japan, with its history of low interest rates, stocks can have lower returns and still retain their attractiveness.

Generally, interest rates are a pretty good predictor of what types of investments are attractive in each country. If rates are low, it makes the stock market more attractive because in addition to dividends there is also the possibility that a stock will appreciate. So because Japan is traditionally a low interest rate country—usually in the 3 percent range—Japanese stocks are not overvalued even when the P/E ratio is high.

But P/E ratios also signify, albeit roughly, how expensive a company is relative to profits and sales. The fact is that Japanese companies, if measured by the price of their stock times the number of shares outstanding, sell for a lot more money than American companies. For some reason Japanese companies are expensive.

The value of Toyota Motors, as measured by its stock price, is about $44.01 billion. General Motors, with annual sales that are about twice as large as Toyota's, has a stock market value of just $26.4 billion, about the same as Microsoft Inc., the software company that has sales of just $2.3 billion. (In 1991, General Motors lost twice as much money, $4.5 billion, as Microsoft had in revenues.)

Nintendo, the big Japanese maker of electronic games, is val-

ued at $14.56 billion on the Tokyo exchange. US West, the big
regional telephone company, is valued at $14.46 billion on the
New York exchange. But US West has sales of almost $10 bil-
lion, about triple the sales of Nintendo. And as a regulated utility,
US West has better prospects for sustained growth than Nintendo does since the market for electronic games fluctuates with
the business cycle. (*Business Week* Global 1000, July 15, 1991.)
And Japan Airlines, a medium-sized airline, has a stock value
equal to all of America's airlines combined, including its much
larger rivals, American Airlines and United Airlines.

What these figures show is that the Japanese, in general, value
their companies more than Americans and even Europeans do.
As a result, they tolerate much higher P/E ratios. That means
the Japanese market was not necessarily overvalued before the
fall, it was just valued in the traditional Japanese way—which
by Western standards is very dear.

VALUE BY PERFORMANCE

Finally, Japanese stocks could be overvalued if they were performing poorly when it came to profits and sales. But 1989 and
1990 were strong years for Japan with the economy growing at
a rate of more than 5 percent, twice the rate of growth in the
United States. In 1989 and 1990, Japan was the industrial
world's growth leader. Even in 1992 when the Japanese economy went into "recession," its growth still was pegged at 1.5
percent and its unemployment rate at 2.2 percent. By Western
standards, where recession means economic contraction, Japan
was not in a recession at all.

But not only that, even with a weak dollar, which should make
Japanese exports more expensive and therefore less competitive
on the world market, Japan Inc. was still accumulating record
trade surpluses. And those surpluses are continuing to build. In
1991 they topped $100 billion, a world record. In 1992 they were
expected to top $120 billion, far more than any other nation has
ever earned.

That much cash loaded into the bank accounts of Japan's
biggest companies should not hurt their stocks. On the contrary,
it should help them. With big cash reserves, dividends can be
paid and investments can be made even if sales tumble for a
year or two.

Looking at these facts, it becomes clear that Japanese companies in 1989 and 1990 were not overvalued when measured on any basis. They were not overvalued for their breakup potential (there is none in Japan) nor their P/E ratio nor when it came to the most basic measurement of all—how well their products did in the marketplace. And yet the stock market came down sharply.

THE ELECTRONIC ECONOMY AND THE BRAIN

The point of this is that markets still respond to fundamentals, only not as often. More frequently they rise and fall on extraneous news. The creation of a new technology, a new form of money, as we shall see, and new tradable instruments have all added to the tendency of the world's markets to rise and fall based on emotions. Markets, which are supposed to set prices by weighing demand against supply and factoring in other useful information—new technologies, for example, that might upset the demand for oil, say—are not factoring everything in. The information environment in which we live does not separate the important from the unimportant. It is all wheat, and it is all chaff.

A good analogy to the new global economic grid can be seen in the way the human brain is believed to work. In the brain there are two hemispheres: the left hemisphere where judgment, language, and mathematical reasoning lie; the right hemisphere where pattern recognition and artistic and musical ability lie. The left hemisphere is generally the dominant one, and its rulership is why we live in a world of science, language, toolmaking, and technology instead of a world ruled by art. Left hemisphere dominance is not a matter of choice or cultural predilection; it is biologically determined. At least this is what physiologists think today.

Connecting the two hemispheres is what is called the corpus callosum. This thick bundle of nerves allows messages to flow between the two hemispheres. It allows them to communicate. The corpus callosum enables the judgment and reasoning ability of the left hemisphere to be tempered with the spirituality and artistic sensibilities of the right hemisphere.

In most people the corpus callosum also acts as a filter. Dominance is maintained on the left because not every message gets through from the right. Communication between the two sides is modulated by the filtering effects of this bundle of nerves.

But if you give someone a dose of LSD or send him off to an Indian ashram for twenty years of intense meditation, something happens to the filtering abilities of the corpus callosum, some brain physiologists say. It stops being a filter and instead becomes a data highway. In such a circumstance, when the right and left hemispheres have uninhibited communication, judgment is altered. It is not uncommon to hear the mystic say that "all things in this world are of equal importance"—the flea and the atomic bomb. Hierarchy breaks down in favor of a flat world where everything is of equal significance within the grand scheme of things. Without the filtering mechanism, to mystics everything is of the same value under God's watchful eyes.

In the most objective sense, this may be true, and perhaps the mystics are right. But it is no way to run a railroad or an airline or a global economy. It is no way to shift money from market to market.

Yet in a way that is how the electronic economy works today, as if all things, all types of information, are equal. The global economy, where real or imagined "facts" move markets, functions like a mystic or an individual on LSD. Attention, pure and uninhibited, is drawn not to what is true or important but to everything equally. As a consequence, anything that catches the market's attention can move it.

ELEVEN

THE MONEY EQUATIONS:
How a Handful of Computer "Nerds," Mathematicians, and Nobel Prize Winners Propelled Wall Street Away from Trading Products and into a Realm of Pure Abstraction

umber crunchers, nerds, and pure geniuses have invaded the world's financial markets. They have done so not simply to make money but to figure out very complex conceptual puzzles, to find new ways of managing risks. Stocks, with their daily fluctuations and volatility, with their responsiveness to the markets, have captured the imaginations of these thinkers.

Many of these people see Wall Street not as a crap shoot but as a mathematical puzzle where their ideas about risk and reward, stasis and chaos can be tested in real time. And as this new breed takes over, the products being traded—the products that move markets and make big money—are becoming ever more abstract.

The neural network of money would not be so responsive to news, quick to change, and resilient if it were not for these new abstract products—highly complex packages designed for use on the global electronic grid. Most of them are not really products at all in the way that a Chevrolet is a product. Instead, they are ideas. They are, if you will, ways of harnessing vast amounts of buying power and then moving it across huge distances of space and sometimes even time. They are ways of handling vast amounts of video money.

Conceptually, these abstract products are often outgrowths of real products that have been traded on the futures markets for years. But when they go electronic, they do it with a twist. Rather than trading a contract today for a bushel of wheat to be delivered next year, these new products are usually contracts to take delivery on a financial product. Instead of buying wheat on the futures market, the new products that are traded are contracts to buy stocks, specific ones or all the stocks on the entire stock market, in some cases, and even such esoteric items as foreign currencies and future interest rates. Futures contracts on interest rates did not exist in 1971. They did not really get into the market until the late 1970s when Citicorp invented them in Tokyo. Today, there are outstanding contracts for $3 trillion worth of them, a little more than half of the gross national product of the United States.

DERIVATIVES MAKE THEIR DEBUT

These new products by and large are what are called "derivative" products because they are derived from something else. A tradable option, for example, is not really something in and of itself. It is a right or, more precisely, it conveys a right. Buy an option and you are buying the right to purchase a specified stock or stock group, currency, or even bond at a predetermined price sometime in the future. Those rights can be traded, and they have a value that is separate, though related, to the value of the underlying product. Options are traded on the futures markets, stock markets, special options markets, and electronically between investors.

Though complex, these products can be traded with lightning speed. There are immense profit (and loss) opportunities inherent in the market for products like options because they are intensely volatile. As a consequence, the market for tradable options has grown from essentially zero in 1973—the year the Chicago Board Options Exchange opened for the first time—to a market where more than $170 billion changes hands each day. One hundred and seventy billion is enough money to purchase about 1.7 million average homes.

Some of these products are quite intricate. Take tradable options for the Standard & Poors 500 index of stocks, for example. This product can be likened to a multitiered abstraction. The product's bottom level is a basket of stocks, the five hundred New York stocks that make up the S&P index. That is a solid enough base since contained within those five hundred stocks are some of the biggest, most important companies in America.

But the index does not really trade its very substantial foundation. One share in the S&P 500 is not really made up of five hundred stocks. Instead, it is made up of fractions of each of those shares. If one S&P index share actually contained five hundred shares of the underlying stocks, the price for an index share would be several thousand dollars. Instead—and this is the first level of abstraction—because each index share is composed of fractions of five hundred underlying shares, the index sells for only a few hundred dollars. In July 1991 one share of the S&P 500 index cost just $374. For traders, buying the index is a convenient way of betting the entire market.

Now let's talk about the second level of the abstraction—an option on those S&P 500 index shares. These options, though traded on the Chicago Board of Trade, really change hands in video space since the CBOT operates what it calls the Retail Automated Exchange System, or Raes. Raes is an electronic exchange where index options as well as 178 other products can be traded with a few easy-to-use programs and the click of a mouse. For a fee and the right licenses, you can trade options electronically via Raes. Once you have the correct codes you can gain access to Raes through any telephone line, although some traders bypass phone lines and instead put a pizza-pan-sized satellite dish on their roofs.

TYPES OF OPTIONS

There are two basic kinds of options: call options and put options. If you buy a "call" option, you have the right to buy a specific index, stock, currency, or bond at a prearranged price anytime before that option expires. Usually, options have a life span of one to twelve months. But some options are written for longer and some for shorter periods of time.

"Put" options are options to sell a stock or other product at some specified time in the future for a specified price. They are the counterpart to call options. If you sell a put option, you either have to have the stock, index, or bond on hand, or be prepared to buy it and hand it over when the option is called.

Options are at the heart of the new video economy. If you buy an option on a stock, you are betting that it will go either up or down sometime in the future—a reasonable assumption and one that electronics or a global economy has not changed.

TRADING OPTIONS

Options are a type of futures contract. With them you are buying the right to purchase something in the future. But they are also different from traditional futures contracts. With a futures contract for corn, for example, the last owner of that contract is obligated to take delivery on the corn. But when you buy an option, you are not obligated to buy the underlying product. You can just walk away.

Let's say that you think the stock market in general will rise. It is July 5, 1991, and the S&P 500 index is selling for $374. If the market rises 5 percent by the end of the year, that share should be worth about $392.70.

But why tie up your money buying an expensive stock? Why not just buy an option to buy that stock?

Let's say you bought a six-month option to buy the S&P 500 index at, say, $380. That means that at any time between July 5 and January 5 you have the right to purchase an S&P index share for $380 from the person who sold you the option. If the stock really does climb to $392.70, you can exercise your option. At the precise moment that you exercise your option and buy the stock for $380, you can simultaneously sell it for $392.70 on the stock exchange. For your efforts you will make $12.70 a share, less whatever you paid for the option. If all you had to pay was the price of the option, which is far cheaper than the price of the stock, you could have bought a broad range of options and still spent less than the price of one real share of stock. And some of these options would be winners.

But what happens if the stock goes down and you bought an option? If you bought an option to purchase a share of the S&P 500 at $380 and the stock begins to fall, you can either try to sell your option to someone else before it expires, or you can simply walk away from the deal. You can let your option expire. All you lose when you let an option expire is the price of the option.

VALUING OPTIONS

But how much should you pay for an option? And how do you value them if you want to sell them on a portfolio of stock you already own? Or on a portfolio of stock you are prepared to buy? How do you determine the value of a "right"?

The method of how to value options has proved to be a good tool for valuing other products as well. In fact, the equations that led to valuing options are said to be the most widely used equations in finance today.

Back in the late 1960s a nascent quant was studying what is called Capital Asset Pricing Theory. The quant in question, Fischer Black, was a young professor of mathematics at the Massachusetts Institute of Technology.

Black, a tall, soft-spoken intellectual with steel-blue eyes, who is often described as cool, even aloof, is famous for his abrupt—even one-word—sentences. Black looks more like an engineer—someone who perhaps designs rockets or at least jet planes—than a typical Wall Streeter.

Black had earned his Ph.D. in applied mathematics at Harvard and was working part-time on a number of big computer projects for Arthur D. Little, the consulting firm in Cambridge, Massachusetts. In those days computers munched punch cards and were slow, cumbersome beasts, but back at the Institute, as MIT was called, mathematicians, physicists, and engineers were dreaming big about computers, chips, and networks.

Simply programming computers was not challenging enough for Black. He wanted to apply their power to real-life problems. Though he had no formal training in finance, Black was fascinated by it. It was mathematical and abstract, but it was also based on the pragmatism of real life. And there was the possibility of making profits by melding together mathematics and money.

Capital Asset Pricing Theory was what first interested Black in finance. It was mathematically elegant and simple, and yet it worked in the real world. The theory had its roots in the work of Harry Markowitz and William Sharpe, which began in the late 1950s and continued through the middle 1960s. Though their work was considered obscure at first, Markowitz, Sharpe, and another economist, Merton Miller, won the Nobel Prize for Economic Science in 1990.

Markowitz, a tall, courtly, soft-spoken man of immense charm and warmth, grew up in Chicago where he studied music, enjoyed chess, and was a whiz at math. He received his Ph.D. in economics from the University of Chicago. He worked at the Rand Corporation in Santa Monica, the think tank set up for the Defense Department by Herman Kahn, the nuclear weapons strategist. Kahn, a three-hundred-pound mathematician with an ego as large as his girth, was one of the first people to apply game theory, statistics, and mathematics to military strategy. In the process Kahn built Rand into one of the most important government-funded research centers in the country and widened its scope to include economics, sociology, futurology, applied mathematics, population, and more. Though largely defense related in its outlook, Rand had a reputation for bringing together some of the most creative thinkers in a wide range of fields.

At Rand, Markowitz experimented with computers. He began by writing programs designed to assess portfolio risk. The exercise—it was purely an exercise since Markowitz himself was not an investor—was to develop the "optimal" portfolio. Questions like that—developing optimal formulas, for economics or nuclear weapons strategy—were Herman Kahn's forte. Kahn, the strategist and amateur economist, was perhaps the first American to forecast that Japan would become an economic superpower, perhaps the sole economic superpower.

While he was at Rand in 1960, Markowitz also met William Sharpe, a slight man with a blond goatee who had studied at Berkeley and was working on his Ph.D. at UCLA, a couple of miles away from Rand. Sharpe became engrossed in Markowitz's work on the optimal stock portfolio and developed his Ph.D. dissertation around some of Markowitz's notions.

From Rand, Markowitz went to teach at Baruch College in New York, and Sharpe went on to teach at Stanford University in California. But they stayed in touch, exchanged papers, and developed their research. Each in his own way tried to come up with a mathematical model for the optimal investment portfolio. Their goal was to find mathematical ways to lessen the level of risk in an investment portfolio while maintaining the possibility for reward. They thought that by applying mathematics to the stock market they could achieve these long-sought-after goals. Little did these modest men know they would contribute greatly to changing the world of money.

The Markowitz model, as it was named, was based on the notion that risk could be minimized not so much by shrewd stock picking—as most people in the late 1950s and 1960s still believed—but by scientific diversification.

The Markowitz model mathematically described ways to distribute risk in an "optimal" portfolio by diversifying investment among a number of different products, such as stocks, bonds, and futures contracts. It also proved mathematically what many savvy investors knew intuitively: Diversifying a portfolio by industry group—utilities, high-tech, and manufacturing, for example—could also lessen risk since the factors governing these stocks are different.

According to Markowitz, the laws of statistics dictate how much diversification is optimal. A portfolio of twenty stocks selected from different groups gives you about as much protection as is theoretically possible. Adding one hundred more stocks to the portfolio does not change the risk/reward equation by much, but choosing which twenty stocks to buy is critical.

While it is true that one stock may go up while another goes down—so overall yield is lessened—the chances of everything crashing at once in a diversified portfolio is not as likely. In theory, plotting the optimal portfolio could be done by computer if you knew the risk factors governing each component in that portfolio.

The Markowitz model was able to quantify risk, for the first time. In the model it was called "beta." The size of beta was supposed to convey an accurate assessment of risk. For instance, if beta for a portfolio was 1.2, it meant that for every 10 percent up or down that the stock market traveled in general, the portfolio would travel 12 percent up or down along with it. A portfolio with a beta of 1.2 was two percentage points riskier than the market itself.

If a portfolio had a beta of 2, the portfolio would travel up or down by 20 percent when the stock market in general rose or fell by 10 percent. There was a greater possibility of reward if a portfolio had a beta of 2, but there was also a heightened level of risk.

USING THE BETA PRINCIPLE

The principle of beta suddenly gave investment managers a new tool. If a portfolio had a beta of, say, 2 (which meant it was twice as risky as the market in general), then that portfolio would have to deliver twice the return of the market to justify the added risk. But if the return was less than twice that of the market in general, the money manager was not doing his job. The risk/ return equation was out of whack. By using beta in this way, Markowitz thought, a portfolio manager could continuously adjust his portfolio so that the reward was commensurate with the risk. If the manager was unable to get the return to at least equal the risk, he should move to another profession. The key here is not just picking the stock of well-managed companies, however, it is picking stocks that conform to certain mathematical rules.

The equations a manager had to solve to use the Markowitz model and to create the ideal portfolio were daunting. For example, to build a portfolio of just fifty stocks, less than the average number a fund usually holds, requires that the fund manager perform 1,225 calculations. A state-of-the-art computer, back in the late 1950s and early 1960s when Markowitz was doing his work, required thirty-three minutes of computing time to solve these equations. Back then, that much time on an IBM mainframe cost about $300. (*Institutional Investor*, November 1990, page 84.)

The Capital Asset Pricing Theory is now used in investment houses around the world as the scaffold on which investment portfolios are built. It is so widely used that trillions of dollars have been traded based on how the equations turn out. It has nothing to do with quality or with what companies make. It has nothing to do with how long or short term a manager thinks. It is simply mathematics.

The model has been lauded as just so much common sense. In an article in the *New Republic* in December 1990, just following the award of the Nobel Prize, Robert Samuelson, an economist, chided the Nobel commission for having given a prize to three economists who discovered the obvious. The only trouble is that at the time their discovery was made, it was far from obvious.

The Markowitz equations are now so commonplace and computer time is so cheap that a version of the theory is sold by *Money* magazine. For $199 a subscriber can buy the program and use it on his personal computer for managing a small private portfolio the same way the big investment firms use it to manage their multi-billion-dollar funds. While it took thirty-three minutes to run the equations back in the early 1960s, the average personal computer can now do the calculations in just a minute or so.

The elegance of Markowitz's ideas captivated an entire generation of financial theorists. By using beta—and a second quantifier called "alpha"—risk could be rated even more precisely. Alpha referred to the risk level of an individual stock. By computing the two of these quantifiers together, portfolios could be built like intricate Chinese boxes—a solid though boring utility stock balancing a volatile but high-flying entertainment stock; a government bond balancing a portfolio of higher yielding second mortgages; and so on. With these equations risk was distributed and trading took place in an effort to match the total rate of return to the relative size of beta. The biggest users of these new tools were the nation's biggest investors: state pension funds, union pension funds, and insurance companies. These big funds control about 60 percent of the nation's stocks and bonds.

THE END OF STOCK PICKING

By constructing portfolios that were no longer based on individual stocks and the companies they represent, a process of divorcement began in the financial community with tremendous repercussions. Stock pickers—men and women who patiently studied companies, visited sites, talked to managers, and cared about a company's health—were pitted against quants who were interested only in a portfolio's total return. To achieve ever greater returns, portfolio managers had to trade in and out of stocks with increasing frequency. Quants, using mathematical models, had divorced the investor from his traditional role of bringing capital to a company in return for a share of the profits and a share of the company's net worth. Instead, it became the job of an investor to pile up overall returns.

.   .   .

But there was another wrinkle, as we shall see. With the invention of megabyte money, interest rates began to soar. That meant if you were creating portfolios from a menu of investment options, interest rate investments, such as bonds, were increasingly competing for your investment dollars. Companies were forced to offer the same kind of return a money market fund might pay or risk having the price of their shares collapse (as investors shifted investments). Collapsing share prices could result in a takeover.

With interest rates in the 1970s double what they were in the 1960s and going as high as 21 percent, companies were forced to think in shorter and shorter time frames or risk watching their stock prices collapse. For the first time it was no longer important how a company made money, only that it was able to do so. Selling off portions of a company, borrowing money in the capital markets and then paying it out to stockholders as dividends, even using profits not for new investment but to purchase a company's own shares of stock, all became common practices used by companies to keep their stock prices high.

The era of long-term investing ended sometime in the 1970s, and we are still recovering. Switching in and out of risk groups—under the guidance of the equations—became the newest investment fashion. The company mattered less than its stock. What that meant, from the perspective of the big picture, was that ability to trade rapidly grew in importance.

VALUING OPTIONS

But let's get back to Fischer Black and options.

Black examined the Markowitz equations and was impressed. If mathematics could be used to build portfolios with one risk factor balancing another, then it had other uses in finance as well. To conduct his work Black had an advantage Markowitz lacked: In the late 1960s computers were becoming cheaper, faster, and far more widespread; computers at universities were available to the faculty although the PC was still a decade or more away. And punch cards were being replaced by real keyboards.

For a mathematician like Black, options were a fertile intellectual playground. There was tremendous uncertainty associated with them as well as volatility and risk, especially for naked options (those that are sold on stocks, money, or bonds you do not own. When one of those is exercised, you must scramble to buy the underlying product in a hurry and turn it over to the option holder). With all options, naked and covered, Black knew that whoever devised a way to diminish the risk could make a lot of money. He or she would have to. That was the nature of markets in general.

THE OPTIONS MARKET

Options have been traded in one form or another for hundreds of years. In the nineteenth century, long before there were computers, brokers traded what were then called "privileges." Back then you could buy a put or call privilege, just as you can today. The difference was that in the nineteenth century there were only loosely organized over-the-counter markets for privileges. These markets were between traders who knew one another and who operated usually within the same city. With the advent of the telegraph, the geographical range for trading privileges was extended a bit, but it was still a small, loosely organized market confined to New York and Chicago. The great railroad baron and philanthropist Russell Sage was one of the nineteenth century's biggest options traders.

When Fischer Black became interested in options back in the late 1960s, an informal market for them still existed. They were considered a very iffy investment then, appropriate for reckless investors with a stomach for risk. If options had betas, they would be sky-high.

The big problem with options, before Black, was knowing how much they were worth. How do you value a right? If you know how much that right is really worth, then you know when to buy, sell, or hold it in your portfolio. If you know what it is worth, you can have a market. And if you have a workable method for determining how much that option is worth, then you also know when it is too expensive or a bargain.

Black knew—and most savvy investors also knew—that when you put a value on something as ephemeral as the right to purchase a stock or currency or bond for a predetermined price sometime in the future, you must begin by taking account of the current value of the underlying asset.

If shares in Walt Disney trade at $50 each (or German marks

cost 50 cents each), that figure is an important factor in the way you value an option. So is the "strike" price, the price at which you would want to exercise your option. If the current price of Disney is $50 and you are betting it will go up 5 percent to $52.50 within six months, then you are interested in knowing how much options will cost with a strike price *below* $52.50. An option with a strike price above $52.50 would be worthless to you since you are betting that $52.50 is the top of the market. A strike price below $52.50 will give you a profit if you exercise your right to buy the stock and simultaneously sell that stock to someone else on the open market.

Of course, market trends must also be factored into the picture if you are valuing options. Suppose Disney shares are at $50 and have been climbing. If you are interested in an option with a strike price of $45, one that expires in three months, it's not going to be cheap. Why would anyone sell you an option that already contains a profit in it when he or she can just as well sell the stock on the open market and make money? In the market the only incentive is money. For currency options the same rules apply.

On the other hand, if the price is at $50, an option to purchase the stock at $55 will be cheaper since there is always some uncertainty about how high the market will go. If you own the stock and you can sell an option on what you own, it is an easy way to make a little extra money. And if you are betting that the stock will not quite make it to $55, you are also betting that the option you sold will never be exercised. For you, the money you receive for selling your option is found money—something to lessen your risk or, to be more poetic, ease the pain of uncertainty.

And, of course, there is always time, a factor that must be accounted for, especially in valuing something with an expiration date. As options run their course, they can lose value, particularly if the market is going in the opposite direction from the way the option is written. And options can also lose value over time simply because the advantage in a timed transaction tends to shift from seller to buyer as the seller's asset approaches the moment when it must self-destruct. Since an aging option offers you less time to resell it if the market turns against you, older options often lose their appeal unless the market is on their side.

Fischer Black had to factor all these variables and more, such as the price and volatility of the underlying asset, into his equations. He also had to do it in a way that was both simple and elegant, the two most often used adjectives in the mathematician's vocabulary. And, of course, the equations had to be built to run through a computer. They had to be precise and give hard results that a trader could use.

FISCHER BLACK INVENTS AN EQUATION

To come up with a way of valuing an option, Black went the long way around. He and his colleague, Myron Scholes, tried to build a mental model of an option. They called this a "synthetic" option. In it, they reasoned, they would have to take into account interest rates in addition to the above-listed factors because the money used to invest in any financial asset would not receive interest payments. Lost interest payments are a cost of investing and are also a threshold. If an investment yields less than current interest rates, why take the risk of investing at all? Just leave your money in the bank.

The formula that Black and Scholes came up with goes like this:

$$C = SN[D] - Xe^{-rt}N[D - \sigma\sqrt{T}]$$

The Black-Scholes model, as it was called, works like a little machine. Its five forward gears (mathematical inputs) spin at different speeds to produce a single result: the value of an option. When it is used, the model tells a trader exactly how much to pay.

The inputs are:

S—the current price of the underlying asset, such as stock or currency;

N[·]—has to do with the probability that the term in brackets will be worth less than it ought to be.

D—a term composed of other mathematical terms:

It is a wheel within a wheel that functions like the fine-tuning mechanisms on an old radio dial. D adjusts the equation so that the value of the option changes along with the price changes in the underlying stock or other asset;

X—the strike or exercise price of the option;

r—the interest rate;
σ—the asset's volatility, a term that resembles beta in the Markowitz model.

To grease the wheels of this mathematical machine Black also threw in some extra bits:

$$\frac{\ln(sx) + (r + \sigma^2/2)T}{\sigma\sqrt{T}}$$

T—the time until the option expires in months;
1n—a natural logarithm that also functions like the fine-tuning knob;

The Black-Scholes model is a relatively simple equation, not much more sophisticated than college calculus, really. (There is no test at the back of this book.) Its simplicity made it an easy equation to program into a sophisticated hand-held calculator or into a computer.

Like any equation, this one can run either forward, to solve the question of value for an option if all the other variables are known, or it can run backward. When it is run backward and the value of the option is known, what the trader needs to know is the volatility of the option or the price of the underlying stock, and so forth, all useful checks a trader can use to determine the value of his investment.

A MARKET IS BUILT AROUND THE EQUATION

The Black-Scholes equation proved to be a very powerful tool, and around it an entire industry was built. The equation, which was published in an article in 1973 in the *Journal of Political Economy,* coincided with the opening of the Chicago Board Options Exchange, called the CBOE. The exchange was the first organized options exchange in the country supervised by the Commodities Futures Trading Commission, which in turn is supervised by Congress. At first it just traded options on stocks, indexes of stocks such as the Standard & Poors 100 and 500, and other products like bonds. But later it expanded. The CBOE also set uniform dates for options to expire—the Saturday following the third Friday of the month. And it set uniform lifetimes for options as well—from one month usually up to a year. It also organized a clearinghouse, called the Options Clearing Corporation. The clearinghouse is where sellers of options are matched with buyers and where the accounts are tallied. It is the exchange's "back room" and the reason people use exchanges in the first place—to be certain that each seller and buyer is genuine, that they are matched, and that all debts are paid.

Within a year of its inception the CBOE moved from a corner of the Chicago Board of Trade to its own trading floor across the street on LaSalle Street. The trading floor, all twenty thousand square feet of it, was designed without a pillar or post so that each trader could have a clear view of all the action around him. It was also the first exchange floor designed for computers. And because traders move around a lot when they are not behind their screens or on the phone, the ground was covered with the same knobby-rubber tiles that are used in industrial kitchens. When it was built, the floor was designed to handle as many as two hundred thousand options trades a day.

A year after that, in 1975, the American Stock Exchange began trading listed options. That same year the Philadelphia exchange began trading them, including options on currencies. The following year the Pacific Stock Exchange, in San Francisco and subsequently Los Angeles, opened its options trading department.

From there, options trading went global. In 1976 options markets opened in Montreal, Toronto, Sydney, and, in 1978, London. Tokyo followed shortly after.

By 1978 two hundred types of options were traded at the CBOE and hundreds more at exchanges around the world. Options on mortgages, called Ginnie Maes—Government National Mortgage Association—were being traded alongside hundreds of stocks. Also traded in gargantuan numbers were options on U.S. Treasury bonds, municipal bonds, British pounds, Canadian dollars, German marks, Swiss francs, gold, silver, copper, oil, as well as more mundane products such as corn, soybeans, cattle, and hogs. The value of all these diverse types of options could be computed using the Black-Scholes model.

Because business was growing so fast, the CBOE moved once again. Twenty thousand square feet of trading space was simply not big enough to house the growing exchange, its floor brokers, and technology. In 1984, eleven years after it was founded, the

CBOE built a new building; again, it was just across the street from the old building and still on LaSalle Street. But this time it had the biggest trading floor in the world, more than double the size of the previous one.

Prior to the advent of the exchange and the Black-Scholes model, there was negligible trade in options in this country. After the exchange was launched and the formula was published, options trade grew very rapidly. More than 200 million options contracts—about half covering stocks and about half covering more exotic products such as currencies and mortgages—were written in the United States in 1990. A single contract might cover thousands or even tens of thousands of shares or millions of dollars' worth of foreign interest rates or foreign currencies. Thanks to the model, buying options on a stock or currency, once considered a very risky business, became a way to hedge against the risk of owning stock. Black-Scholes turned investing on its head.

Because of the model, more money is now spent purchasing stock options than is spent purchasing stocks. The options exchange, which is less than two decades old, trades twice the dollar volume of what the two-hundred-year old New York exchange trades each day. In Chicago, which is where the world's biggest futures as well as options exchanges are located (if anything has a "location" in electronic space), three-quarters of the exchanges' business now involves trading financial products rather than the traditional products sold on those exchanges like pork bellies and soybean futures.

Options prices remain volatile investments, but the model makes that volatility manageable because it helps traders automate their decision-making. The model, loaded into computer workstations, is fed with data coming directly from the markets so it can digest new assumptions—changes in interest rates, the tick of the clock toward an option's expiration date, fluctuations in underlying stock prices, and so on. It computes these changes and signals the trader when it is time to make a move. But since everyone in the $170-billion-a-day options market is using the same equation, in one form or another, victory goes to the swift. And swift means technology.

CUSTOMIZING THE EQUATIONS

The model is continually undergoing customization and refinement. New wheels are attached by traders, mathematicians, and professors working for various brokerage firms. A version of the model now computes options on Treasury bills; another computes the value of foreign currencies. With refinement the model is versatile enough to figure out the value of almost anything. For instance, how much is an option worth on a Boeing jetliner? In the late 1980s when Boeing's backlog was long, airlines swapped their options with one another to buy Boeing jets. If Lufthansa needed jets in a hurry, it could buy TWA's options. The Black-Scholes equations told them how much those options were worth.

Warrants are another area where the Black-Scholes model works its magic. Warrants are a type of option, usually with longer-term expiration dates—ten years is not uncommon—or even no expiration date at all. Trading them used to be about as sleepy a business as trading municipal bonds. A few wild investors might phone their brokers once or twice a month to inquire about the market for warrants. The broker would in turn phone the one or two New York firms that traded warrants and a day or two later advise his client to neither buy nor sell. Warrants were to be kept, the adage was, sometimes forever.

Traditionally, warrants have been used as "sweeteners" to make an offering of preferred stock or bonds a little more attractive to investors. They are a cheap way for a company to increase the potential yield on one of its bonds, by offering to sell the bondholder a quantity of stock at an attractive price sometime in the future. And, of course, they have been increasingly used as incentive pay for the nation's top executives. A warrant granted to a chief executive might have a ten-year life. If the stock goes up during the warrant's term on this earth, the executive stands to make a killing. If the stock goes down, he's sitting on tons of worthless paper. The executive's job, in a company that issues warrants, is to make the stock rise.

Since Black-Scholes can value warrants, warrant trading moved into the big time. Even Michael Milken, the imprisoned junk-bond king and billionaire, traded warrants. His company, Drexel Burnham Lambert, which underwrote junk bonds for companies, often stripped the warrants from the bonds they sold.

The warrants were traded separately. Milken even set up what were called "strip funds" for trading warrants. Today, hundreds of millions of dollars' worth of warrants are traded each day. The Black-Scholes equation, extended outward for a longer term and rejiggered for warrants without expiration dates, works as well valuing warrants as it does valuing conventional options.

And the equations have other uses as well. They can even be used with bonds. The theory goes that if you buy a company's bonds, you are in effect taking an option on the company, since, if the company goes bust, which is increasingly likely these days, the law says stockholders lose all while the bondholders, as creditors, get the company. If that is the case, then buying corporate bonds is the same as taking an option on the company as a whole.

From this conceptual perspective the Black-Scholes model suddenly becomes a highly useful tool for the bond market, too, especially the junk-bond market that deals in low-grade corporate debt. Corporate debt can be plugged into the model the same way that option prices are fed into it.

For bonds the model works this way: The total outstanding debt of the company becomes its "strike price" because if the company cannot pay its debt, that figure is the price at which the creditors (bondholders) can seize it.

The expiration date becomes the date when the firm's bonds come due. The value of the underlying asset is simply the breakup price of the company if all its parts are sold. The market volatility of these assets can be factored into the equation along with interest rates.

It may seem cumbersome to run bond prices or airline options or dollar prices or Treasury bill prices through the model, but not with computers. It actually takes very little time. And when all of these numbers are put into the Black-Scholes machine, out pops value. In the bond market, traders suddenly have a new way of determining if a company's debt is a bargain or is too dear.

And there are many other applications of the theory as well. Some economists have called Black's little equation the most successful theory in all of economics.

FISCHER BLACK JOINS THE STREET

Fischer Black stayed at the Institute until February 1984, when he went to work for Goldman Sachs & Company, one of Wall Street's most prestigious and most technology-driven firms. Black joined the firm to devise new mathematical ways to cut risk in trading stocks, options, and other products. Myron Scholes went to work for Salomon Brothers in August 1991.

Black, who earns more than $1 million a year at Goldman Sachs, published a new research paper in July 1990 in the *Journal of Finance* that is expected to have wide-ranging applications. In it he went back to his roots. He borrowed heavily from the Markowitz model of Capital Asset Pricing Theory but applied its portfolio-balancing idea to exchange rates.

The new theory, which also contains wheels within wheels, has no doubt already been converted into a software program that is loaded into and running on the computer workstations at Goldman Sachs's currency trading desk. The formula treats currencies the same way Markowitz treated stocks: It assigns risk and allows traders to build portfolios that are safer.

More and more, as traders enter electronic space from their computers, they are conducting their business with the aid of Nobel Prize–winning equations. They make their decisions by touching the cursor arrow to the icon on the screen. Traders do not necessarily know what the equations are doing or how they work, just as most drivers do not know how the engines of their cars operate. Nevertheless, these equations increasingly are behind the movement of money. The equations, not the traders, are the drivers as finance becomes more high tech.

TWELVE

MAKE WAY FOR THE PROGRAMS:
How Computer Programs Were Developed to Hedge Risk and Manage Money

Options are at the heart of the megabyte economy because they offer an inexpensive way for investors, big and small, to take positions in companies and to hedge their risks. They are an extremely versatile instrument, and though options are volatile, the equations of Fischer Black and Myron Scholes can give investors important signals early enough so that their level of risk is diminished. With a PC and a few well-written software programs, an investor can claim profits from options.

But though options are a huge part of the electronic economy, they are just one part of a much larger futures market. The world's futures markets, which are now larger than the world's stock markets, are also truly global and electronic.

Until 1972 the futures markets were primarily commodities markets. That is why the American markets are located in Chicago, which was the hub of America's intranational trade. Chicago was the nation's market city. Farmers brought their wheat there, and ranchers sent their beef there by railroad. The big iron mines sent barges full of iron ore there to be sold. It was where the nation's railroads, rivers, and lakes all came together. It was where the airlines established their first domestic hubs.

The futures markets developed around Chicago's commodity

trade. There, speculators bought up contracts from farmers on wheat that had not yet been harvested and cattle that had yet to make it to the feedlot. They would buy contracts for delivery six months later, and in the meantime, speculators would trade those contracts a hundred times.

Because the speculators were allowed to bid for commodities alongside the slaughterhouses, foundries, and grain mills, the Chicago futures market functioned smoothly. If there was a bumper crop of wheat and prices fell, speculators rushed in, bought up the surplus wheat, and warehoused it.

Intervention from the speculators kept falling prices from collapsing and kept the markets calmer and more orderly than they would otherwise be. Speculation worked the other way around, too. When wheat was scarce, the dealers would empty their grain elevators and sell their surpluses at auction. That sudden rush of a new supply prevented prices from rising out of control. Supply and demand worked their magic in Chicago, giving American farmers a cushion against plunging prices and consumers relief against rising prices.

For a hundred years the noisy Chicago "pits" were where these transactions took place. They were hot in the summer, cold in the winter, and always clamorous. And they have always been among the world's truest "auction" markets.

While Chicago is the world's center when it comes to the futures business, it is not the only place, by any means, where the world trades its trillions of dollars' worth of futures contracts each year. Chicago does have the Chicago Board of Trade, the largest exchange, the Chicago Mercantile Exchange, and the Chicago Board of Options Exchange, but there are other exchanges around the world as well.

New York has the Comex, for Commodities Exchange. It also has the NYCSCE, the New York Coffee, Sugar & Cocoa Exchange; the NYCTN, New York Cotton Exchange; and the NYME, New York Mercantile Exchange. It is also home to the NYFT, New York Futures Exchange.

Kansas City has the Kansas Board of Trade, called the KBOT. And there are huge futures exchanges in London, Zurich, Tokyo, Paris, Frankfurt, and elsewhere. These huge markets have all evolved together and are all competing for business and collaborating on products with one another. All of them now trade financial products such as interest rates, options, foreign

currencies, stock indexes, and so on. They trade financial contracts alongside pork bellies, gold, silver, platinum, and soybeans. To the trader all commodities behave more or less the
same way, whether they are metals, grains, or megabyte money.

FUTURES CONTRACTS GET AUTOMATED

The Chicago Mercantile Exchange is where the concept of trading futures contracts on money was invented, in 1972. Back
then, Leo Melamed, a lawyer, science-fiction writer, and trader,
began thinking about money as a commodity and about how to
trade it.

He had read what economists were writing then: The dollar
was overvalued, and as a result, American exports were being
hurt. In his orientation and outlook, Melamed was a monetarist.
He believed money was at the heart of the economy and that
its quantity determined prices. But he also believed money was
a commodity, something to be traded and haggled over in a
fashion not much different from the way farmers haggle over
the price of rice.

Melamed was also a strong believer in the free market. Though
he was a lawyer and not an economist, he was a disciple of
Milton Friedman, the Nobel Prize–winning economist who
taught at the University of Chicago. Friedman was both a genius
and a dynamo. In the late 1960s and early 1970s Friedman
gathered around him in Chicago a group of like-minded intel-
lectuals that included Melamed. As Friedman's critique of liberal
capitalism gained adherents and his notions about the central
importance of money as the determinator of prices and growth
gained favor, he traveled the world advising heads of states and
ministers of finance in countries as different as India, Chile,
and Israel.

Melamed was a dreamer, but he was also a pragmatic man.
He reasoned that if the dollar really was overvalued, as economists and policymakers were saying, then a speculative futures
market for currencies would have a beneficial effect on its value.
If the dollar was traded the way wheat or soybeans were traded,
he reasoned, there was no way it could remain overvalued.

Melamed assembled a group of egg, butter, and metal traders,
and a few other eccentrics as well. One of his group, Henry
Jarecki, was a Chicago psychiatrist interested in the markets,

in speculation, and in making money. Another, Bert Norton, was a bridge-playing buddy of Melamed's without any futures market experience. Both now are very wealthy men.

Melamed's decision to trade currency futures was based on the change in the nature of money, as we shall see. When the dollar was freed from gold and allowed to float freely in value in 1971, it was just a short intellectual step from the egg and butter pits to the dollar pits. After all, to a trader, how different were dollars from bushels of wheat?

To make his argument, Melamed hired Milton Friedman to write a position paper on trading foreign currencies at the Chicago Mercantile Exchange. Friedman showed how dollars were commodities, and he suggested how a futures market for currencies could be organized.

Partly on the strength of that paper and partly because of the change in the nature of money brought about by the end of fixed exchange rates, the Chicago Merc, as it is called, granted Melamed the right to trade money.

THE DOLLAR MARKET OPENS

Today, largely as a result of Melamed's efforts, about $800 billion worth of dollars, marks, and yen changes hands every day in the cash and futures markets of the world. That amount is roughly twenty-five times more money than is exchanged each day in all international trade transactions.

That money is mostly involved in nothing more than making money. It is an ocean of money. One day's worth of trading is more than all Canadians, together with all their industries, mines, and businesses, earn in a year. One day's worth of trading could buy the total output of the Boeing Airplane Company—everything from its helicopters and cruise missiles to its 747 jetliners—for the next eighteen years. It is money enough to purchase outright the nine biggest corporations in Japan—overvalued though they are—including Nippon Telegraph & Telephone, Japan's seven largest banks, and Toyota Motors.

MELAMED'S MONEY PIT

Leo Melamed's invention was incorporated as the International Money Market. The IMM, as it is known, was set up at the

Chicago Mercantile Exchange with its own trading pit. The IMM has its own list of members who have purchased the right to trade there.

Strangely enough, the pit where money is traded in Chicago really is a pit. It is a round ring, about thirty-five feet in diameter at its widest, that slopes downward in a series of concentric steps. Each descending ring of steps is slightly smaller than the previous one. The ring itself is not much different from the ones where sumo wrestlers collide or cockfights are held except that at its center, instead of clay or sand, there is technology.

The IMM pit at the Merc is definitely one of the most important nodal points on the world's electronic money grid. Wires coming up through the floorboards of the exchange in Chicago are like nerve bundles rising up through the base of the skull. They are filled with a steady stream of vital financial information that moves across switches and synapses in torrents. The Chicago node, in turn, is connected to the other big nodal points in New York, London, and Tokyo. Through these fibers the world trades its currencies, bouncing them off satellites and sending them under the seas. Connected to these thick bundles of nervelike wires are perhaps one hundred thousand computer terminals around the world that follow all traders' moves and instruct them on what to bid and what to offer.

On a busy day five hundred traders can be crowded together on the steps of the IMM pit. They are shouting their bids and offers into the air in what is called "open outcry," an anachronistic system. Open outcry, as its name implies, means that a bid or offer is good only as long as the shout can be heard in the air. As a result, the noise of the repeated bids and offers is deafening.

Within this clamorous environment traders make their deals. An order pops up on a screen, it is brought to a trader, and the trader gestures, yells, and grunts to get attention for his offering or bid. Orders stream into Chicago and the pits from investors around the world.

THE FUTURES MARKET EXPANDS

But dollars are not all that they now trade. Beginning in 1976, Melamed brought interest rate futures to the IMM. These are not really interest rates, per se, but U.S. Treasury bills and three-month Eurodollar deposits. A three-month Treasury bill pays interest at a fixed rate. Own one and you own a rate of return. Buy one and it is the same as if you lent your money to a relative or friend. In this case the relative is Uncle Sam, and he is obligated to pay interest on the loan you have made to him. You can sell the loan you have made to Uncle Sam to someone else who needs a stream of interest paid at a steady rate over an agreed-upon time. Or you can swap your interest rate with that owned by someone else. Get a lower rate when you swap, and your partner must come up with some cash. Trade a shorter term for a longer one, and you pay your partner a sum. Computer programs value these trades, using a variant of the Black-Scholes model. After all, a bond, Treasury or otherwise, is a lot like an option. It has an underlying value, it fluctuates in the market, and it has a defined life span. These programs let you know at every moment the market value of what you own and the optimal price of what you want to buy.

Buy or sell one of these Treasury bills in the IMM futures pit, which you can do in $1 million units, and you can pick up some bargains: a 9 percent interest rate on $1 million, say, could cost you just 8.375 percent. Look down at the computer screen, where Black and Scholes are working hard, and you can tell that the spread on that transaction is good.

At the Chicago Board of Trade, which is just down the block from the Merc, the market for U.S. Treasury bonds has grown even bigger than IMM's pit at the Merc. On a good day at the Board of Trade, $50 billion in Treasury bonds can change hands. For the traders who get a fraction of a cent on every trade, the numbers add up. Many fortunes, including Melamed's, were made in the money pits.

At the Merc, about $2.3 trillion in futures contracts on the Standard & Poors 500 index of stocks also changes hands each year. About $2.4 trillion changes hands each year on the S&P 100, which is a separate index. Another trillion or so changes hands in municipal bonds. Trade in traditional futures products such as oats, hogs, cattle, and copper now makes up only about a third of all the business done on the futures exchanges.

BALANCING ONE RISK AGAINST ANOTHER

But why have these markets grown so large? Partly it is because electronics has enabled one market to use another as a way to cut risk, a strategy called "hedging." Partly it is because the different markets, futures and cash (such as the stock market), are run by different sets of rules. These rules, as we shall see, make it advantageous for investors to make deals across a number of different markets. And partly it is because new software, such as those based on the Black-Scholes model, have enabled traders to develop ways of swiftly moving money from market to market in a vast global money-making game.

Let's examine just one of the rules.

If you buy stocks on the New York Stock Exchange, you can do it either by paying cash (which is why it is called a "cash market") or by borrowing from your broker. If you buy stocks on credit, you have to open what is called a margin account. The size of your margin account is set by the Federal Reserve Board in Washington, which oversees the banks and the money supply, among other things. For more than twenty years the Federal Reserve has required deposits in their margin accounts equal to half their investment. Investors have to have sufficient money in their margin accounts to cover their losses.

In practice, margin accounts work this way: If you want to buy one hundred shares of Company X and those shares cost $10, for a total of $1,000, you have to deposit $500 with your broker and then you can borrow the rest of the money from him to buy the stock. Your broker pays you money market interest on your margin account and charges you a little above that rate when you borrow. Brokers can make big money from their margin operations.

If the value of your stock purchase begins to fall so that your losses eat into your margin account, your broker can issue a "margin call." By doing so he forces you to either put more money into the account or sell your stock.

By setting the margin requirement so high, the Federal Reserve has kept the cash market full of cash—liquidity, economists call it. The market would have to crash by 50 percent on a single day before all margin accounts were wiped out and investors were forced to scramble for money to cover their losses.

That day has not yet happened, although October 19 took us almost halfway there.

Until the early 1970s, if you wanted to buy stocks, you had to abide by these rules. There was no other way. Stocks existed in one domain of the financial system while futures products existed in another. These two domains were completely separate. Different committees in Congress oversaw each of those markets, which, unfortunately, they still do.

The futures markets, however, has traditionally operated by a different set of rules from the stock market. The futures market also has margin requirements, but they are different from those that the Fed sets for stocks. The clearinghouses for the futures markets set each market's requirements. The clearinghouses are where all trades are tallied up at the end of the day and where the money actually changes hands. It is through the clearinghouse that winners pay losers what they owe. Though clearing houses set margin requirements for futures contracts, their decisions are overseen by the Commodities Futures Trading Commission, which in turn is watched over by Congress.

For the Chicago markets (although it is an anachronism to call them the "Chicago" markets since they can be accessed from anywhere in the world) the margin rules invite more speculation than the New York markets do. The requirements on the futures exchanges require only that an investor put up a bond big enough to cover one day's losses. The bond is deposited by a commodities broker at the clearinghouse. The size of the bond, compared to a stock margin account, is generally small— usually just 5 percent or 10 percent of the price of the commodity contract that is being traded, and with all but a few products it is closer to 5 percent than 10 percent.

But the futures market does not really need security deposits as big as the stock exchanges'. Since most commodities are limited as to how much they can go up or down in a single day, the bond an investor puts up is usually more than adequate to cover any single day's loss. If the losses begin to mount, the bond is cashed, and the proceeds are paid directly to the clearinghouse that settles the account.

In the futures system no money has to be borrowed. Although accounts are adjusted daily so that the bond is always sufficient to cover any loss, the only money a speculator needs before he

can obtain a futures contract is the price of the bond. Since the
futures markets move fast and are very volatile, the bond can
often be extinguished after one day's trade. The only person who
has to pay the actual contract price is the one who wants to take
delivery on the commodity when the futures contract expires.

When geography mattered, different rules governing the futures and stock markets were not important. These two sets of
rules also did not matter very much when the products traded
in the two markets differed.

But all that changed in 1972. After Leo Melamed set up the
IMM, a blurring of the borders between the markets began to
occur. First, foreign currencies and U.S. Treasury bonds were
traded on the futures exchange. But then, beginning in 1982,
stock index funds began to emerge like the Standard & Poors
500 index and the separate S&P 100 index.

These indexes, in a sense, are products of both exchanges,
and they can be purchased under either of the exchange's rules.
For the smart investor, that adds to these products' versatility.
With a flick of the mouse money can be moved from one product
to another and from one exchange to another. Even after hours,
when the clamor of the pits has died down, traders can exchange
contracts on all the products they trade on the floor through
Reuters' Globex automated electronic trading system, through
its Instinet system, and through other automated exchanges as
well.

But here is how the rules might affect participation directly.
If you bought the S&P 500 index on July 8, 1991, you would
pay $374 on the New York Stock Exchange. On that same day
you could also buy a futures contract on the S&P 500 index
with a delivery date of September 1991 for $386. Or you could
buy an option on that index at the Chicago Board of Options
Exchange for $8.95 with a strike price of $385, also for delivery
in September 1991. On any given day the price of this product
would vary, sometimes ever so slightly, sometimes widely, across
each of these three exchanges. Not only that, but the cost of
purchasing these products would vary, too.

For instance, if you bought the index in New York, you would
have to put $192.50 into your margin account immediately. If
you did, you would own the stock outright. But if you bought
an option on the stock instead of the stock itself, you would have

to put down only $8.95, the full option price. You could trade that option just as easily as you could trade the stock, and depending on the volatility of the market, you might make or lose more money with an option than with the stock itself. You also might decide to exercise the option and buy the index outright and then sell the stock on the cash market.

Generally, since volatility in the options market is higher than on the stock market, your risk/reward potential is also greater with options.

Or you could buy the stock index on the futures market. Since margins on the S&P 500 are higher than they are on other futures products—the outcome of intense bickering between the New York and Chicago exchanges—the margin requirement on index contracts is 12 percent. That means you would have to put up only $46.32, which you could lose in a single day or which might build up in value if the stock and futures markets were to rise.

These disparities among exchanges have led to wonderfully inventive hedging possibilities, as we shall see. But with the maturation of the futures market, something even bigger has happened.

Because variants of hundreds of the same product can now be traded across many different exchanges, all the markets have become intertwined. Futures, cash, and even the smaller regional exchanges have become closely linked together. Private electronic networks tie together traders during the exchanges' off-hours. Electronic exchanges and simpler electronic bulletin boards also tie traders together with their counterparts around the world. And with Leo Melamed's invention of currency futures and his subsequent invention of interest rate futures, money itself has moved onto the exchange as a commodity to be traded.

To be sure, the pits still exist in Chicago, with their separate culture, just as the white-shoe firms of Wall Street still exist as separate entities. But the noise of the pits coexists with the quiet hum of computer screens. New technologies have not so much replaced open outcry as they have enabled traders to create new pits and have expanded the markets from the region surrounding Chicago and the Midwest to the world. How else could Melamed have built a business where $500 billion changes hands every day?

And new technology has not so much displaced the brokers on Wall Street as it has given them new tools and new strategies. But while it has enabled them to hedge their investments and develop new ways of making money, it has put the individual investor at a market disadvantage. How can someone with a small portfolio gauge risk and assess deals as swiftly as the computers at Goldman Sachs or Morgan Stanley? It just is not possible.

For the average man or woman, the price differences and rule disparities among Chicago, New York, and the regional and global exchanges must seem like a confusing hodgepodge. And they are. London, New York, Tokyo, and Hong Kong trade many of the same products but under very different rules. Some want money immediately, some not for two weeks. Some sell shares, some sell what are called "share receipts." Trillions of dollars trade in and out of these markets every week.

The way these markets, with their particular histories and cultures, have been wired together without planning or foresight makes their actions fraught with contradictions, paradoxes, and insufficiencies. But to the mathematician with an eye trained in finance, these disparities and illogical relationships are precisely where money can be made. Harmonize the markets, subject them to the same rules and regulations, and there would no longer be the possibility of arbitrage—which is to say, there would no longer be the opportunity to buy a product on one market and sell it on another to take advantage of the momentary differences in price between them.

For the mathematically inclined these disparities are also an invitation to devise new formulas for hedging risk by spreading it around the world through a vast web of interconnecting markets, all trading different variants of the same underlying item. Why pay cash when your company needs money if you can buy it on the futures market by putting up a 5 percent bond? And that way you can get your money when you need it. It is precisely those opportunities that geniuses like Leo Melamed seized upon when they opened new markets. But by doing so they also increased the size and complexity of the markets dramatically. With the increase in size came a dramatic increase in volatility as well. For the numbers cruncher, the wiring together of different markets became a way to make vast sums of money.

THIRTEEN

COMPUTERS RUN THE SHOW:
The Invention of Portfolio Insurance and
How It Contributed to the Debacle on
Wall Street

H ayne Leland is a numbers cruncher. Like so many
of the brilliant minds behind the innovations on Wall Street,
this reclusive intellectual was attracted to mathematics and
physics before studying economics. Leland was raised in Seattle,
where he attended the Lakeside School, the same prestigious
private high school where William Gates, the founder of Microsoft, studied.

Like so many innovators of his generation, Leland attended
Harvard, graduating with a Ph.D. in economics. For years he
taught finance at the University of California at Berkeley, where
he still lives. (At one time he even lived on a houseboat in San
Francisco Bay, a most unlikely home for a financial genius who
devised an entirely new class of investment product.)

It was there, at Berkeley, in a quiet campus setting far from
Wall Street and the Chicago pits, that Leland invented portfolio
insurance in 1976. Portfolio insurance is a method for hedging
investments through arbitrage—buying on one market and selling on another—and it uses all the tools of the modern electronic
economy. During times of limited volatility, the practice actually
works. It really does limit downside risk. But when there is panic,

as there was during the market meltdown in October 1987, it only contributes to the market's fall.

With two partners Leland set up Leland, O'Brien & Rubenstein in Los Angeles, selling portfolio insurance programs to be run on the computers of the world's biggest fund managers. Mark Rubenstein, one of the partners, received his Ph.D. from UCLA, and was hired as a professor of finance at Berkeley, where he met Leland and helped him refine his equations.

John O'Brien, the other partner, studied at MIT and at UCLA. A consultant who had put in many years on Wall Street, he became the marketer of the firm.

THE GROWTH OF PORTFOLIO INSURANCE

The business has grown remarkably. In 1976 portfolio insurance did not exist. Today, portfolio insurance is guarding more than $100 billion in stocks around the world. Aetna Insurance, Bankers Trust Company, Morgan Bank, and Wells Fargo Bank have all licensed the programs from Leland, O'Brien & Rubenstein which they modify and sell.

Portfolio insurance starts with the Black-Scholes equations, but it also takes advantage of the disparities of price between the options and the cash markets. For instance, if you buy the entire Standard & Poors 500 index for $374, why not take out a little insurance? For just a few dollars more you can buy a "put" option on the index. Put options give you the right to sell a stock or an index at an agreed-upon price sometime in the future. So if you buy the S&P index for $374, why not buy a put at, say, $372? If you took that position, it would mean that no matter what happens in the stock market, your losses would be a maximum of $2 on each share of the index plus the price of the option. Not a bad way to limit risk.

But what about the upside? If you insure your portfolio this way, there is no limit to your profit potential, although you must deduct the price of the option from your winnings. Since options are now sold on almost all stocks, you can even set out to insure your entire portfolio with an option on every stock.

But buying put options can be expensive, especially when the market is volatile and prices are heading downward. That is because the value of a put option increases as the price of the underlying stock falls. After all, with a put you are locking in a floor price, and that becomes increasingly valuable in a falling market. If the stock sinks below that floor, the option still entitles you to sell the stock at the agree-upon price because the poor fool who sold you the option agreed to buy the stock from you at the prearranged price. To do that the buyer must either be crazy, which is sometimes the case, or else he is getting a sufficient price to cover his risk.

SYNTHETIC OPTIONS

Leland found a way around the high price of options. In the program he developed, which can be modified to accommodate the rules of any of the world's big exchanges, he created what is often called a "synthetic put." It is similar to the mental model of a "synthetic option" that Black used when he was doing the first work on his equations. The synthetic put is a construction that pays its purchaser interest. It does so by buying U.S. Treasury bonds, so it is not really a put option at all. It takes advantage of the disparities between the markets and the different ways different products behave. By doing this Leland was able to devise something that behaves like a put but is far cheaper to buy.

The equations behind synthetic puts and portfolio insurance are quite complicated, but they can be tucked away inside a computer program that contains all the information about an investor's portfolio. The computer can also keep track of the changes in volatility of the market in general as well as the stocks in an investor's portfolio in particular.

When it is switched on, this big program keeps track of the portfolio and all its variables. But rather than buy only options, the program also buys Treasury bonds (part of the synthetic put). Treasury bonds are virtually risk free, and they offer a constant yield. Treasury bonds also vary in price but are subject to risk factors that are different from those of stocks or currencies. Adding Treasury bonds to a portfolio immediately lowers its overall risk—its "beta." And because Treasury bonds can be purchased on the futures market with just a 5 percent margin requirement, the cost of obtaining Treasury bonds is not excessive.

MIXING UP PRODUCTS TO CUT RISK

The portfolio insurance programs (there are now competitors to the ones developed by Leland) mix up products from three markets—options, stocks, and cash—the way a washing machine mixes up socks: vigorously and swiftly. Never before was this possible. Without computers it just could not be done. Without computers and close linkages between the markets, there was no way to assess risk in real time and to analyze a portfolio quickly enough to hedge against risk. As we have already seen, it took Harry Markowitz thirty-three minutes on a 1960s vintage mainframe computer to analyze the beta of one stock portfolio. And that transaction cost about $300.

In today's markets, with today's cleverly built portfolios, even thirty-three minutes is too long to prevent disaster. In October 1987 thirty-three minutes represented an overall market decline of about $55 billion. Portfolio insurance programs running on workstations or souped up PCs complete their calculations in fractions of seconds. As they do, they tell the trader what changes to make in their portfolios.

In today's markets, on a regular basis, computer workstations have to crunch numbers several orders of magnitude greater than Markowitz needed to do his Nobel Prize–winning work. They have to compute risk factors across three or more markets, across time zones and around the world. They have to run hundreds of equations through their microchips within a fraction of a second. They have to take account of the differences in regulations between exchanges and between countries. If they cannot do this, they are useless to the masters of the megabyte economy.

Computerized portfolio insurance has had its share of criticism, however. During the big selloff of 1987, the programs looked at the data and were stumped. The only action they could take was to sell. Selling in a rapidly falling market only exacerbated the plunge. Although Hayne Leland claims that a mere two-tenths of 1 percent of all stock sales on October 19, 1987, were due to portfolio insurance, critics of the programs, such as Charles Schwab, claim that the big insurance programs initiated the fall and then fed it by selling stock, exercising and then selling options, and by buying government bonds.

SO WHAT EXACTLY IS BEING TRADED?

Portfolio insurance is only one way to hedge risk through arbitrage. Some methods that have been developed remain proprietary. Fischer Black, for example, developed a proprietary program for Goldman Sachs & Company that uses his model and trades stocks and other products across a number of markets to reduce risk and increase the possibility for gain. Other companies have done the same, widening their portfolios to include stocks sold not just in the United States but in Europe and Japan. Some of them also include Japanese and European bonds, currencies, and interest rates in dozens of different countries.

The global electronic economy has made this possible. But in the end, what exactly is being traded? These computer programs are not trading stocks, at least in the old sense, because they have no regard for the company that issues the equity. And they are not trading bonds per se because the programs couldn't care less if they are lending money to Washington, London, or Paris. They are not trading currencies, either, since the currencies the programs buy and sell are simply monies to be turned over in order to gain a certain rate of return. And they are not trading futures products. The futures markets are only convenient places to shop. The computers are simply making transactions. They are moving tokens across the megabyte economy.

These programs are trading something that is very abstract and complex. In one sense, all they are trading are ghostly images that symbolize buying power, images that store labor, wisdom, and wealth the way a computer stores numbers.

But they are also trading mathematically precise descriptions of financial products (stocks, currencies, bonds, options, futures). Which exact product fits the descriptions hardly matters as long as all the parameters are in line with the description contained in the computer program. For stocks, any one will do if its volatility, price, exchange rules, yield, and beta fit the computer's description. The computer hardly cares if the stock is IBM or Disney or MCI. The computer does not care whether the company makes nuclear bombs, reactors, or medicine. It does not care whether it has plants in North Carolina or South Africa.

In a way these programs are not all that different from those in the nose of a cruise missile. The missile is given a detailed description of the terrain it must fly over, assembled from satellite data gathered from high overhead. The data is translated into ones and zeroes and put in the missile's computer.

When the missile is launched, its sensors—sensitive compasses, laser gyroscopes, radar, and infrared—scan the terrain below. The scanners constantly try to match what they pick up with the digitized map deposited in the nose cone. The missile flies its course by matching up the terrain below, gathered by its sensors, with the terrain described in its computer. As long as these two descriptions are in synch, the missile stays on target. Using this technology, accuracy can be pinpointed within a few feet in a six-hundred- or seven-hundred-mile journey.

But this is not flying really. It is matching one set of digitized descriptions with another via an elaborate computer model. It is moving rudders and adjusting thrust electronically to keep the two descriptions in line.

Even though all this happens in real time, in the real world, and causes real damage, as proved in the Gulf War, technically it is really more a simulation of reality than reality itself. Change the landmarks on the ground that were picked up by the satellite, and the missile is lost. Its sensors can only compare one set of descriptions with another. They cannot really navigate, they cannot improvise. Destroy the terrain map in the memory, and the missile cannot make it to its destination.

The same can be said about computers. They are programmed to sift through the world's rapidly fluctuating markets where billions of transactions worth trillions of dollars are completed each day. As they scan this vast terrain, they are looking not for individual items but for certain recurring patterns that fit those stored in their memories. They are trying to find strings of numbers that resemble the descriptions programmed into them by the quants at the firm. They are looking for bonds yielding X percent over Y many days to offset a broad-based portfolio of stocks selected for their alphas. They are trying to match preprogrammed descriptions of ideal portfolios with the numbers they see in the real world. They are trying to match the map with the terrain.

But if you brought these ideal portfolios a bright new offering, they would not know how to assess it. The programs, which balance the portfolios of the nation's biggest pension funds, are only trying to minimize their risk while maximizing their gain. They do it by switching on the autopilot and switching off judgment.

While the big portfolio managers use these techniques and proudly point to them as indicators of their sophistication, they are at the same time falling into one of economics' most basic conundrums: the fallacy of composition. This little theorem posits that the actions of individuals, while prudent, can be damaging to the society as a whole. The example that is usually referred to in the textbooks has to do with savings.

In a depression, the textbooks say, the prudent action is for individuals to save as much money as they can. After all, who knows how long each of these individuals will be able to keep on working? And if they are dismissed, they will have to rely on their savings. But from the perspective of the society, the worst action individuals can undertake during a depression is to save all their money. In a depression the economy needs to be stimulated, and to do that, individuals must spend.

The fallacy applies to the electronic economy as well. With all this high-tech gear moving money from market to market and product to product in an all-out effort to diminish risk, the society's overall level of risk is intensified. After all, when capital avoids investment in new companies, when its time horizon is forever being shortened, and when the individual instrument— stock, bond, option, or futures contract—is less important than the overall manner in which a portfolio is balanced, then the capital markets are no longer performing their role in society. Rather than bring capital to new companies and rather than bring money to the government to finance its programs, the attempt to develop riskless portfolios moves investment away from those who need it. The types of returns these portfolios require and the short time frames through which the investment managers see the world cause the entire economy to perform for the short term.

Risk-averse portfolio managers demanding high returns increasingly cause companies to eat their seed corn. No wonder General Electric, Ford, and IBM buy billions of dollars' worth of their own stock to keep the price high rather than investing that money in new research and development. In the short term such actions pay off. After all, those companies use portfolio managing programs, too. But what about tomorrow? How will these companies compete?

Many market economists—the ones who create the programs—see this phenomenon and are not worried. These thinkers, like Alfred Rappaport at Northwestern University's Kellogg School, think publicly held companies have one responsibility: to return value to the stockholders. To Rappaport and his colleagues, many old-line companies—Kodak, for instance—should slowly dismantle themselves, selling off their interests piece by piece. The proceeds from these asset sales should go to the stockholders until the companies themselves are extinct. From this perspective the electronic economy makes vital sense. Companies dismembering themselves look good on the computerized maps in the investors' nose cones. They pay rich rewards, their stock prices remain high, and they have virtually no investment in the future in research and development. This sort of company would be all payoff, and the computers would fight one another to buy it.

But what about the fallacy of composition? How would the nation fare as a whole if companies ran themselves just for the quants? If companies saw the maximization of shareholder value as their only responsibility? If they ignored customers, employees, the "national interest" in order to focus on making their stock more attractive to the computers that pick them?

The answer is obvious: If companies were run just for the shareholder, it would be a disastrous to the country as if everyone saved during a depression. Perhaps more. Kodak, General Motors, Ford, and other major companies that are not growing swiftly enough for the short-term investor would simply be broken up and sold off. That is the way the quants skew the markets. And that is the way the electronic economy is skewed in general.

The machines of the information age are not contemplating investments. They are only trying to match random numbers strewn across the global landscape. They are looking at quick fixes and high rates of return. When something fits their terrain maps, they buy it. They don't question the overall impact of such a move. They don't wonder about how their actions will affect the overall economic organization of society. They are not programmed to do so.

Back in the laboratories of high finance, in the offices of Harry Markowitz, Fischer Black, Hayne Leland, and others, researchers are devising new formulas and new strategies based not so much on the future but on the past. They sit in their offices looking through printouts and running numbers through their workstations in an attempt to capture value.

It is an abstract land, a land of description rather than reality, where the real and the financial economies barely touch. It is from this remote station in life, a kind of financial Tibet, that the mathematicians of Wall Street dream. It is from this remote outpost of economics that trading strategies are born.

FOURTEEN

OPPOSING FORCES:
How the Electronic Economy Is Adding to Instability Not Just in the Economic Sphere but in the Social Sphere as Well

Chaos does not usually develop suddenly; instead, it proceeds little by little. The chaotic collapse of the stock market on October 19, 1987, was preceded by months, even years, of growing instability. What leads to the breakdown of order is often a series of small insults. Each of these insults may not be jarring enough to put the system out of whack, but taken cumulatively, they are a devastating force. Chaos comes the way water boils. It begins with tiny, even hesitant, bubbles before its full fury is unleashed.

Chaos also develops exponentially the way water hyacinths grow across a pond. These lovely white flowers, with their wide, padlike leaves, reproduce themselves every day. At first the pace of their growth seems slow, until finally they fill half the pond. Then, the next day, the pond is completely overrun.

These images apply to the new electro-economic world, which is, after all, being constructed on very shaky ground. As the electronic economy takes shape, it must accommodate conflicting and often contradictory forces—forces that no one completely understands. It is a new world order based on information, but information is always shifting, going out of date, being revised, updated, and amended. Information is often pregnant with what can only be called insults to stability.

The new world is one in which localism—local markets, currencies, and rules—must contend with globalism. It is a world where governments have less power and the private sector more, where governments participate in markets—by borrowing money—but can no longer control them.

It is difficult for the average man and woman to create a world view that fits this new era because the volume of information they receive is overwhelming. In the past there was religion, the family, neighbors, and friends to help explain and give meaning to events. In the past the pace of change was slow, and life could be divided neatly into the same categories that were taught in school: biology, chemistry, medicine, civics, economics, math, and so on. There were absolute standards of right and wrong, and men and women who tried to embody them. In the past changes occurred, but, as they say, they took their own sweet time getting here. All of life's assumptions could not be overturned in a day; there was permanence, not chaos; sharp distinctions, not fuzzy logic and vague terminology. In the past cultures and cultural assumptions about truth, beauty, art, right and wrong, religion and rock 'n' roll did not butt against one another. Cultures were isolated; they did not intermingle or compete to the extent they do today.

In the electronic economy there is no such thing as stasis, no point that is fixed, no assumption that is not related to a host of others, and no idea that cannot be revised. It is a world of images moving across hundreds of millions of computer and television screens, across time zones and language lines and around the world in an eerie global syncopation. The space shuttle Challenger disaster, the October 19 stock market crash, the collapse of the Berlin Wall, the World Cup Soccer game, the invasion of Kuwait, the Gulf War, the Soviet coup—all were seen simultaneously by billions of people and influenced the ups and downs of global companies and the economy.

THE IMPERMANENT WORLD

It is a world of complete *impermanence* where, according to a July 16, 1990, *Time*/CNN poll of people eighteen to twenty-nine years old, there are no leaders or heroes that stand out. A world where the future is vague, undefined, and marked by anxiety. Where young people want nothing but to be left alone to earn a living and, as *Time* magazine stated, let the "people in authority authoritate."

In 1968, Marshall McLuhan wrote that "we have extended our central nervous system itself in a global embrace, abolishing both space and time as far as our planet is concerned." (*Understanding Media,* 1968) But in that book and later in his life McLuhan worried that the nervous system we have extended is rather raw and jumpy and without mechanisms to dampen it when it becomes perturbed.

Like Hyman Minsky, the sagelike economist at the Jerome Levy Economics Institute who wrote *Stabilizing an Unstable World Economy,* McLuhan feared that the newly constructed electro-economic system that girdles the globe tends more toward chaos than stability, that it would create a world where people cannot keep up with change and—in an effort to preserve what little of themselves they still have—a world where escapism and retreat are the only interests pursued with passion.

THE EXTENDED NERVOUS SYSTEM

The nervous system that we have extended outward is a network of terminals and computers nestled in homes and offices, factories and government buildings, libraries and universities, briefcases and desktops, all around the world. It is an array of wires, fiber-optic switches, lasers, microwave relays, satellites, telephone lines, modems, monitors, TV screens, broadcast media, satellite-linked newspaper printing plants, icons, network-serving devices, ATMs, mainframes, minis, PCs, enhanced telephones, and Wall Street trading devices. It is a system that is always juiced with electricity, always calculating and manipulating ones and zeros. It calculates time in billionths of seconds, and it is getting swifter. It is global and glowing, pervasive, and has its tentacles in just about every home in the developed West, nearly every home in the East, and in every neighborhood in the Third World. Access to the megabyte economy is never more than a few feet away. Mankind's sensory and nervous system extensions, as McLuhan liked to call these new technologies, are everywhere.

One of these networks, now called Internet, began as an American scientific- and defense-related network linking a few dozen scientists and their computers in the United States. In its infancy in the early 1960s, when it was known as Arpanet, for Defense Advanced Projects Agency Network, scientists in the Defense Department and at universities around the country and at the Rand Corporation in Santa Monica casually exchanged information about computer design, software configuration, aeronautical engineering, mathematical models, and other technical questions relating to America's defense and technology needs. From its inception the network helped scientists communicate with one another and helped them solve difficult technical problems.

Today, Internet has grown into scientific and technical networks that are no longer limited to defense. It comprises more than two hundred different national and international computer networks linking scientists, engineers, students, and professors in thirty-five countries. It links together supercomputer research centers in the United States with similar centers elsewhere. The network connects 370,000 computers where data can be entered or retrieved, and it has more than 3 million users who are in constant communication with one another.

Each month 3.2 billion "data packets" are exchanged between network users. The volume of information traveling on Internet is growing by 25 percent a month. Most parts in the system can send 2 million bits of information a second (8 bits make up a character or letter); some parts can move 1 billion bits a second. Typically, the system breaks up the transmissions every 100 nanoseconds. And the average speed of transmission is half the speed of light. Internet is one of several thousand such networks.

Computerized networks, such as Internet, travel through wire or fiber-optic cable, or are beamed by satellite around the world. They are controlled by their own computers, called "servers," and by other computers called "hosts." Servers feed the network, and hosts run it.

Data networks are far more efficient than telephone or telegraph networks, especially for financial transactions. The server computers on a network can take a long communication between two or more computers, "cut" it up into small batches called data packets or "envelopes," assign each of these envelopes a destination along the network, called an address, and then electronically transmit the envelopes to their destinations, with other envelopes for other addresses sandwiched in between.

By slicing up the communication into bits and pieces like so much sausage cut with a knife, network-serving computers can fill up any pause in a communication with data bound for somewhere else. The network is designed to operate like a Los Angeles freeway with a steady stream of cars constantly entering and leaving it from the side streets and surface streets below. Superfast switches along the network shift and shunt the data from computer to computer, sending it to millions of different destinations. These switches can turn on and off billions of times a second. All of the world's thousands of data networks are ultimately connected.

THE BANKING NETWORK

To see how these networks interact, let us look at one that is both ubiquitous but invisible: the bank clearing network.

On a normal day America's fourteen thousand banks transfer about $2.1 trillion over their local data networks. This is a staggering sum, more than one-third of the gross national product of the country for a year. In a day enough money goes from bank to bank to cover the salaries of about 100 million working Americans for a year, to pay for seven years of defense spending, to neutralize seven years of balance-of-trade deficits, or to reduce the national debt by half.

Banks transfer these huge sums of money along their data networks primarily to settle checking account balances—yours, those of your friends, and those of America's companies. Some of these highways are even used to settle balance-of-payment transfers between countries. If the networks could not do their jobs quickly, huge imbalances would accrue between banks that receive money and those that are supposed to pay out. If banks were not able to process checks quickly, they would be in the dark about how much money they had on hand. In the simplest terms, they would not be able to cash your check or tell you if you were overdrawn at the bank.

Without a rapid system to process the 2 billion checks written each day, all other monetary interactions within the economy would be slowed down as banks were forced to wait to see what their overall obligations were. They would have to wait until mail trucks, limited to 55 miles per hour, transported paper checks and bills between banks and around the country or until airplanes, limited to 550 miles per hour, delivered checks by air freight. Yet even with these electronic networks and with messages traveling along them at nearly 100,000 miles per second, the average data speed on the banking network, our private banks can have collective checking account imbalances with one another running up to $100 billion or more a day. And because the banks with the deficits generally have to finance those deficits, even if it is only overnight, they have a powerful incentive to develop networks that are efficient and quick.

Banks use their electro-economic networks to settle their accounts with the Federal Reserve Board and its twelve regional Federal Reserve banks. The regional Feds are where private banks keep their legally required reserve accounts and where they go for overnight and short-term loans. Banks might also use these networks to buy and sell billions of dollars' worth of Treasury securities, which they can hold in reserve, and to transfer money overseas.

The regional Federal Reserve banks monitor their members' transactions along the major networks. They watch banking balances, scan the network for large transfers, look for illegal money laundering, and generally try to gauge whether their policies and rules are being followed. Fedwire, which is run by the Federal Reserve from New York, is the biggest of these dedicated banking networks and is the official network for clearing domestically issued checks. It is also used to conduct transactions with the Federal Reserve Board and the Treasury Department.

There are other networks as well. For example, Chips, Clearinghouse Interbank Payments System, which the banks own and which is based in New York, transfers large sums of money to settle accounts between them. A big loan from a bank to a corporation might be transferred around the country on Chips, cut up into small data envelopes by the serve computers, addressed, spliced in between a smaller series of transactions, and sent on down the line. Bankwire, a smaller service also owned jointly by the banks, gets the overflow from Chips and Fedwire.

"The efficiency of these networks is vital to our ability to compete overseas," said Richard Van Slyke, a professor of engineering at the Brooklyn Polytechnic Institute.

Van Slyke, a large man with sandy blond hair and blue eyes, exudes well-being. He has that devilish gleam in his eye that says, "I know something you don't." And well he should. He is an expert on computer cryptology, coding data (especially financial data) so that no one can eavesdrop on the transmission.

According to Van Slyke, our banks and our financial markets are now competing on the basis of their technology; that's where they gain their efficiencies. Not only do these networks allow banks to process checks and move money more rapidly and therefore have more money on hand, but they cut costs.

To get information onto Fedwire, each bank must first gather up all the checks its patrons have deposited in each of its branches. Then operators pass these checks through machines that automatically read the account information written on the bottom of the check in magnetic ink. Next, the operators manually key in the handwritten amount of the check.

Once they are in the system, the computers take care of the rest. For example, they assemble the thousands of checks written by account holders of Chemical Bank in New York, say, and payable to account holders of Bank of America in California. These combined claims from a myriad of accounts become one large claim against Chemical Bank that is then sent electronically to Fedwire, where it goes to the regional Federal Reserve bank in San Francisco. In San Francisco the computers balance the claims against Chemical Bank with the claims by Chemical Bank against Bank of America. The computers in each of the banks are notified, and funds are transferred. This evening ritual takes place millions of times a night as the nation's fourteen thousand banks settle their accounts.

"In New York alone, every day, 3 million financial transactions worth many billions, even trillions, of dollars take place through these electronic networks," said Van Slyke. The computers hardly lose a cent.

Soon the check-clearing network will be completely automated with new machines that are being developed by IBM, DEC, Unisys, TRW, and other computer companies. These new machines can read, interpret, transfer, and even store the handwritten amounts written on the check. They scan checks with high-speed video cameras as checks pass down a conveyor belt. These cameras and computers even enhance the image and convert it to a data code the computers can read. The new computers can also store the complete color image of the check (be it a sailboat, a New England winter, a California gray whale, Mickey Mouse, an illegible scrawl, an endorsement, and so on) and send that image around the country.

To store the color images on both sides of a check now requires, according to IBM, fifty thousand characters of memory, about as much memory as it takes to store ten pages of simple black-and-white text. And considering the billions of checks written each day, the cost of storing all these images in full color is tremendously expensive.

But researchers have developed special mathematical formulas that reduce the information displayed on the check, the handwriting and the picture, into long strings of numbers. These algorithmic equations, which are the key to compressing data, storing it, and then retrieving it, can now be patented.

IBM's new algorithmic system can read, understand, and store the handwritten amounts on a check using only five thousand characters of memory, a tenfold reduction. New storage techniques allow a semiconductor no bigger than a credit card to store 1 million characters. As a result, banks will soon be able to manipulate check images so they can be called up on the color monitor of a personal computer at home, on the color terminal at the bank, or even on an automatic teller machine. In years to come billions of these color images will be transferred around the country, silently, day and night, as the capacity of the data networks increases to what are called "gigabyte" speeds, billions of bits of information a second. This means that one network could transfer each second the full-color images of almost a million checks to any destination in the nation or the world. These high-speed, high-capacity networks would drastically shorten the time it takes for a bank to process its accounts and thereby melt away the large $100 billion imbalances between banks that occur each night. By cutting down these huge overnight imbalances and the big interest rate charges that go with them, the banking system would become far more efficient, cheaper to run, and perhaps even safer because more money could be moved to where it is needed faster.

NETWORKS THAT TALK TO ONE ANOTHER

The network that brings you your money over Fedwire interacts with dozens, even hundreds, of other financial networks. Information from your account can then be automatically sent to the Cirrus check-cashing network, which is owned by MasterCard, so that you can withdraw funds from your account at eighty thousand automatic teller machines located around the country. You can also borrow money from your MasterCard account on this network or from your other credit cards simply by inserting the right card.

MasterCard's Cirrus network, located in Denver, is connected to the NYCE automated teller machine network in New York, the MAC network in New York, the Yankee network in New England, the STAR in California, and the national Plus network owned by MasterCard's competitor, Visa International. Each of these networks can "talk" to any other network. Through some banks these networks can be accessed from a personal computer at home to pay bills, read balances, transfer funds from one account to another and from one bank to another. The data can also be accessed from automated teller machines and from computers inside the bank. Some of these networks can be accessed from abroad, where they not only transfer funds but change them from one currency to another.

You may be standing in front of your branch bank in New York, but when you insert your ATM card into a Cirrus terminal, it sends the impulse to Denver before it goes to a computer inside your bank. Distances no longer matter.

"The computers you are using automatically select the best electronic route—fiber-optic highway, satellite, land telephone lines—whatever is fastest and cheapest," said Van Slyke.

They also transform your transaction into a special secret data code that the managers of the Cirrus network hope no computer hacker can break. All this, including the encryption, happens automatically in the few seconds it takes to complete your transaction.

If you have your paycheck electronically transferred to your account, you are able to withdraw those funds instantly as they move from your employer's bank to a financial data transmission network, such as Fedwire or Chips, then into your bank's computer, and finally through the Cirrus, Plus, or NYCE network to the automated teller machine you are using. These networks, crammed with data, are always in motion. They are always exchanging information with one another and always moving money.

And where does one network end and another begin? "That is the wrong question to ask. All the networks are linked," said Van Slyke. "Ultimately, they are all connected." There is really just one network, and a gifted hacker—given enough time—can enter them all.

Banking networks are also linked internationally. If you receive a check from a foreign bank and your account is at a major money center bank such as Citibank or Chase Manhattan, that check is cleared against the issuing bank through a network called Swift, for Society for Worldwide Interbank Financial Telecommunications. Swift, located in Basel, Switzerland, has thousands of member banks around the world that use this service to instantly transfer money from bank to bank.

Swift is linked, in turn, to a number of local banking networks in countries in Europe, Asia, Latin America, and even Africa. Banks in these countries have ATMs that offer services similar, and in some cases superior, to ATMs in America.

Banks also put secondary information, such as loan payment records, onto electronic networks. This information is purchased by companies such as TRW and Dun & Bradstreet. The computers at these companies are programmed to automatically attach a credit rating value to the information they receive electronically from banks, other financial institutions, and department stores located around the country. Then the rating companies sell the information they receive back to the banks from which it originally came. The rating companies sell lists of the people with good ratings to banks, and the banks solicit them for loans, credit cards, or home equity mortgages. If any of the "prequalified" people on the list accept a loan, the funds are moved into their account automatically, a payment file is started, and the process begins anew with all the networks chattering. And this continual extension of credit is done entirely by machine.

So sophisticated are these new network systems that the approval time for the credit purchase of a new automobile has been condensed dramatically. In the 1970s it took a week or so to have a new car loan approved after it was referred to the local bank's secured loan committee. Today, loan approval can come less than a minute after a salesman makes a call from the showroom to the computerized offices of General Motors Assistance Corporation, Chrysler Credit, G.E. Credit, or any of the other big finance companies. Approval is granted or denied without human intervention.

WHERE THE NETWORKS CONVERGE

As sophisticated as these networks are, they are still vulnerable, and their vulnerability comes from their very source of strength. Computer hackers discovered long ago that because all networks meet and converge, there are really no secure boundaries between them.

They have devised ways to guess personal identification numbers—called PIN numbers—with random number generators and other secret access codes, said Van Slyke. They have learned how to shut down entire networks by transmitting faulty data in the form of viruses, worms, and Trojan horses. They have learned how to generate the same random numbers that data encryption specialists use to protect information. And they have penetrated such seemingly secure networks as IBM's own proprietary computer network that links its top executives.

At best, the boundaries between these networks are semipermeable—as are all boundaries in the new electro-economic economy—and the entire system, considering the amounts of money it is responsible for, is extremely fragile.

FIFTEEN

COMPLEXITY AND THE MARKETS:

How Even the Most Exquisitely Complex and Sophisticated Systems Are Also Fragile

M illions of computers threaded together through tens of millions of miles of cable make up the neural network of money. That complex system resembles a snowflake, an elaborate fiber-optic pattern of connections with nothing at the center. It is complicated, complex, and, paradoxically, both strong and fragile.

Just consider the level of complexity with which we are dealing. The big commercial financial networks have hundreds of thousands of computers all talking together at once. These terminals are often sending the same data in different forms and formats and with different interpretations. I.D.E.A., the big British financial information firm in London, sends out reports from its analysts on the direction of the bond market that often contradicts the reports sent out by Bloomberg Business News. And Bloomberg's online analysts may make radically different interpretations about where the dollar is headed from the analysts at High Frequency Economics, a daily fax service in New York.

This information and other information is sent out along the world's data highways. Once this information is sent, it moves like light bouncing off the walls in a funhouse made of mirrors.

All the nervous, on-the-spot interpretation, communication, and talk is multiplied into near-infinity.

These enormous streams of data, once released, do not simply go into the void. They are acted upon. Each node on the data highways of the world is interactive. A brain sits at each terminal, ready to press buttons, analyze information, and make trades depending on what shows up on the screen. Each flurry of information, price, and interpretation jars the entire system and affects millions of players in the electronic economy.

Just consider the size of the big commercial systems: Reuters has two hundred thousand interactive terminals; Telerate has eighty-five thousand computer terminals; ADP, a rival financial information service, has sixty-eight thousand terminals; Quotron has seventy thousand terminals and other devices; and Bloomberg, fourteen thousand terminals.

Financial companies often have desks full of terminals. They may have Bloomberg, Reuters, and Telerate all going at once. They may also have their own proprietary services: Each broker at Merrill Lynch's hundreds of branch offices can dial up Merrill's own analysts' reports on the screen as well as any of the reports from the commercial services Merrill buys.

Such a level of electronic complexity is staggering. Underneath our streets and through our airways trillions of bytes of information pass each second through a complex series of routing computers, signal repeaters, and incredibly quick switching devices.

But that is not all. The world's financial and banking companies are connected to the global network through their own internal networks of mainframe computers, computer workstations, PCs, supercomputers, pocket terminals, and automated teller machines. These private internal networks, such as the one Merrill Lynch operates, have tens of thousands of computers and terminals interacting with one another. Information sent from one company's branch office to another is often coded, addressed, and then routed along public telecommunications lines. Spliced in between data going from one Salomon Brothers office to another may be data flowing from one of Salomon's rivals, such as Morgan Stanley & Company. Yet secrets from Solly's trading floor are not intercepted by Morgan because the coding is different. For that matter, in between each packet of information from Morgan Stanley may be data from the Pentagon or news reports sent for broadcast on a radio station network.

Though they are not all used for financial transactions, the nation's number-two computer maker, Digital Equipment Corporation (DEC), has an installed base of 6 million networked mini- and mainframe computers, all chattering to one another at once. In 1991, DEC made a deal with Microsoft Inc. to provide software for this massive network so that information from one computer can be transferred to another with a few keystrokes. Each of the computers on these networks is slightly different. Each has different information stored in its memory. Some have unique protocols designed especially for the needs of a single company. Some speak slightly different languages. Some use slightly older versions of the same computer language. These languages are continually upgraded, modified, and corrected.

Each of these number-crunching machines, loaded with software, is in a state of constant interaction with the rest of the network. That means information originating in one box is sent along public and private data highways to another box, perhaps hundreds or even thousands of other boxes. In the process a virus may enter the system, reproduce itself, and foul up the flow of information. Viruses are computer programs designed by mischievous or even malevolent programmers to cause havoc, for example, to reproduce until they have filled a computer's entire memory. Some viruses, the worst ones, are designed to wipe out the contents of a mainframe's memory or destroy its programs or even the software that runs the network. In a recent and very alarming study, one-third of all companies in America reported that their computers had been attacked by a virus within the last year. While viruses are man-made, problems can also happen by accident.

FEDWIRE GOES CRITICAL

One famous incident that may foreshadow others occurred along an important leg of the financial network on November 21, 1985. On that day the Bank of New York in Manhattan installed a new software package on its mainframe computers.

The new program was supposed to connect the bank to the Federal Reserve Board's securities desk through Fedwire and the Automated Clearing House. Fedwire and the Clearing House are electronic data networks used by banks to settle their accounts with one another and with their regulators. Fedwire, which runs on an IBM System 370 mainframe computer, is operated by the New York Fed, one of the twelve regional Federal Reserve banks. The New York Fed has three identical IBM 370s at its data center. Fedwire processes an average of 150,000 transactions between banks each minute. Citibank, the nation's largest bank, can clear as much as $50 billion in checks through Fedwire in a single night.

The Fedwire system has ten thousand nodes—banks, savings and loans, credit unions, and other institutions that issue or receive deposits and checks. That means that almost all the major banks in the United States (and some foreign banks as well) deal with the Fed through Fedwire. On an average day $1 trillion passes through Fedwire as banks exchange checks and borrow from one another and from the Fed itself to cover their overnight shortfalls. Fedwire is also the method that banks use to deposit their reserve funds at the Fed to protect against bad outstanding loans. The Fed monitors the way banks deal with one another by watching what happens on Fedwire and at the clearinghouses.

The Bank of New York is a large money-center bank that has a lot of dealings with the Fed's securities desk. Through that desk the Fed buys and sells government bonds and notes to settle accounts between banks and regulate the economy. When the Fed is buying, its payments add money to the banking system, which puts downward pressure on certain interest rates. When the Fed sells these bonds and notes, it takes money out of the system and puts upward pressure on some interest rates. Banks also trade securities among themselves through the securities desk.

Each evening when banks settle their accounts with one another and with the Fed, 2 billion checks pass through the system over the Fedwire network. But on November 21, 1985, the Bank of New York's new software package had a glitch. For most of the day the Fed delivered securities to the Bank of New York as planned. But the Bank of New York's faulty software package kept it from receiving payments electronically from customers and from other banks. The Bank of New York paid its outstanding bills, but not one penny came in.

In a system as big as Fedwire, with so many checks clearing

in a night, a problem at a single bank is enough to throw the entire system out of whack. While the rest of the system functioned smoothly, the node on the network that was the Bank of New York built up a huge imbalance. By the time the problem was discovered late that night, the Bank of New York owed the other banks on the Fedwire system $23 billion.

Twenty-three billion dollars is real money, to say the least, a scant billion less than the American Express Company grosses in a year, a sum just 15 percent less than Boeing's annual sales. The Bank of New York built up that imbalance in just one day due to the software glitch. But software problem or not, the bank still had to make good on its obligations to the other banks.

The Bank of New York had to raise a lot of money in a hurry. It had just one place to turn: the Fed. It was forced to borrow $23 billion overnight from the Fed until the problem was corrected the following morning. That money was lent to the Bank of New York at an overnight rate of about 5 percent—a little over $3.1 million in interest payments for the night.

The problem affected just one bank on the network, but the imbalance was still huge. What would have happened if the bank's software problem had spread? Or if the problem had been caused deliberately by a virus inserted in the nation's bank-clearing system by a computer hacker or "financial terrorist"? Or, as Paul F. Glaser, chairman of Citicorp's corporate technology committee, asked in *Innovation and Technology in the Markets*, edited by Daniel R. Siegel, "What would have happened if the bank had not solved the software problem for several more days? What if the database had been destroyed, unable to deliver offsetting instruments? What if a clearing and settlement bank had gone bankrupt in the middle of the crisis?"

Instead of an imbalance of a "mere" $23 billion, it might have grown far larger if any of those contingencies had occurred.

Had the breakdown been nationwide—and a problem in Fedwire's software could have caused that—imbalances worth perhaps $1 trillion could have accrued during the night. To cover those imbalances, money would have had to be borrowed. But from whom? Not even the Fed has that much money on hand. A disaster that large would take weeks, perhaps even months, to sort out. The costs would have been catastrophic.

Disrupting the network is one thing, but what if the banks' electronic files were destroyed due to a computer error or a virus?

Reconstructing those files by hand from paper records stored in warehouses around the country could take months.

According to Richard Van Slyke, the nation's financial networks—and some individual banks—have almost certainly suffered from similar disasters and failures. But when they occurred, the banks did their utmost to keep the incidents quiet. After all, if a high-tech robber drains automatic teller machines around the country with counterfeit computer cards—which has already occurred, said Van Slyke—it is not something the banks want to advertise.

WILL THE BACKUP SYSTEMS WORK?

Most financial organizations have backup systems for their computers and networks. The Fedwire system is designed so that every few hours an exact copy of its database is made and sent to another computer. If Fedwire's computer fails, the system automatically switches the network over to one of the two remaining IBM 370s at the New York data center.

But even with those backup systems there can be problems. The entire Fedwire system went down three times between August 1987 and September 1987. After IBM and the Fed's technicians reset the system, its "up time" was extended from an average of 97.2 percent in 1987 to 99.98 percent in 1990. But then disaster struck again.

On August 16, 1990, Fedwire went down again. This time it was not due to the computers. On that day a power failure cut off service to New York's financial district, which included all of the Fed's computer systems. Just as planned, a backup generator was switched on, but the generator was water-cooled. The tragedy that day was that one of the ten-inch water lines used to cool the generators also failed. Hardly a high-tech problem. Without the water the generators could not be used. Fedwire had to be turned off.

Fedwire was not down for long, but it took a week before it could operate at full capacity and resolve all the imbalances that occurred. During that week there were days when Fedwire had imbalances of 15 percent—as much as $150 billion was in the wrong accounts.

In August 1990 the General Accounting Office, the investigative arm of Congress, recommended that Fedwire be strengthened. Not only were there physical weaknesses in the system—its computers could be physically sabotaged without much trouble since the computer rooms were not secure, the report said—but the software used by the Fed to manage the system was not adequate to the task. Fedwire's software was not protected against sophisticated hackers and saboteurs. The system's electrical power, as illustrated by the broken water pipe incident, was also not very secure.

The fact that Fedwire was not secure poses no small problem. With $1 trillion traveling through the system each day, a malfunction (accidental or otherwise) could paralyze the country. In that event none of the nation's ten thousand banks would know how much money they had on hand, how much they owed to other banks, and how much was owed to them.

Two international versions of Fedwire, Swift (Society for Worldwide Interbank Financial Telecommunications headquartered in Basel, with Stratus computers located in Belgium) and Chips (Clearing House Interbank Payments System, with IBM mainframes in New York) have had their share of computer malfunctions despite elaborate backup systems. And each time malfunctions occur, imbalances are built up.

In all there are twenty-one major electronic networks around the world designed to move money. These systems move about $3 trillion a day. None of these systems is more secure or safer than Fedwire. Such are the perils of the information age.

PROTECTING THE FINANCIAL SYSTEM'S SMALLER "NODES"

Fedwire, Chips, and Swift are big quasi-public systems. But what about the smaller private systems that are connected to it and to one another through the neural network of money?

Charles Schwab & Company, the big discount brokerage housed in San Francisco, runs its operations off a souped-up ten-year-old IBM mainframe (not unlike Fedwire's) from its headquarters on Montgomery Street. But it also has a backup computer on the East Coast that follows each move of the San Francisco mainframe and receives copies of its database periodically. The East Coast computer can take over if there is an earthquake, fire, or sudden malfunction in San Francisco.

The New York Stock Exchange, American Stock Exchange,

as well as the nation's futures markets all have backup computers scattered around the country. Citicorp, the big New York–headquartered bank, has its mainframe computers located in a Chicago suburb. The bank's "money" may be in Manhattan, but its electronic "vault" is in Illinois. Citicorp, which is also the nation's largest credit card issuer, has its card operations headquartered in Long Island City, New York, but the computers that keep track of the transactions of its 25 million cardholders are located in South Dakota.

Other companies have moved their back room operations offshore. Backup computers hum for American financial and banking companies in Ireland, Jamaica, the Dominican Republic, Hong Kong, Tokyo, and even Haiti.

DEALING WITH COMPLEXITY

Even so, there are weak links. First, adding backup computers greatly increases complexity along the network. Imagine how complicated it is to have not just one highly complex computer network but a network and its "shadow" operating. Sending copies of databases across the country or around the world for safekeeping can be risky. Data can arrive garbled, or it can be intercepted. A fully backed-up system is really like operating two systems: a primary network and its slave.

But if there were a major meltdown, would these backup systems really work? Or would they create chaos, overloading the lines with duplications of files already in transit? And would their files be recognized as the real thing by the computers on the receiving end? Data recovery experts at consulting firms such as Booz, Allen & Hamilton, McKinsey & Company, Arthur D. Little, and others, caution that the nation's backup systems are not up to the task should there be a real "crunch."

We know how the system operates when one or two computers go down. Fedwire had a fully backed-up system, and still 15 percent of its transactions were unaccounted for, causing billions of dollars in imbalances. But what if several systems went down at once? The result, most likely, would be catastrophe.

Backup systems could be improved to handle accidents adequately. But they still could not avert intentional sabotage.

Between 1988 and 1990 a group of computer hackers who

call themselves the Legion of Doom entered computers owned by the BellSouth network; they designed programs that figured out passwords at each security gate along the company's data highway. Designing a program to figure out those codes granted them access to restricted areas in the network. The company has programs that sweep through its databases to see who has entered, so the Legion members were caught, arrested, and then released.

The former legionnaires now run a company called Comsec Data Security to help other companies defend against electronic intrusions. But if the legionnaires could enter BellSouth's secure databases, what about Salomon Brothers' databases? Or Morgan Stanley's or Security Pacific's? Could hackers enter databases owned by Citicorp to alter credit card balances? Could they change account balances or send out electronic payments to their accounts from Sumitomo Bank? Could hackers disrupt Chips or Swift or Fedwire? If they can't today, they will be able to tomorrow.

In 1988 a Cornell graduate student, Robert T. Morris, Jr., a second-generation computer maven, tall and thin with a scraggly beard, created what is called a "worm" program. Morris's father—also tall and bearded—was one of the developers of computer cryptography. For various government departments, including the spy agencies, the senior Morris developed supersecret ways to encode data. He was a legend in the computing world for his uncanny ability to construct mathematical puzzles and strings of mathematical formulas. These logarithmic formulas were able to conceal order at the outer edges of randomness.

Unlike his old man, Morris the younger was not working for the government but for himself. He devised a devilishly clever worm program—so-called because it "burrows" into a computer, invades a protected system, lies in wait, and then reproduces itself madly at a predetermined time. Morris sent his worm into Internet, the scientific computing network that links hundreds of thousands of computers, supercomputers, and research centers around the world into a data exchange network.

Within hours after its release young Morris's worm invaded and disabled six thousand computers linked together on Internet. Only a few of the targeted computers, such as the one run by the supercomputing center at Carnegie Mellon University, were protected against the worm. Luckily, Morris was only out for glory, not to ruin the system or extort money. His worm program was designed to self-destruct. Even so, Internet was out of commission for hours. Had Morris been more vicious, Internet could have been disabled for months, and years' worth of scientific research could have been ruined.

Over the last few years hackers have broken into the military computers of Israel's defense ministry, not an easy task considering the overall level of security in that country. They have spread viruses through the computer system run by IBM that links its more than 330,000 employees together in a worldwide net. One group, the nuPrometheus League, broke into the computers at the Apple Computer Company; they first stole the source codes for the Apple Macintosh computer and then distributed them through commercial online databases.

These codes, which were closely guarded secrets, allowed people to duplicate Mac programs or write programs for the Mac on their own. When the nuPrometheus League distributed the codes for free to programmers, they breached Apple's copyrights—not to mention its security system. As a consequence, programmers everywhere acquired access to Apple's proprietary research.

There are many other examples of hackers disrupting service, including the case of Logisticon, a company that makes programs for managing corporate inventories, not the most exciting line of work. But when Revlon Inc. did not pay Logisticon's bill, the company entered Revlon's computers and disabled the inventory management program it sold to Revlon. Revlon was forced to shut down for a day.

Other problems also make the neural network of money vulnerable. When a transducer failed in an AT&T switching station in lower Manhattan in August 1991, it shut down an important telephone and data switching station. The failure not only curtailed talk, but, since it was the link through which air-traffic controllers talk to one another, it forced all the airports on the East Coast to shut down. That then idled planes from around the world and, in turn, idled passengers on connecting flights. With the failure of those devices, worldwide air traffic was disrupted for nearly a day.

CONCENTRATED TECHNOLOGY LEADS TO SPEED AND VULNERABILITY

Aside from its vulnerability to accident or sabotage, the blown AT&T transducer points out another vulnerability of the system: All the technology of the megabyte economy is highly, highly concentrated. For example, a single undersea fiber-optic cable between the eastern United States can now carry 85,000 simultaneous telephone and data transmissions. A single satellite can carry about 135,000 simultaneous transmissions. That is an enormous amount of data to flow through a single device either underneath the seas or in the heavens.

Such concentration makes a great deal of sense economically. It does not cost very much more to launch a complex satellite or to lay an ultra-high-capacity cable than it does to put in older technology. (Not that many years ago the maximum number of simultaneous transmissions an undersea cable handled was sixteen.) But what happens when that satellite fails? When its solar panel is struck by a tiny meteor? Or when the undersea cable is destroyed? With that much concentration a single disaster could stop the flow of communication between continents for months. Similarly, what happens when Fedwire—with its $1 trillion in daily transactions—is invaded by a hacker's virus? The whole system could shut down.

Other data systems are equally concentrated. The information system for clearing credit card charges run by Visa International has been doing more than $1 billion per day in business since 1989. Visa runs the Cirrus automated teller machine network, and it does clearing for dozens of smaller credit card companies. If Visa's computer went down for just a few hours, it would be enough to show up on the Commerce Department's data on retail sales. If payments were disrupted or cash was unavailable on Cirrus during the Christmas holiday shopping season, for example, it could cause riots.

The point of this is, of course, that the neural network of money is highly capable, a real technological advance, but it is also fragile, and its highly concentrated nature magnifies whatever frailties it has. As a consequence, a local disaster could become a global disaster. A system failure at a single critical switching station could idle communication around the world.

A virus sent into the system by a graduate student at a local university could immobilize an entire network.

The global system needs more backup capacity, as the 1990 GAO report said about Fedwire. For instance, in 1989 a backhoe operator digging pipes out of the ground near the Chicago airport accidentally dug up and snapped a fiber-optic cable connecting the United Airlines reservation system with the rest of the world. For an entire day it was as if United, the nation's second largest airline, had ceased to exist. No one could make a reservation, check a seat assignment, or cancel a flight. That problem could have been prevented, said Richard Van Slyke, had United simply installed a second cable that exited the building from the other side. Salomon Brothers and some other financial houses have just such an arrangement. But, unfortunately, not all of the nodes along the world's electronic network of money are so well defended. For a hacker with a newly designed virus, any un-defended entrance point is an invitation to invade the entire network.

SIXTEEN

THE CENTERLESS WHOLE:
How the Global Electronic Market Is
Fueled by Fads and Fed by Rumors to
Create Shorter Time Horizons and More
Volatility

N etworks, by definition, do not have centers, which makes them difficult to control, police, and govern. In an electronic network every point or node is equidistant from every other point. Each node communicates its good or bad news, its zeros or ones, with every other node at half the speed of light, the speed at which, according to Einstein, time collapses and ceases to flow.

A world of electronic networks is a world where data can flow without restriction across national borders, through security barriers, around the globe, almost without regulation. The information it conveys—money transfers between banks and between countries, the purchase or sale of stocks, bonds, and currencies, orders for products, TV programs, the news, gossip, cartoons, rumors—all intermingle as the server computers cut and splice and address the ones and zeros that are pumped through the lines.

These transfers of information are extraordinarily difficult to monitor and trace. Every bit of communication is moved through the network, from point to point, in the most direct and most economical fashion, which means that throughout the day, minute by minute, data may be disassembled, reassembled, and

shunted along completely different paths. The networks themselves are formed and reformed constantly as they change their
shape to accommodate traffic.

This is a complicated world, one in which a great deal of
mystery and significance lies beneath our streets, in the power
lines and cables inside our walls, inside the plastic and metal
boxes on our desks, and in electronic components in our homes;
one in which each letter in a word is sent along a different
pathway in the computer network; one in which each zero in
the number 1 billion may take a different route to the market.

THE END OF EQUILIBRIUM

In a networked economy the old economic ideas of "equilibrium"
are gone, vanished, outmoded. How can there be equilibrium—
which economists define most simply as the balance between
supply and demand over time, a balance between economic
inputs and outputs—when the supply of information always
increases? When each analysis adds to each subsequent analysis? When information alone can create purchasing power and
define value? When the data that people use to make their buying and producing decisions is revised by the minute? When
Wall Street's case of nerves can cause a 508-point drop in the
Dow, costing $500 billion, and no economic fundamentals have
changed?

How can there be equilibrium when real and financial economies are so different in size? When the formerly fixed boundaries between nations, trading partners, companies, competitors,
and collaborators have all been breached? When the battle between American and Japanese chip producers is fought not on
their home turfs but in the design and engineering studios of
other countries such as Switzerland, Britain, and Israel? When
money is private and can be created not just by the federal
government but by credit card issuers and banks? When government can no longer control exchange rates?

And how can there be equilibrium when the size of the pool
of money changing hands globally every day dwarfs the actual
value of the goods traded? When countries grow nationalistic
and protectionist just as they lose control over their own destinies? How can there be equilibrium if money becomes transformed from something solid and substantial, with demonstrable

equity value such as silver or gold, into something new, strange, and ethereal?

PREDICTABILITY IS LOST

Peter Schwartz, a futurist and consultant in Berkeley, California, who was head of strategic planning for Royal Dutch Shell in London, said in an interview that a networked economy is an unpredictable economy where the "significance of people's perceptions—the intangibles—can begin to matter more than the facts themselves." To economists such as Hyman Minsky, to futurists such as Peter Schwartz, and to theorists such as Marshall McLuhan, this network of networks increases everyone's chances for gain and loss dramatically.

One reason the electronic economy is perpetually out of balance is that whenever data travels over a network, it is magnified. Magnification in this sense does not mean that it is made louder, brighter, or bigger. It means that the data assumes a greater degree of significance the more it is perceived. The significance may have nothing to do with anything intrinsic. Often, just the fact that the data has been distributed—that it is seen by someone, as Peter Schwartz says—is what makes it important.

Take, for example, the economic figures released by the government. These include information on the gross national and domestic products, the trade deficit, consumer spending, inflation, and many other figures. The stock, bond, and foreign exchange markets usually react to these figures when they are released. They react even though the figures released by the government almost always have to be revised a few weeks later and sometimes revised again months after that or even a year after that. In many cases the revisions are greater than the original estimates. Sometimes the sign, plus or minus, is even wrong. In these instances even hard-boiled investors rely not on the data itself but on how they think other people will perceive that data. As bad as the data is—and every year economists complain it gets worse—it continues to move markets.

According to Francis Schott, former chief economist of the Equitable Life Assurance Society, "The trade statistics are particularly noisy, and as an economist I try never to make too much of those figures when they are released. However, in advising my company, I must consider them because the mar-

kets do." In other words this information is significant because
it is released; it is not released because it is significant.

Every time new information makes it way onto the electronic
global grid—whether that information is "noisy" or not, true or
false—it modifies the assumptions of nearly everyone connected
to that grid. It causes everyone on the network to consider not
only the significance of each new morsel of data served up but
how everyone else on the network will interpret it and react. As
Francis Schott said, the trade statistics may be poor indicators
of the true trade picture, but they must be considered because
investors attach meaning to them.

"As a result of the influence of people's perceptions, a system
as complex as the global economy will always have a variety of
possible outcomes," Peter Schwartz wrote. His point was that
like subatomic particles in physics, which are governed by what
is called the Uncertainty Principle, the economy is also altered
by the way we observe it. (*International Economy*, March/April
1988) According to Schwartz, "Information is always contami-
nated by people's beliefs and is never really complete."

Mood, which is difficult to quantify, emotionality, sentiment,
confidence, and fear, all cloud the lens through which we see
information. Forecasts that are supposed to rely on the data
usually are wrong. And because networks have no centers, no
place to filter out the true from the false, information that makes
it onto the global grid is first considered true before it is discarded
as false.

Those forecasts that are "messier," that allow for the influences of other factors, may often be more accurate, but with
sentiment so hard to gauge, it is a wonder that forecasters like
Schott, who has often been quite accurate, can foresee anything
at all.

THE WAVE-PATTERN ECONOMY

Information networks can be thought of as highly complex assemblages of standing wave patterns. These standing wave patterns resemble the almost motionless wrinkles on the surface
of a swiftly moving stream as it flows around a group of rocks.
The standing wave pattern is usually fairly stable, but it also
oscillates a little as each new bit of information is added—a new
statistic about trade, news of the death of a country's elder states-

man, the intention of a company to issue a bond, a change in consumer confidence, and so on.

Each new bit of data added to the network is like a pebble thrown into the stream. The pebble disrupts the overall pattern as the news of its impact is communicated outward in a series of concentric circles. But when that news is fully absorbed, the original pattern slowly returns. While most new data interferes with the pattern a little, it doesn't have the power to alter it permanently.

Each of these patterns, in turn, influences other patterns around the world. Trade statistics showing a big increase in the United States' deficit might cause traders to sell dollars and buy yen, disrupting those markets somewhat. A pickup in consumer spending might cause other traders to sell bonds and buy stocks, causing those patterns to shift based on new information added to the mix.

But over time these variations don't amount to that much— bonds go up or down a few basis points, stocks rise or fall a few points, a product sells and then languishes on the world's shelves. The rocks embedded in the standing wave stream still hold firm.

Yet every once in a while, on a day like October 19, 1987, quite unpredictably the entire network becomes so agitated that even the rocks on the floor of the stream are jostled. Such an event changes the standing wave pattern irreversibly.

Wars and revolutions can cause these shifts. So can the collapse or long-term run-up of a market or a new interpretation of the law.

The biggest changes, which are chaotic, are beyond the ability of most forecasters to predict. They are difficult to forecast because they are heavily influenced not just by the events but by the way people view them.

No one foresaw the October crash, which was highly influenced by people's perceptions. No one predicted the three-month collapse of Japan's Nikkei stock index or the demise of the savings and loan industry or Iraq's grab for Kuwait's oil or the Soviet coup.

Since nearly all networks are connected, and all computer terminals and modems around the world serve as sense organs for the global information grid, the causes of a catastrophic event are broader than ever before and therefore more difficult to fore-

cast. Information, misinformation, leaked information, guarded
information, misplaced information, and noisy information all
influence events. As a result investment advisers such as Francis
Schott must increasingly act on the basis of what they think
other people think. They must give their advice by taking into
account how others will react to the wide range of data that the
information grid serves up. Instead of analysis, the new world
demands intuition.

"In the case of the Federal Reserve," said Schott, "I must
think about how the Fed will react to the economic data that is
released by the government and then how the markets will an-
ticipate how the Fed will react to that data. Sometimes it's a real
guessing game."

DOWNGRADED GOVERNMENTS

And what about governments in this networked world? They
have been downgraded when it comes to running the economy.
The trend that has been going on for more than a decade is for
governments in every country to sell off their holdings and at
the same time borrow more in the capital markets.

On the governments' part, selling off assets is an admission
that in a global economy centralized control creates entities
which move far too slowly and respond far too awkwardly to the
quickly changing international environment. It also shows that
the power of government is decreasing at a rapid rate relative
to the private sector.

It may take social scientists quite some time before they fully
understand the role of government in this new world. Government, business, commerce, and trade are all being redefined as
globalization proceeds with dispatch.

The convergence of those two trends, a future more difficult
to predict and government less able to act, is alarming. It may
signal a future where there is too little central authority to stop
a calamity before it occurs. The world may lack sufficient control
mechanisms to curb chaos when it begins.

TECHNICAL FACTORS

The immensely complicated neural network of money, with its
millions of nodes and billions of transmissions, links markets

everywhere in a dance of commerce and trade. Eavesdrop on conversations at a Wall Street restaurant, and you are as likely to hear traders talking about New York's markets as about Tokyo's exchanges, the Philadelphia Stock Exchange, where options are traded, or the Chicago futures markets. Decisions on what and when to buy or sell a product have nothing to do with geography. Traders with PCs, workstations, modems, and a few passwords can trade anywhere.

Traders are hunting for returns. Less and less do the fundamentals matter. The world is now driven by "technical" factors—that is, models, computer or otherwise, that tell traders when to buy or sell. Some of these models, like the ones developed by Harry Markowitz, have won Nobel Prizes for their creators. Others, such as the Black-Scholes model for trading options, are contenders. But there are other quirky factors, to say the least, that move markets. These are the human factors.

Technical factors frequently have little regard for how much research and development a company is undertaking and how many patents or copyrights it owns. They also rarely take into account the strategic moves a company might make. It took a Japanese company, Sony, hunting for a strategic alliance, to recognize the value in the film library owned by Columbia Pictures Inc. and in the record library owned by CBS Records. Sony bought both companies outright. It took another Japanese company, Matsushita, to see the value in the film library of MCA Inc. and its Universal Studios subsidiary.

Before the takeovers, Wall Street's computerized gnomes traded stock in Columbia and MCA with apathy. The computer programs on Wall Street did not see the value the strategists at Sony and Matsushita did. Nor did Wall Street's technical models like the unpredictability of the film business. The models want steady results, a quarter at a time, and are not interested in the longer term.

Generally, technical models measure little more than the risk/return ratio on an investment or on an entire portfolio, as the Markowitz models first did two decades ago. These models also work in real time, as events happen, and continually recompute the risk/return ratio. Some of the more complicated models give buy and sell signals derived from interviews with experts. Others monitor the market as a whole and compare prices on one exchange to prices on another. Some models even take account of the overall economy—where interest rates are, what the government's leading indicators say, the rate at which debt is growing.

DUBIOUS MODELS

But some of these models—some of the more dubious ones, that is—attempt to do more. For example, four thousand investors subscribe to the *Elliot Wave Theorist,* a $200-a-year newsletter that gives buy and sell signals based on a complicated numerological formula that attempts to measure the mood of the masses. The *Elliot Wave Theorist* is also available electronically on fourteen thousand Bloomberg Business News terminals around the world. The *Theorist* is produced in Gainesville, Georgia, by Robert Prector, a reclusive refugee from Wall Street.

Though the *Theorist* failed to call the 508-point stock market collapse in October 1987—instead, it predicted the Dow would reach 3,700 sometime that year—it did announce the long upward movement of the market beginning in 1982 and several turnarounds in the market that occurred subsequently.

The *Theorist* also announced that a "top" to the market (not just the stock market but all markets, including the futures and real estate markets) had been reached in mid-1991, just prior to the mini-collapse of November 15, 1991, when the Dow fell 120.30 points, its fifth largest decline ever.

On Wall Street there was significant awareness that the *Theorist* had predicted the market's top. Traders became nervous. A number of traders and analysts were also aware that wave enthusiasts everywhere (not just those associated with the *Elliot Wave Theorist* newsletter) were predicting the end of the ominous "fourth cycle," after which the market would fall dramatically. That market fall would be so dramatic, said David Allman, director of research at the *Elliot Wave Theorist,* in an interview, that the market would trade at about half its November 1991 rate sometime in 1993. A Dow of 1,500 is what he predicted—down from about 3,000.

If nervousness and defensive investing have returned to the trading desks of Wall Street, Lombard Street, and the Ginza, the *Elliot Wave Theorist*'s "technical analysis" has helped to make it so.

Of course, there may actually be something to the *Elliot Wave*

Theorist's analysis, though it is certainly not scientific. But it does have enough adherents to move markets.

The wave's rationale goes back to a mystically oriented accountant in the 1920s named, not surprisingly, R. N. Elliot, who was influenced by the writings of a California yogi. The yogi taught that there was a cyclical quality to life, a nice thought that is still open to debate. Elliot fit numbers to that yogi's idea. The numbers he chose, called the Fibonacci numbers series, is a repeating series that was discovered by a thirteenth-century mathematician who was trying to figure out the progression and rapidity with which rabbits reproduce. The mathematical progression of the series, which can be topologically graphed as a spiral radiating out from a central plane, has some elegance to it. But it is about rabbits, after all, not markets.

No matter. Once Elliot got hold of it, the Fibonacci series seemed to fit his idea of a constantly repeating series of stock market cycles, which he then modestly termed the Elliot Wave.

Without any empirical evidence, many important Wall Street mavens have been following the theory. (No one really knows positively when one cycle ends and another begins. And the *Elliot Wave Theorist* admits that some significant errors have been made based on that one point, especially failing to predict the October 19, 1987, collapse.)

Some technical traders, many with MBAs from the best schools and some even with Ph.D.s, buy and sell based on where the Wave is headed. Other intelligent economists and analysts must be polite to these Wave enthusiasts because they pay the consulting bills. And because Wave advice goes out to thousands of paper and electronic subscribers, a call from the *Elliot Wave Theorist,* no matter how implausible the theory may be, can move the markets. That means otherwise rational investors must be ready to react to what the "irrational" is saying. At times, such as on Novewber 15, 1991, that thinking was pervasive.

There are other "technical" models, too. There are newsletters based on astrology, numerology, and other very tenuous material. There are analysts who try to map mass psychology, and psychologists who try to analyze mass markets. There are also "inferential" thinkers—analysts who clip small-town newspaper stories seemingly at random and then report on what patterns they see in the news. Some of those technical analyses flash on traders' screens when a call about a market is about to be made.

These rather dubious "technical" analyses exist side by side with other technical analyses that are based on science and economics properly applied and sometimes misapplied.

It is a jumble out there. The thought waves of the megabyte economy are not only congested but also very confused. Though investors have always sought help from outside the mainstream, the difference now is that the electronic system takes whatever fad or hysteria is in the air and spreads it globally. As a consequence, fundamental factors—the strength of a company, the resiliency of a country's economy, the size of its film library—may at times mean less than the pseudoscience of astrology or the Elliot Wave.

Even so, most old-guard economists believe markets are rational. In fact, among most economists it is simply a given—a basic tenet of their thinking. They conceive of the market as a "price discovery mechanism." That is the notion they are selling to Eastern Europe as they help those countries construct market economies, and it is based on the idea that with enough interested bidders, the price of anything will soon reflect its real value.

But that notion negates the quirkiness of everyday humans. It neglects the superstitious nature of the way many traders trade and many buyers buy. It neglects the influence of such preposterous ideas as the Elliot Wave, astrology, and sheer intuition as market movers.

When David Allman sends out a Wave call that causes thousands of otherwise rational people to buy or sell an asset, what has really changed to make that asset suddenly more or less valuable? The answer is nothing. Though markets often behave rationally, they do not always do so. The spread of technology has created an incredibly efficient system for buying and selling products. But it does not add one whit of rationality to the process. If anything, it makes it easier for markets to move for the most improbable and panicky reasons.

MARKETS THAT ARE TOO EFFICIENT

When the stock market dropped 120.30 points on November 15, 1991, Lawrence H. Summers, the chief economist at the World Bank who is on leave from the economics department at Harvard University, said in an interview that "the markets often react to events far more than the fundamentals suggest they should."

That was a diplomatic way of putting it. What he meant was that nothing happened to the world on November 15, 1991, that made it substantially different economically from the world of November 14. No major company went bankrupt, no new statistics were released by the government, no big mergers were undertaken, and no massive deals fell through. Except for the market's moves, it was a pretty normal, even boring, day.

Yet suddenly the value of corporate America had taken a 4 percent drop. Similarly, there was nothing very much different economically between the way the world looked on Friday, October 16, 1987, and the way it looked on Black Monday, October 19, 1987. The world's electronic economy simply went into conniptions.

The world's markets react to whim and fancy. That has made them far more volatile than at any other time. Such volatility is good (and profitable) if you have the right programs running on the right computers and are able to drastically shorten your investment time horizons from months to weeks, days, and sometimes even minutes. But that change has been very damaging to the underlying real economy (where most of the world works), which thrives best on long-term planning and stability.

Volatility really is increasing. Robert Shiller, an economist at Yale University, has applied statistical methods to analyze price changes in the markets. His conclusion is that volatility is far larger today than in the past and that the price swings which underlie that volatility are greater than what can be accounted for by any underlying changes in the value of the real assets. What Shiller pinpointed as the cause of the increased variability in stock prices is trading for trading's sake: speculation. Increased speculation in the markets is what is driving the markets. A good portion of that speculative hunt for gains is motivated by rational analyses, but a significant amount is propelled by irrational fears, hopes, and expectations.

One implication of Shiller's findings is that the electronic marketplace is not as good as it once was as a mechanism for discovering real value. It may be good for speculation, and it may be good for bringing untested and often wacky assumptions to light, but it is not good at discovering value. After all, the real value of companies changes only slowly; it does not change minute by minute. And companies do not suddenly gain or lose 4 percent or 20 percent of their value in less than a single day.

In other words, the electronic economy may be masking rather than discovering the real value of our corporations and other assets. The electronic market may be failing in its most important task.

That is a frightening thought. And if it is correct, there are very serious consequences. For example, if the megabyte economy is a speculative economy where trading has replaced the orderly (though noisy) price discovery mechanism, then anyone using the market as a price gauge is using a gauge that is faulty. That means most investors do not really know the value of America's (and the world's) corporations.

If real value in the market is hidden, then speculative trading is a much better strategy to follow than investing. If the value of General Motors or IBM is hidden behind the electronic buzz of speculation and the noise of "technical" factors, then whoever is lucky (or smart) enough to discover the real value of those assets can rush in and scoop them up, hold them briefly, and then sell them when everyone else catches on.

Markets have always contained a speculative fringe, but traditionally, long-term investors held the broad middle ground. Traditional markets were created for moving capital to companies with good ideas in return for a share of the profits. Traditional markets were supposed to be transparent, with the value of a company reflected in the price of its stock. But speculative markets treat stocks as if they were commodities where trading is the way to create profits. By definition, speculators are short-term investors. When they dominate a market, they change the market's character, and transparency goes away.

Electronics have made the stock market, particularly the American stock market, cloudy. The real values of the companies traded on the big exchanges are obstructed by the frenzy of speculation and the myriad of ways in which products can be traded. How does anyone know what Chrysler is worth when traders around the world are exchanging its options, warrants, bonds, and common and preferred shares of stock at electronic speeds? Can the company really be worth 40 percent less from one year to the next? Can investors who buy the stock really know so little about the company that when its debt is downgraded (no surprise to those who have followed Chrysler's woes), the stock plunges nearly 20 percent in a day? The only reason for that kind of reaction is that most technically oriented investors know a lot about stocks and very little about *companies*.

Perhaps that is why so many Japanese—and, to a lesser extent, European—investors have come into the United States to invest since the electronic economy began. They know our companies better than our own investors do, and they place a higher value on our assets than we do.

From a speculator's point of view the American companies that have been bought over the last few years are nothing more than large agglomerations of underperforming stocks. Few investors—and no American company—wanted to buy CBS Records (despite Bob Dylan, Michael Jackson, and fifty years of rock, folk, and jazz); MCA and Columbia Pictures (despite their film libraries); RCA Records (despite Elvis Presley); part of Time Warner Inc. (despite its film, book, and photography libraries); McDonnell Douglas (despite its technology and manufacturing expertise); Genentech (in spite of its patents and experience in genetic engineering); Macmillan Publishing (with its long list of titles); and dozens of small computer and software development companies with scant earnings but long lists of patents and copyrights. To American investors schooled in speculation, these companies had little value. To European and Asian investors, these companies were brilliant jewels.

MARKET "ADJUSTMENTS"

Another piece of evidence that the electronic markets are failing at their most basic task has to do with the increase in large market "adjustments" over the years. Seven of the ten largest daily price changes on the New York Stock Exchange since the end of World War II happened since 1987. The years since the 1987 crash have been more volatile than all the years preceding it.

So many big stock markets changes centered in such a short span of time suggest that the markets are not responding to the ups and downs of the greater economy. Between 1945 and 1987 there were four deep recessions. Since 1987 there has been only one, and it has been relatively shallow. But the markets weathered the four recessions prior to 1987 with equanimity compared to the way they have reacted after that date.

For the markets it no longer seems to matter whether the economy is headed into a recession or a period of prolonged growth. All that matters is whether the trading day offers electronic speculators the prospect of making money. And though newspapers and the electronic media are obligated to give reasons for each market rise and fall, the evidence seems to suggest that there usually is no reason at all. The value of companies is not discovered by the market, only the value of a stock. Just as the real and financial economies have become divorced, so for the most part have companies and their stocks.

The electronic markets may be hampering rather than helping the economy as a result. The markets are highly volatile and increasingly speculative. They are also extremely expensive. For instance, according to research undertaken in 1987 by Lawrence H. Summers when he was at Harvard, the corporations listed on the New York Stock Exchange had a combined income of $310.4 billion, while the receipts of the firms with membership on the NYSE—the ones that are actually allowed to trade those companies' stocks—totaled $53 billion for the same year. Add to those fees the costs that companies must pay to keep their stocks listed and traded—reporting, presentations to securities analysts, and payments to consultants, accountants, and others to put the companies in legal compliance with the market rules—and the costs of participating in the "official" market increases that sum to $75 billion. According to Summers that means *the markets* today consume about 24.2 percent of total corporate profits. That is only a little less than the $133.8 billion the corporations paid in taxes.

SHRINKING TIME HORIZONS

So who is winning in the megabyte economy?

Clearly corporate America—the country's real-economy companies such as GM, Ford, and IBM—are the losers. These companies have had their time horizons shortened, and they have been buffeted unceasingly by the volatility in the stock, bond, and international currency markets.

Since 1971 and the demise of the Bretton Woods system, they have been victimized by rising interest rates, rising commodity prices, and the continued demand from investors for profits that match the expectations of the computer models. They have also been hit hard by rising prices.

Over the years, especially during the 1980s, real-economy

companies have been hit by wave after wave of corporate take-overs, with the stock market conspiring in those takeovers by camouflaging rather than revealing true value. These companies have also been handed a big bill from the firms that sell their stocks for the thrill of participating in financial markets that are rigged against real-economy companies. Companies that produce goods but exist in a world dominated by finance have been hurt badly.

Workers have also been hurt. Since 1971 wages have remained flat in real terms because American companies, forced to provide greater profits to satisfy the demands of the markets, have failed to invest in productivity-enhancing machinery.

Old-line financial companies have also lost in the electronic economy. The role of banks, savings and loans, and finance companies are being taken over by smaller, more mobile, and nimbler competitors. Banks continue to have huge overhead costs associated with originating and servicing mortgages and other loans, with those loans now usually bundled together into portfolios that are sold in the markets. Banks and savings and loans, determined to compete, entered markets about which they knew very little and have watched their losses mount. In finance, too, the idea of building and holding a portfolio—loans, in this case—has been replaced by the notion of transacting business. Loan portfolios need to be administered; loans that are sold do not.

The government is also a loser in the electronic economy. The Federal Reserve, though powerful, cannot determine policy if it goes against the wishes and whims of the market. The Fed is a large and important financial factor, but it is only one of many large factors in the world.

The regulators, too, have lost. While trying to maintain distinctions among markets—futures, stock, options, and so on—they have instead created arbitrage opportunities for quick traders. By exploiting the differences among the markets, computers and their masters can amass great fortunes. The regulators, forced to watch powerlessly as they fight their turf wars, are relegated to inconsequential actions such as debating whether one product is an option or a futures contract. While they conduct their debates, market participants continue carrying out their abuses.

America, more than any other country except Britain, is the

loser. Our large, open markets have made our real-economy companies especially vulnerable to the ups and downs of the electronic economy. In a world with multiple currencies, where telecommunications has enabled production to be far-flung and global, jobs have migrated offshore. America, the most advanced economy, is the most globally diverse, with more of its profits emanating from abroad. As a consequence, with the majority of trade now for parts instead of products, the trade imbalance has become a structural component of our economy. That means every export contains imports, making it nearly impossible to have balanced trade.

But there are some winners in the megabyte economy. The firms that have a share of the $75 billion or so in fees from trading stocks are big winners. So are the traders. And the firms that design the tools that make the market work—software, telecommunications equipment, and computers—are among the few who have also won big.

SEVENTEEN

THE SOCIAL COSTS:
When the Economic Unit Is the Globe, Where Do People Fit In?

It is no mere coincidence that along with the integration of the world's economy into a seamless electronic whole, there is an upturn in ethnic rivalries and violence and civil unrest. In 1992 there was war in Yugoslavia and in the former republics of the ex–Soviet Union. There were riots in American cities as different as Los Angeles, San Francisco, and Atlanta. Images of those wars and riots on CNN and the other media brought home just how powerless some groups remain in this highly integrated world economy.

Computers talk the same language; they understand one another. They share data, track products and money, and move investments anywhere their programmers say they should. But what about the people? What about the workers in Watts displaced by workers in Korea or Mexico or India? Or the citizens of Armenia, suddenly vying for power with their neighbors? Or the citizens of Russia, once cocooned by the state but now in full competition with a world economy that its leaders have forced them to join?

For these people, a world that is rapidly integrating, that is becoming one, is a world full of fear. For them, a world where markets are linked and the "means of production" are globally distributed is one in which powerlessness has replaced a strong sense of local or even national control, and fear supersedes a sense of security.

The changes we are witnessing today did not simply arrive fully formed. They are part of a wrenching, longer-term shift away from the nation-state and toward the world-as-a-whole as the fundamental unit of economic activity. This trend, which is fraught with contradictions, filled with competing interests, and plagued by setbacks, is nevertheless moving ahead. And short of nuclear war, nuclear accident, plague, or a massive chemical spill, it will continue to move ahead at an increasingly rapid pace.

Among those who have studied this shift in detail are Charles Kindleberger, an extremely erudite and insightful economist and historian at the Massachusetts Institute of Technology; Peter F. Drucker, the Austrian-born management guru at the elite Clairmont Graduate School near Los Angeles; the late Arthur Burns, a former chairman of the Federal Reserve; John Kenneth Galbriath, the urbane Harvard economist, historian, and social critic who served in a number of Democratic administrations; Kenichi Ohmae, the economist who heads McKinsey & Company's Tokyo office; and Jib Fowles, a futurist at the University of Houston. There are dozens of other economic historians who have studied this process of integration as well. These thinkers have come up with an interesting view of the way the world has been changing and drawing closer together over the last hundred years or so.

During the Victorian era, a century or so ago, the world's economy was very loosely linked. According to Drucker, at that time most people were involved in purely domestic pursuits. In Britain—the most advanced nation at the time—and in Belgium and the United States, where the statistics from that period are reliable, 80 percent of the population earned its living by working either as farmers, domestic servants, or skilled workers—tinkers, livery workers, cobblers, blacksmiths, construction workers, and, increasingly, manufacturing workers. The rest of the population was engaged in services such as retailing, teaching, government work, or transportation.

These figures translate into a world where most transactions were purely domestic in nature. Though the figures are difficult to calculate (Charles Kindleberger thinks the estimate is too low), it is safe to say that only about 5 percent of all purchases had an international component to them. But even if we take Kindleberger's concerns to heart, the probability is that no more than a maximum of 7 percent to 10 percent of all transactions had a global component to them a century ago.

Chances are that when the average Victorian man or woman in the United States went to the general store and purchased thread, needles, seed grain, alcohol, calico cloth, spices, fruit, magazines, tomato paste, pasta, canned salmon, and various other sundries, every one of those goods was produced domestically. In those days if there was an exception, it was most likely the cloth that was imported from England.

Most industrial products—railroad rails, iron ore furnaces, ships, telegraph sets—would also have been produced domestically. Only a very few large, industrial items would have been imported at the time: locomotives from England, trolley cars from Germany, diamonds from South Africa or Russia. Everything else, nineteen out of every twenty purchases, would have been for products made at home.

To be sure, countries traded during Victorian times. Steamships were built, tracks were laid, and canals were dug. During the late Victorian period, world trade expanded by as much as 7 percent a year. Victorians were enterprising people. But the base from which they expanded was very small indeed, and the volume of trade, compared to today, was minuscule.

Even so, British financiers invested in building the railroads in the United States and in Peru and Argentina, and those countries then imported British railroad equipment. German financiers invested in Tanzanian diamond mines and imported German mining technology. But even with such relatively large investments overseas—here and in the colonies—most of the world's economy remained as separate islands only tangentially linked by slowly moving steam- and sail-powered ships, trains and (beginning in 1844) the telegraph.

The telegraph, incidentally, laid the foundation for the world economy when, in the late 1870s, all of the British Empire was linked to London telegraphically. As a consequence, according to Jib Fowles, the futurist, "the long process of global standardization began, standardization that would culminate in computer codes, programming languages, and microchip design. After all, a bale of cotton—whether from Egypt, California, or the American South—or a ton of coal had to weigh the same if London traders using telegraphs were arranging for sales and for deliveries around the world.

"After the invention of the telegraph, for the first time," Fowles said, "time zones were standardized around the world. Rather than having each village set its own time, which they did by declaring twelve o'clock the time when the sun was directly overhead, the telegraph led to the establishment of eighteen world time zones. Without standardizing the world's time zones, you could not run railroads, have telegraph messages returned promptly, schedule shipping or manufacturing, or efficiently trade stocks or commodities. With the invention of the telegraph and the wiring together of the British Empire in the late Victorian period, the world for the first time began to do what we are now all doing: marching to the same tempo. The telegraph also laid the basis for the electronic economy and global capital markets because traders and investors could track their investments with only minimal delays."

WHEN ECONOMIES WERE SEPARATE

Still, the relative isolation of each nation's economy from others had two initial consequences. First, growth was slow, ideas moved uneasily, and trade between countries was inefficient. In those days, France really was France, and Spain really was Spain. There was no American Ford, IBM, Unisys, or General Motors, or their equivalents, operating there, and certainly no Fujitsus or Nissans operating in any other country. A few companies had international representatives to sell their wares, and some other organizations, usually chartered by the government, traded goods internationally on behalf of several companies.

But the second consequence of this isolation was that the economies of the world, prior to World War I, were relatively insulated from one another's ups and downs. The financial panics in the United States during the 1870s had virtually no effect on Europe. Conversely, Europe's booms and busts did not affect the United States very much. If Europeans were in the midst of a period of belt tightening, it didn't hurt manufacturers in the United States or Canada very much because most of their sales were domestic. Because international capital flows were small (although growing), the crash of a stock market in one country would not starve other countries for investment funds or cause investors to sell stocks in one country to pay for losses in another.

THE LINKS BECOME CLOSER

After World War I, the integration of the world's major economies increased dramatically. Unfortunately, the impetus for this growing level of involvement was war. Countries fighting alongside one another financed each other's efforts and increased trade to provide for each other's armament needs. America lent money to Britain and France, and shipped millions of tons of food and war materiel to its World War I allies.

According to R. Buckminster Fuller, the mathematician and designer who developed the geodesic dome, it was the high-strength steel alloys used to make the long-range guns on Dreadnoughts, England's battleships, during World War I that drew the world closer. Those guns required iron from Minnesota, cobalt from Africa, tungsten from South Africa, and nickel from Nevada. The brass shell casings used in the war required copper from Nevada and Chile, and the bullets required Nevada's lead. Wartime vehicles used rubber from Malaysia and Brazil.

The Great War paradoxically brought the world closer together. It also was the first instance where trade on a worldwide basis had to be tightly coordinated, not just for finished products, like radio sets, but for intermediate products, like the vacuum tubes that went into the sets. In that war, raw materials were shipped to one country for processing, to another for manufacturing, and to a third for final assembly.

After the war, with the patterns of trade and integration deeply established and new technologies proliferating, integration continued at a rapid pace while industrial growth also moved ahead. By the mid-1920s the United States was producing more than 1.5 million cars a year, importing rubber and exotic metals and exporting finished vehicles. By 1925, 40 percent of the American workforce was engaged in manufacturing; domestics became scarce (replaced by washing, sewing, and vacuuming machines), and farmers left the farms, also replaced by machines. By the mid-1920s the industrial countries had established fully developed manufacturing societies complete with engineering schools, research centers, and management schools, all with standardized accounting methods.

By the mid-1920s American companies were manufacturing hundreds of little canvas-covered airplanes and airplane engines each year; more important, they were exporting them. General Electric was selling generators overseas, and Westinghouse was selling Pullman cars and railroad parts through their own distribution channels overseas. Evinrude and Johnson sold outboard motors in Africa and Europe. To keep these products running, spare parts had to be shipped overseas and channels of distribution to local mechanics and parts stores had to be established.

And communications technologies were also rapidly spreading. After World War I, telephone lines were strung across America, Europe, and underneath the seas. Companies raised capital for those efforts in the world's budding capital markets in London, New York, and Frankfurt. And for the first time, after World War I, homes were included as part of the communications grid. Telephones entered the home and so did radio, with tremendous economic and social consequences.

Copper for these cables had to be found, dug, and refined. Effective insulators for overland and undersea cables had to be discovered. Oil to power the machines of transportation and production had to be lifted from the ground, and refineries had to be constructed.

In the 1920s out-of-the-way places—such as Odessa, Texas; Monterrey, Mexico; and Jakarta, Indonesia—were linked to the increasingly oil-hungry world by telegraph, telephone, ship commerce, pipelines, and multinational exploration crews. By the late 1920s long- and shortwave radio signals carried messages between the continents.

Soon, a handful of multinational companies emerged: Ford was manufacturing automobiles on two continents by the mid-1920s; Firestone began producing tires in Europe and the United States at about the same time; Texaco explored for oil in the United States and the Middle East; Gulf, based in Pittsburgh, explored for oil in Kuwait; Britain's Lever Brothers and America's Johnson's Wax were making and selling household goods around the world; Bosch, a German auto parts manufacturer, set up shop in the United States, along with Britain's Rolls-Royce, Germany's Bayer, and Switzerland's Nestlé. By the end of World War I, people had learned the rudiments of conducting business globally.

INVISIBLE TRADES

The 1920s saw ideas also begin to be traded in a big way. Edison's movie projectors, developed in New Jersey, were licensed for manufacture by companies in England. Movie studios in Hollywood collected royalties from places as far away as Tokyo, Tashkent, and Peking. American truck manufacturers built diesel engines under license from Germany's Dr. Diesel, and manufactured dyes and chemical products patented by Bayer and I. G. Farben. United States Steel in Pittsburgh paid companies in the Ruhr Valley to use their patented processes for making steel, and companies around the world paid Alexander Graham Bell to produce versions of his telephone.

By the late 1920s at least 20 percent of all economic transactions had an international component to them. Radios had tubes with exotic metals inside; cars had tires made of rubber; metal-working lathes and cutting tools from Bridgeport, Connecticut, were used around the world; and Ford, Boeing, and Douglas began to export passenger airplanes. Companies everywhere were licensing patents and copyrights as the global market was beginning to form.

Twenty-plus percent may not seem like very much, but it was enough to create deep links and deeper dependencies. When the world was only 20 percent linked, it had its first truly global shock—the Great Depression—beginning with the near-simultaneous collapse of the New York stock market and Germany's default on its World War I debts.

During World War II, according to Drucker, efficiency and integration proceeded even more rapidly. For example, the United States, with one-fifth the population of its combined wartime allies and foes, was able to field an army equivalent in size to those of all the belligerents. But more important, the United States was still able to outproduce not only all its foes combined but its allies as well.

AFTER WORLD WAR II

Since the conclusion of World War II, integration has become even more prevasive. During the postwar era, American companies transformed themselves into multinationals, distributing not only their marketing acumen but their production technology as well. According to R. Buckminster Fuller, after World War II, America's single largest export was its industrial and manufacturing base.

That is not an exaggeration. No country has shifted more of its productive resources abroad. Today, on average, American companies derive about 22 percent of their profits from their overseas operations. Those operations include manufacturing, research, and marketing. Japanese companies, by contrast, derive only 5 percent of their profits from overseas operations. Most of their profits still come from exporting.

IBM, Ford, General Motors, Hewlett-Packard, Digital Equipment Corporation, Johnson & Johnson, Westinghouse, General Electric, H. J. Heinz, and a long list of other companies have research laboratories and production facilities abroad. IBM's Swiss research center has even won a Nobel Prize for its work in superconductors.

Since World War II, American companies have been cutting back the percentage of Americans working in their overseas operations. IBM's European operations are staffed predominantly by Europeans. In Japan, where Mobil Oil is the number-two oil company, only a handful of Americans work in the company. A multinational company today is not only broad-based and far-flung but also staffed by a widely divergent group of people.

Foreign multinationals are following the same pattern as their American rivals. Nissan, Toyota, and Mazda have California design studies; Thomson, the French electronics company, conducts research in the United States; Matsushita, Sony, Fujitsu, Phillips, and Siemens conduct research in the United States and manufacture their products here. Computers track every move these companies make.

Since World War II the world has become even more deeply connected. Today, 60 percent or more of all economic transactions have an international component to them. And even that estimate may be too low. Today, 60 percent of all economic transactions take place as a result of the global electronic economy.

There are really very few products that have only one nation of origin anymore. Nearly every major product is a multinational effort—clothes, cars, and even fast food. Even so-called domestically made cars—Chryslers, Fords, and General Motors vehicles—have, on average, only about 70 percent of their parts made in America; the rest come from their affiliates in Mexico, Canada, Korea, Europe, and Japan. In fact, most trade today is not in finished products at all but in intermediate goods—the turbine blades instead of the jet engine; the computer chip rather than the computer; the transmission rather than the automobile. And most of that trade is conducted from one overseas division of a multinational company to another overseas division of the same company. IBM builds its PCs in Florida, Britain, and Japan, with parts, such as disk drives, chips, and wiring, made by IBM's subsidiaries and affiliated companies in California, Europe, Singapore, Malaysia, and Japan.

The Boeing 747, which began life in 1971 as 97 percent American, is now only about 70 percent American made. Almost every new, complex technological undertaking is a global effort from the start. The Boeing 777, a new long-range twin-jet passenger plane, was conceived as a multinational undertaking involving hundreds of foreign companies.

Since the conclusion of World War II, hundreds of American and foreign companies have formed global alliances and joint ventures. Hundreds of American companies, from RCA's consumer electronics division to Amdahl, the giant computer maker, have been taken over by foreign firms, have sold large shares of themselves to foreign companies, or have formed technology development alliances.

IBM has alliances with Japan's Fujitsu and Germany's Siemens. It also has an alliance with Apple Computer, which in turn has an alliance with Japan's Sony. Ford owns a piece of Japan's Mazda, and the two companies develop cars together. But Ford is also developing a utility vehicle with Japan's Nissan. General Motors owns part of Isuzu, and Chrysler and Mitsubishi have several joint ventures going. But Mitsubishi also has an alliance with Mercedes-Benz, and Mercedes has an alliance with Porsche. Mitsubishi produces cars that go head-to-head with all three companies. In these relationships capital is transferred between divisions electronically, ideas are shared via computer terminal, and E-mail travels everywhere as the global workshop expands.

Since World War II the world has become very confusing, with companies competing in one market while cooperating in another. Joint ventures and alliances have created an intricate set of relationships that are a challenge even for the best business minds to follow. One company, Asea Brown Bovari, which produces power-generation equipment around the world, started out as Swedish, merged with another company, and moved to Switzerland. Asea, a globe-girdling giant that many other companies, including IBM, are trying to emulate, has adopted English as its official language. All of its far-flung divisions are linked electronically in what it calls its "matrix" system of management. By tapping a few keys, managers anywhere in the world can learn what their counterparts are doing, how much they are spending, and what projects they are bidding on. By tapping into the matrix, Asea's bean-counting accountants can determine precisely its worldwide financial position.

NO NATIONAL PRODUCTS

There are very few purely "national" products and very few purely "national" transactions left. How can there be? Banks today extend you a mortgage and then resell that mortgage to Japanese or European investors. American automobile lenders bundle up their installment loans and resell them to overseas investors. Insurance companies in England invest in American venture capital funds. German and Japanese pension funds buy Manhattan real estate, and Mexican industrialists build condominiums in Florida and take over American companies. The world is increasingly connected.

Just open up the back of your television set, the top of your computer, the engine compartment of your car, or the contents of your clothes closet, and you will see the true extent of globalization. Look at your stereo sets, fax machines, tires, or furniture, or simply inquire where the beef was grown that is nestled between the buns of your fast-food hamburger, and you will see how pervasive globalization has become. When it comes to what Karl Marx called the "means of production," there are no national entities left.

GLOBAL ECONOMY IS THE ONLY ECONOMY

For the average man or woman the emergence of such a tightly linked global economy has been invisible. These changes move like the hands of a clock, too slow to see if looked at directly but unrelenting in their pace when viewed intermittently over time. But they also move at the speed of light—the speed of the electron—too fast to see even if viewed straight-on.

As a consequence the world we now inhabit is markedly different from the world of a decade or two ago. The jobs we hold, the way we work, the companies that employ us, and the sectors in which our country excels have changed. In the span of a decade or two a host of old and comfortable patterns have been completely dislodged. As the functional economic unit becomes the world instead of the nation-state, the structure of nations and the notion of sovereignty must change. "My notion is," said Jib Fowles, "that the world is beginning to resemble one gigantic hive."

But it is not just we Americans who are feeling the pace of change quicken. Billions of people across this earth are grappling with this shift in the parameters of reality. In the fifty years since World War II, Japan has been transformed from an Asian state unfamiliar with democracy, plagued by wave after wave of political unrest and a history of rulership through violence, into a model of democratic decorum.

Britain, world-ruling and fiercely independent at the beginning of World War II, is now just another member of the European Community, no longer an island but connected to the mainland through an undersea tunnel and railroad, instant telecommunications, membership in a European parliament, and, soon, membership in a pan-European central bank.

The stress of these changes has been intense. Countries connected to the global electronic economy, like the millions of computers connected to a network, are becoming part of the vast and highly integrated global workshop and economy. But as they do, their citizens rebel against the inevitable loss of identity and national sovereignty. Men and women around the world chafe at becoming just another interchangeable part of the new world economy—an accounting "input," a unit of labor. As a result, a new "tribalism" has emerged. From the ex–Soviet Union to Bosnia and Canada, people are demanding the right to express their ethnic identities.

No one really likes to be a cog in the international economic and business machine. People do not want to be factored into the global equation as a depository of raw materials (the Middle East, Mexico, and Canada), a market or a pool of industrial and production talent (Europe, Japan, and the United States), a place to locate a research lab (Switzerland and Israel), or a future market (the ex–Soviet Union and the Third World). Communities around the world that are linked electronically to this newly integrated world system are increasingly uncomfortable with their loss of control over their own destinies as they integrate into the global workshop.

Marshall McLuhan, the late Canadian social scientist, was one of the first to observe how these two competing economic influences—globalization and the uneasiness that comes from the loss of local and national control—would manifest themselves. Along with the globalization of the economy, McLuhan said, comes a countervailing trend toward parochialism, localism, nationalism, chauvinism, ethnocentrism, fundamentalism, and racism.

McLuhan said that globalism, telecommunications, air travel, the modern media, and computers were changing the way we analyze problems, organize companies, structure countries, value one another, and even use our five senses. Indeed, McLuhan's Canada is a good example of the dichotomies that are developing between the global economy and the local community. For example, the Canadian government had relatively little trouble signing a free-trade agreement with the United States that would deprive Canada of many of its most cherished national rights when it comes to trade and the economy. The Canadian federal government, the provincial governments, and its labor unions and political parties supported Canada's further integration into the American economy and the world economy. Free access to American capital, markets, and technology were powerful inducements to Canada's business community even though it meant that their home government could no longer protect them. For these companies the risks were clearly worth it.

But when it came to the purely local and largely symbolic issue of the Meech Lake Accords, which would give French-speaking Quebec more autonomy and the French language more clout while keeping Canada a single country, the country's leaders balked. Outside of Quebec, Canada's English-language chauvinism and anti-French feelings have become even more intense as Canada joins the global economy. Provincialism and ethnocentrism are on the rise in Canada as globalism looms overhead.

This "up-and-down trend," as the *Economist* newspaper once put it, is happening worldwide. In countries everywhere the two trends compete: integration into the global grid, on the one hand; greater local identification, on the other. Could it be, asks the *Economist,* that it is time to say "good-bye to the nation-state"?

McLuhan predicted that there would be an increase in ethnic identification accompanying globalization. As a consequence, ethnic and linguistic rivalries within Canada may eventually force the country to dissolve as a nation-state, just as it becomes even more integrated into the global grid. As a fragmented entity with a diminished economy, Canada's global clout and bargaining power would only be lessened. The ability of its separate ethnic communities to survive independently would be in doubt. Canada would thereby join the international economy not as the nation it once was, occupying a huge portion of the world's geography, but as a cluster of companies, communities, talents, and resources linked electronically and structurally to other such entities around the world and with its laws harmonized with those of the United States through the free-trade agreement.

Such a state, however, is abstract, vague, and ethereal. A cluster of productive interests is not much for its citizens to identify with. It is hard to sing a national hymn or sacrifice one's life to the multinational economic interests that support you. It is hard to be loyal to the economic band that supports you when it is controlled by people at various points around the world.

In a world where the functional unit is the globe, people tend to identify more deeply with their own races, religions, cultures, neighborhoods, villages, towns, and cities than with the planetary economy as a whole. If for some reason they fail to identify with their own localities and ethnic identities, then they are lost to the loneliness of alienation, a term Karl Marx coined in his critique of capitalism over a century ago.

This, then, is an emerging pattern. On the big issue of joining the new world system, no country remains opposed for very long. Britain, France, and Italy gave up a great deal of their economic and political sovereignty to join the European Community, which is dominated by their ancient enemy, a unified Germany. Canada gladly gave up its sovereign rights and joined the United States in a free-trade agreement. Mexico, which has made anti-

Americanism into a quasi–state religion, allowed its president, Carlos Salinas de Gortari, to come to Washington with a plan to link the two economies legally, with very little protest from his constituents at home. Every nation in the Western community of nations, seeing the big picture, went along with barely a whisper of discontent and official discord. But on the local issues of race, ethnicity, and local control over local institutions, they stand firm.

The big trade treaties and agreements, and the ones that will be arrived at in the future that will include the newly liberated countries of Eastern Europe and the Soviet Union, represent nothing less than the demise of the old nation-state system and the rise of an entirely new form of shared sovereignty. It is a new world that is organized along networked lines.

SOCIAL UPHEAVAL

A high price is to be paid for the demise of the nation-state. "What we are seeing now," said Benjamin Weiner, a former foreign service officer who is president of Probe International, a firm that advises businesses and governments on political risks around the world, "is the growth of ethnic rivalries. Ethnic rivalries are replacing politically motivated terrorism as the biggest threat to business. We are seeing it in every region of the world" including the Soviet Union, Africa, Canada, Yugoslavia, and, Weiner added, the United States.

When Britain joined the European Community to become just another nation among many, it lost a certain difficult-to-define measure of its historic identity. Corresponding to this loss came the rise of the racist skinhead culture, an increase in the number of attacks against Britain's Pakistani, Indian, and black populations, riots by the minority communities in Britain's northern cities, pressure to limit further immigration especially from Asia, former British Prime Minister Margaret Thatcher's brief retreat from pan-"Europeanism," and the advent of a new breed of murderously violent British soccer fan.

Nicholas Ridley, who resigned under pressure as a senior member of Thatcher's cabinet in 1990, summed up the nationalist sentiments that accompany the loss of sovereignty when he said in an interview with *Spectator* magazine that West Germany was "trying to take over Europe" and that the French were behaving like the Germans' poodles. "I'm not against giving up sovereignty in principle," he said, "but not to this lot. You might as well give it to Adolf Hitler, frankly."

To be sure, other socioeconomic factors also have intervened to disrupt British culture and to squeeze its different social classes and ethnic groups economically. But the loss of sovereignty is not a trifle in the equation. It has been disquieting to the British, just as it will be disquieting to other countries as they begin to understand what globalization means.

In France the rise of Jean-Marie Le Pen and his right-wing racist Popular Front party has coincided with France's growing participation in the European Community and its slow loss of control over its own economic and social affairs as globalization proceeds on both an economic and cultural level, along with the rise of European regionalism. The French feel their culture has been assaulted by the international, largely English-language, media and by the new international economy. The country has become increasingly chauvinistic as it loses dominion over its own affairs. Like Canada, the French government decreed that the media must carry a certain number of hours of nationally produced programming. But in an era of videocassettes and satellite and cable television with hundreds of channels to choose from, the concept of "nationally produced programming" is a quaint anachronism—a rule that can never be enforced.

The French have rebelled against this loss of their heritage by giving Le Pen more influence. A decade or two ago, when globalization was just beginning. Le Pen's words would have gone unheeded. No right-thinking Frenchman or -woman would have paid much attention to his calls for purifying French culture and expelling Arabs and blacks from the motherland, but now his party may gain as much as 10 percent of the vote.

The idea a decade or two ago was that France had developed a universal culture with much to offer the world. The thought was that French novelists, philosophers, poets, composers, scientists, and painters were a humanizing influence on the world and that the French language could offer deeper insights into the way the mind was structured and reality was put together than any other language. A decade or two ago the notion was not to retreat from the world but to meet it head-on. The competition was for ideas, the French thought, and here, before globalization, they believed they had a clear advantage. But what country can stand alone against a global onslaught of culture, information, and ideas? Who is strong enough to resist the barrage of data served up each day electronically?

But now even mainstream socialists, who promoted the idea that France had a role to play in the world of ideas, are forced to appease the growing strength of the nationalistic right wing by sounding a more provincial and localist note. They are forced to confront the fact that Le Pen's party is winning local elections. Far from moving into the megabyte economy with confidence, French workers are as scared as any other nation's workers. While companies see only the advantages of a global market, workers see the global threat to their livelihoods and to their wage levels from a vast global labor pool.

PROVINCIALISM ON THE INCREASE

Nearly every country in which globalization is proceeding rapidly is besieged by the rise of provincialism and racism. Even in tolerant Sweden, young people drive by enclaves of largely Asian and Middle Eastern "guest workers" and hurl insults and stones at the foreigners. In Japan one candidate for prime minister, Shintaro Ishihara, has written openly of his contempt for Americans and white society in general in his book, *A Japan That Can Say "No,"* coauthored by Akio Morita, the founder of Sony. Also in Japan, Yoshio Sakurauchi, a senator, called American workers lazy and illiterate, prompting U.S. Senator Ernest Hollings to draw a picture of a mushroom-shaped cloud and underneath it to write, "Made by lazy, illiterate American workers."

In Germany groups of right-wing toughs chase Vietnamese guest workers through the streets of Frankfurt, hurling glass bottles at them. And in Eastern Germany, newly integrated into the West, there are believed to be as many as fifty thousand or sixty thousand neo-Nazi skinheads organizing themselves into violent squads to attack non-German residents in their country. And in the United States there is David Duke and Patrick Buchanan.

The development of the global economy corresponds with a rise in intolerance because for many people globalism is accompanied by a feeling of powerlessness. In the global economy the threats to a community's economic welfare and well-being are vague, foreign, and come from very far away. The unemployed British soccer fans who rioted in Belgium, killing thirty-nine spectators, and who had to be restrained at the 1990 World Cup Soccer matches in Rome were thrown out of work by competition from Korean, Polish, Mexican, and Brazilian steelworkers. They lost their jobs not to their countrymen, which would have been bad enough, but to people from the other side of the world— people whose language and culture they do not understand and about whom they know little.

Unemployed auto workers in Manchester, Birmingham, and Leeds—once the center of the British socialist Labour party, with its universalist ideas of democracy and progress for all workers around the world—now vote more conservatively and more selfishly. The old universalist ideal of giving aid to the needy, shelter to the homeless, and a place to live to the stateless has fallen on hard times as the economies of the world unite. In a world where the workshop is global, the threat to one's livelihood can come from anywhere. In a world where even the wealthy feel under attack, altruism is in retreat.

As a result, unemployed or underemployed British workers (like their French, German, Russian, and American counterparts) do not view the globalization process kindly. Workers in those countries are not reaching out to embrace other workers of the world, as they might have done a decade or two ago. Instead, they see the world's linking of arms as a threat to their families, their histories, and their futures. It is with a deep sense of trepidation that they move into the era of the one-world economy when a British worker—or an American, Canadian, or French worker, for that matter—is pitted against a worker from far away. It is with fear that Americans and Germans watch as people from other continents swallow up their best, highest-paying jobs and devour their markets.

How do you retaliate against competitors from across the globe? How do you even know precisely whom to retaliate against? How does a labor union in one country, where workers might earn $10 an hour, mount a strike against non-union workers on a different continent who might earn $10 *a day*? How can workers keep the companies they work for from moving their jobs overseas?

When workers are threatened and sense that their government's power to protect them is diminishing, how else can they react but by calling for a resurrection of nationalism?

In the United States it is no mere coincidence that a major issue of the 1988 presidential campaign was over whether the flag ought to be protected by an amendment to the Constitution. Many political commentators dismissed this issue simply as a Republican ploy to gain ground in the election by adopting a more strident and patriotic tone than the Democrats. But by saying this, they missed the point altogether.

The flag became an important issue precisely because many Americans, like their counterparts overseas, feel a loss of control over their own lives as a result of the growth of economic and cultural globalism. Foreign competition has not only diminished America's role in the world, it has also put fear into the hearts of its workers. It has made them feel threatened, causing them to work harder and to work scared. Reports about Japanese and German manufacturing prowess and the low wages paid to workers in Korea have not gone unnoticed by workers in Flint, Michigan; Cleveland, Ohio; or Newark, New Jersey. And because they feel the threat from overseas as much as anyone, Americans—like their counterparts in Europe—are also becoming more nationalistic. For them the flag is the symbol of that nationalism, and the proposed (and defeated) amendment to the Constitution was their way of saying that in spite of the global challenge, Americans still want power.

Factory workers in Europe and North America are by no means alone in feeling vulnerable in the electronic economy. Managerial employees in companies around the world are more frequently working for foreign bosses or competing with foreign companies. Increasingly, managers feel like pawns in the international game. When a boss in Frankfurt, Tokyo, New York, or London makes decisions regarding which person to promote or fire in an office in Toledo or Mexico City, no one assumes that the decision is being made from the heart. When a boss in another country decides which offices are to expand, which are to be shut down, which divisions are to be sold, or which staff members should be moved to another city, it takes away from the average man or woman's sense of power and self-worth. We feel as though we are expendable, as though we are commodities that can be plugged into the global information grid on the say-so of an accountant, or unplugged from that grid without any thought as to who we are. Few emotions are more dangerous than the feeling of being powerless.

But the fear (and anger) that grips the citizenry of the world's electronic global state is a very strange one indeed. Ku Klux Klansmen in Louisiana, Illinois, Connecticut, or Texas may still wear white sheets while decrying foreigners, blacks, Jews, and Catholics, but they are far more likely to arrive at their rallies in Toyota, Nissan, and Isuzu pickup trucks than ever before.

Followers of France's Le Pen may attend rallies in Lyon and Paris and yell for the deportation of Arabs and black Africans, but at home, when they switch on their televisions, they are more likely to watch "Dallas" or a CNN news report than ever before.

German nationalists who want foreigners out of the Fatherland, American soldiers off their sacred soil, and ethnic Germans in Poland, Hungary, and Russia absorbed into the German state, are more likely than ever to compose their propaganda on an American-made IBM computer and design their hateful posters on an Apple Macintosh than on a product made in the Fatherland itself. And Japanese nationalists who rail against the white man's arrogance are far more likely to depend on the huge American and European markets for their sales than ever before.

The fruits of globalization are as pervasive as they are banal. How can you really be anti-American when you wear Levi's jeans, anti-Japanese if you drive a Toyota, or anti-German if you fly Lufthansa? It takes a certain kind of cognitive dissonance to do so, to talk against the Japanese while listening to a Walkman or against the Germans while driving a BMW. Yet people do it— decry globalization while enjoying its fruits.

"Through the end of the decade, ethnic rivalries will intensify," according to Probe International's Weiner. Indeed, the focus of Amnesty International's 1990 annual report was on the rise of ethnic rivalries and the brutal suppression of one ethnic group by another.

A SENSE OF POWERLESSNESS

David C. McClelland, a Harvard psychologist and student of mass culture, wrote that people who feel a sense of weakness often seek to gain a sense of strength and power by aligning themselves with some bigger force—nationalism, religion, racism, even a sports team. As globalism progresses and people feel this growing loss of control, they are likely to bind themselves even more tightly to these big—and often ugly—forces and ideas.

Iranians, whose traditional Muslim world was cast aside by Shah Reza Pahlavi's rapid modernization program and its quickly developing links to the United States, Israel, and the countries of the West, sought solace and a sense of empowerment in a fanatical return to their religion. This is a most vivid example of how people react when they sense they lack control over their lives.

But the trend toward the nationalistic and fanatical did not end with Iran. In the first open election in the Arab world in Algeria, which was dominated by the French for decades, a slate of fundamentalist Muslim candidates, with no economic or political program other than their steadfast adherence to their religion, was swept into office. In Egypt the Muslim brotherhood is the biggest threat to the government of Hosni Mubarak. In Israel, where the global links are deep, the sense of dependency on the United States strong, and the threat very real, the coalition government has grown increasingly conservative. Since 1978 the Israeli government has made the long march from secular socialism and the left to the religious nationalism of the right.

In the United States, since 1978, the Democrats have seen their hold on national politics fail as a coalition of conservatives, nationalists, and religious groups have allied themselves with the Republican party. In countries as different as the United States, India, Britain, France, and Egypt, chauvinism is on the increase.

The electronic economy will only intensify this trend toward localism, particularism, provincialism, nationalism, and racism among people whose lives and identities are disrupted by the end of the nation-state. In a worst-case scenario, right-wing Nazi-like movements will develop throughout the world as countries lose power and control, and as the average man and woman feels more threatened by a global economy that is increasingly abstract and remote.

In the worst-case scenario, religious intolerance will also increase, and fundamentalism—in all its guises and in all its different religious forms—will increase as the average man and woman grope for something big and powerful to cling to. Fundamentalism will increase as people's lives are made to seem insignificant by the creation of a single, massive, global economy whose enterprises are loyal to no one, bigger than everyone, and under no one nation's control.

Even in the best-case scenario, the forces of nationalism will grow as Americans want to be more American, Germans more German, and the French more French. Within each of these countries, each region will also assert itself—Southern culture, Western culture, Northern and Eastern culture—as the notion of the nation-state gives way.

Marshall McLuhan saw the deep tension between decentralization and globalization as the essential—but largely invisible—dichotomy of our electronic age. These two forces, precipitated by the rise of satellites, global electronics, and the ease of jet travel, would alter all our institutions, change our society, and create a new economy, he said.

The first victim of these changes would be the old forms of corporate hierarchy and rigidly centralized government. The old notion of an infallible chief executive at the top of an obedient chain of command, protected by (and from) his troops, could not survive the information age. That old structure would be unable to compete in an electronic world where information is disseminated at the speed of light and where notions of up, down, near, and far have no meaning.

McLuhan also predicted that sharply hierarchical organizations would be replaced by flatter structures where telecommunications technology linked all parts of the company into a more organically functioning whole. Like others over the years, he predicted that each operating unit would have to have more autonomy and flexibility in order to compete and survive in the new global environment.

In the new electronically linked world, McLuhan predicted management would change from a hierarchy to a "widearchy," with lateral links, like alliances, and who sits on whose board of directors often would be more important than ownership links. Indeed, Japan's companies, through their Keiretsu system, are networked together in tightly linked business groups, often with minimal cross-ownership but maximum cross-control. A number of American companies, such as IBM, Ford, and Boeing, are said to be developing their own Keiretsus.

COMMUNISM'S END PREDICTED

The second victim of the dichotomy between the forces of economic globalization and decentralization, McLuhan shrewdly predicted, would be communism. Almost three decades ago McLuhan wrote that communism was on the verge of extinction. The Soviet model, he said, with its highly centralized command economy, guarded information, and hierarchies taller than the Kremlin's onion domes, was out of phase with the new global electronic reality.

In 1968 he wrote, "Communism is something that lies more than a century behind us, and we are deep into the new age of tribal involvement." By tribal, McLuhan meant ethnic. Even in the 1960s McLuhan was able to divine that Marxism could not survive. But it took until 1991, when the Soviet Union met its demise—to be replaced by a commonwealth of ethnic republics—for McLuhan to be proved correct.

These captive republics became free of Moscow not just because they stood up to the power of the Kremlin but also because the Kremlin—like all highly centralized governments—was an outmoded institution. As the Russian republic rises from its ruins, it will strive to join the megabyte economy, employ its workers in the global workshop, and conduct its affairs openly in the global economy, no differently from any other country. The Russians know that if they choose to remain isolated from the rest of the world, they will fall further behind. No country and no people cut off from the world's fertile flow of information can maintain economic power for very long. In the electronic world, Moscow is no nearer to Kiev than it is to Los Angeles or Lima, Peru.

And China is no different. The era when a centralized bureaucracy could control a population and an economy as vast and complicated as China's has passed. Two hundred and fifty million households with access to vital information in underground newspapers or taken directly from the airwaves, through international radio broadcasts, off satellites, from voice and videotape cassettes smuggled into the country—and all spread rapidly over telephone lines and through face-to-face gossip of friends—cannot be controlled by a few hundred people in the top echelons of the Communist party.

For China to enter the modern age and grow, it has no choice but to decentralize its control over its population and its economy, and join the international system.

As we watch the new world of the electro-economic network take shape, we will see tensions between globalization and decentralization intensify. Only those companies and countries that are the most flexible will continue to survive intact. Countries (and companies) that are tightly and rigidly controlled from one central command point cannot succeed in the new environment. Global companies led by just one nationality will not succeed. Countries ruled by one ethnic, religious, or narrow political faction will have extreme difficulty. Businesses and governments that are too narrowly controlled will simply lack the flexibility necessary to survive in today's rapidly changing world.

Countries that allow local populations to flourish and to express their ethnic diversity without losing control over the common good will be in the best position to prosper. Others, such as Canada, which allows itself to be caught up in purely domestic struggles about ethnicity, will find itself swallowed up in the global economy, having lost its special, national voice.

EIGHTEEN

STABILIZING AN UNSTABLE WORLD:

How Volatility Can Be Buffered to Prevent Widening Chaos and Upheaval

Since October 1987 there have been three "mini" stock market crashes. But they were mini only by comparison to Black Monday's 508-point drop. The 120.30-point drop of November 15, 1991, for example, was one of the largest in the Big Board's history, with hundreds of billions of dollars being lost in a day.

That was not supposed to happen. After all, in the wake of the October 1987 debacle, the Brady Commission recommended installing "circuit breakers" that would prevent large market meltdowns. But only two circuit breakers were actually ever put in place, and they have been hardly used. The first, a ban on "program trading," was supposed to curb cross-market selling from the futures market to the stock market when stocks fell more than fifty points. The second was to halt trading when the market fell by more than fifty points in a day.

Taken together, these measures are hardly safeguards at all. They do absolutely nothing to dampen day-to-day volatility, nor do they do anything whatsoever to curb the dangerous instability that has been created by the tremendous disparity in size between the real and financial economies. Perhaps, the next time the market cascades, the existing circuit breakers will be switched on. But if the panic is real, every time the circuit breakers are switched back off, the market will tumble again. After all, halting sales for merely an afternoon is not really going to do much to reverse a panic mentality, especially if that panic mentality spreads electronically around the globe in a matter of minutes or hours. The problems in the megabyte economy are much more deep-seated than these circuit breakers can address. The very basic and fundamental mechanisms of trade and the market must be challenged.

POLICYMAKERS' DILEMMA

The problem with taking some of the jarring volatility out of the system is that most policymakers in Washington have stopped asking questions about the markets and about the economy. As long as they are reelected, they are content. Never mind that America is being dealt a harsh blow by globalization and the electronic economy.

There were hearings in Congress after the 1987 crash, and there have been hearings on the need to harmonize the rules governing the futures, cash, and options markets. But nothing conclusive has been done. Washington's regulatory bodies fight over turf while the rules governing different—but linked—exchanges persist.

In other words, since Black Monday nothing has really changed. Nothing has grabbed the attention of policymakers, not even studies by Robert Shiller of Yale University that show volatility in the markets is increasing. Our policymakers have not meaningfully examined the growth in technology and of technically oriented trading, nor have the really looked into the way information travels electronically around the globe. And of course they have not examined in depth the overall security needs of the global financial system.

Few of these policymakers understand or care about the damage done to the real economy by the financial economy. They watch as the standard of living of the average American lies stuck at early 1970s levels, and they see no reason to act. They criticize American corporate leaders for their high salaries and short attention spans, but do nothing that would make it easier for those corporate leaders to think long-term. After all, when volatility and upheaval rule the markets, changing the value of the dollar, upsetting interest rates, playing havoc with stock prices and profits, what else can corporate leaders do but go for short-term rewards? In this highly changeable environment, why should corporate America's elite defer to their company's longer-term interests? (In the volatile battlegrounds of Beirut or Yugoslavia, not many businesses think long-term, either.) And why should they take more moderate pay packages when they know very well they may be pushed out the door at any time? After all, a short-term, take-what-you-can-while-you-can-get-it attitude is rational in an environment where upheaval is the rule.

But our policymakers do not understand where action is required. They do not realize that it is the current electronic environment and its highly strung, volatile nature that is the culprit. Washington believes America's corporate soul has somehow become sullied, tarnished. It does not realize the electronic environment that has been built up over the generations is out of whack. Nor does it realize that Congress has little power over America's soul. But over the electronic environment it has room to act.

Among our policymakers, faith, unfortunately, lies in one simpleminded idea: unfettering the market. And most of our policymakers believe that the market—in its largest sense—is capable of fixing itself. They believe in leaving the economy to its own devices, despite the fact that those devices have failed to keep America's economy growing and its overall standard of living improving. What's wrong with America, these policymakers believe, can only be fixed by even more deregulation, privatization, and competition. That is why President Bush, just before the 1992 election, proposed a moratorium on all new regulation and why Vice President Dan Quayle and his competitiveness team have been trying to remove old regulations. But in a vast, free-form, centerless megabyte economy, deregulation may be the opposite of what is needed.

It is a pity. Deregulation is, after all, what we are selling to Eastern Europe, China, and the rest of the crumbling socialist world. And it is a line that is correct—to a point. The market must be managed and regulated, the fast-growing Japanese know. It must be planned. Through their painful histories, the German, French, and Japanese have come to understand that the market, though capable of working miracles, is also capable of wreaking havoc on their economies.

On its own, the market is the great leveler. An unfettered and largely open market has kept America's standard of living at 1970s levels. It has led to the buildup of debt and the destruction of the savings and loan industry, much of the banking industry, and much of the insurance industry. It has led to crippling competition within the airline industry to the point where in 1992, according to Robert L. Crandall, chairman of American Airlines, 25 percent of seats flown in the United States are flown by bankrupt carriers. The more regulated environments in Europe and Japan have created a situation where it may cost more to fly, but its carriers are healthy.

The unfettered market has also let other countries overtake us. Much of Europe is now wealthier than America, and so is much of Japan. And though wages have been stagnant in the United States, wealth has been transferred from the poor and the middle class to the rich. The top 10 percent of Americans now own more assets than the other 90 percent of America. That wealth transfer has largely resulted from the failure of the unfettered market to create new wealth. Rather than expanding America's overall wealth-producing capacity, the last two decades have witnessed a shift in what we have. The nation's creditors—its class of bondholders and stock owners—have garnered the lion's share of the gains during the Reagan and Bush years, siphoning it from the nation's debtors, working men and women forced into debt to maintain their life-styles.

The countries that have done the best over the last decade or two are those with the most egalitarian distribution of wealth and with governments that regulate the market and plan. By American standards, Japan's income and wealth distribution are so equal, they are downright communist. The same is true for fast-growing Taiwan, Korea, and Singapore.

Korea, which has been growing at more than 7 percent a year and even higher for more than a decade, has gone from abject poverty a generation ago to a living standard that is about half our own through a combination of market economics, planning, and a workforce that shares in the nation's growth. The distribution of wealth in Korea is highly egalitarian. Such distribution of wealth does not mean Korea (or Japan) has no wealthy people, but it does mean there are few poor people. The egalitarian countries have been outspending America—on a percentage basis—on investment. They have been spending tremendous amounts on early and primary education and on a longer school day and school year. And they have the benefits to show for it.

To raise our standard of living there must be investment. But why invest when you never know where interest rates will go or what kind of profits you will need to keep up your stock price? Still, to get productivity growth to where it should be, we must double what we currently spend on our factories and equipment. Japan, with an economy a little more than half the size of ours and with half the population we have, invests more money than we do in its factories, plants, and equipment—not in per-capita terms but in actual dollar and yen amounts. As a result Japanese factories are newer than ours, and the rate of growth in productivity is twice what ours is.

Investing in productivity allows companies to pay workers more while still increasing profits. Japanese automobile workers, for example, now earn roughly the same wages as their American counterparts. Their benefits are also equivalent, though they are paid out differently. But while Toyota, Nissan, Honda, and Mazda struggled through 1991, a difficult year everywhere, and made profits, Detroit lost more than $8 billion. According to James Womack, a professor at the Massachusetts Institute of Technology who assembled a team to study the world's automobile producers, America's problem is not with its technology. Its primary problem is that its economy is volatile and cyclical, with widespread ups and downs. In his study, called *The Machine That Changed the World*, Womack found that those ups and downs are not conducive to investment, nor are they conducive to the type of manufacturing that is currently needed. A cyclical economy is also not conducive to hiring, training, and keeping skilled workers since they are too expensive to keep during a downturn. In Womack's view, the volatility of the American economy, more than any other factor, is the root cause of Detroit's woes vis-à-vis Japan.

One of the most important reasons for Japan's success (and America's loss) is that its more placid economic environment is far more conducive to investment, training, and keeping skilled workers. Japanese factories are more efficient than Detroit's because Japanese managers out-invest their American counterparts, secure in the knowledge that recessions in Japan are rare and mild, whereas they are brutal and deep in America. The result of that investment is that it takes 15 percent fewer hours to produce a Toyota Camry, for example, than it does to produce an Oldsmobile Achieva, though the cars sell for about the same price.

JAPAN PROTECTED

Japan is protected in many ways from the ups and downs and hypervolatility of the megabyte economy because it trades with the world in dollars and trades with itself in yen. Its dollar economy is separated from its yen economy. It can buy world products, such as oil, with dollars and invest in new plants and equipment at home with yen. It can sell Toyotas to the United States for dollars and use those dollars to buy American real estate and build American assembly plants. And because the dollar is the world's reserve currency, it can sell Toyotas to Europe for dollars as well. Those dollars can be invested in Treasury bonds and can be used for other investments in the global economy without altering the value of Japanese assets.

But even if it were not protected, Japan's superior level of planning and investment would pay off. Since it is a less volatile environment, Japanese managers, like their American counterparts a generation ago, are more long-term in their outlook. Since the future looks about the same as the present, Japan's corporate titans know they will not be bounced out the door. As a result they do not need to loot the corporate till by rewarding themselves with millions over the short run, while they worry where they will work over the long run.

The result of all that boring stability is growth in productivity, which means you can pay your workers more, which in turn means a rising standard of living. Paying higher wages also means your workers have bigger buying power, and that enables them to support (and stimulate) the national economy by buying the goods their friends and neighbors produce. And, of course, increased wages enable the government to increase its revenue without raising taxes.

·   ·   ·

Washington has caused much of the problem. Since Lyndon Johnson, no president except Jimmy Carter has cared about the size of the budget deficit. And then there was Ronald Reagan, who transformed the nation from the world's largest creditor to the world's largest debtor. The Reagan Administration alone added more than $1.3 trillion to the national debt.

Congress has done just as poorly. Congressional turf battles over which committees control the stock and futures markets have done nothing to dampen market volatility. The tax law of 1986, which abruptly changed the investment, depreciation, and deduction laws, caused the rapid depreciation of real estate assets (which contributed to the savings and loan disaster). The tax revision act led to the destruction of the venture capital industry and independent financing for filmmakers (one of the reasons the Japanese could buy Columbia Pictures and MCA Inc. so cheaply), and it helped wipe out high-tech start-ups, the engine of growth that pulled America out of the 1982 recession. The 1986 tax revision also wiped out the investment tax credit for industry.

And then Congress repealed most interest rate deductions for credit cards, which hurt our major retailing chains. Add to that the deregulation of the airline business, with its legacy of more than a decade's worth of bankruptcies and upheavals, and the deregulation of the savings and loan industry, which let inexperienced savings and loan managers invest their deposits in junk bonds.

There is also, of course, the White House's inept handling of trade issues, which has led to the downsizing of the automobile, steel, and computer industries, and Washington's wholesale abandonment of regulating brokerage commissions, which led to a mind-set on Wall Street that favors transactions over investment.

Congress and the White House have created a mess. And only they can fix it. Precisely because our private institutions are so weak, Washington still has the wherewithal to force change— not with a few "circuit" breakers but with meaningful policies designed to create an environment where long-term thinking and investing pay off.

It is time for Washington to act. It must implement a number of important programs to stem our nation's decline and stabilize a highly unstable world. Washington must create an environment in which it makes sense to think longer term by taking the volatility out of the electronic economy. If it achieves that goal, investment and productivity growth—and wealth creation—will return to their 1950s levels.

But even more important, if productivity growth and wage increases return to their 1950s and 1960s levels, more money will find its way into the pockets and purses of the average man and woman. A rising standard of living for everyone—something we have not seen in nearly two decades—will go a long way toward dispelling some of the social tensions that now infect our country.

Men and women who not only feel richer but actually are better off will also have a greater sense of power. A rising standard of living, instead of rising debts, can go a long way toward ending the enmity that has developed between groups that feel powerless and overlooked. And, of course, when wealth is generated through increased productivity, more efficient manufacturing, and a brightening of the overall investment climate, it is distributed in a much more egalitarian way than wealth that is generated by one class of people putting another into debt.

DAMPENING VOLATILITY

There are a number of ways to dampen volatility. First, it is time to reexamine the floating dollar. Since 1971 the dollar has been nothing more than what R. David Ranson, the economist, called the "circular argument." It is volatile, mercurial, and wholly electronic. As such it is a speculative instrument, and it hurts investment in the real economy. It also confuses trade. One of the cornerstones of the European Community is its monetary system. By 1997 it is planning to have a single currency. The economists, planners, and designers of the European single market understand that if trade and investment are to flourish, price stability is necessary. With a single currency they will not have to worry about price changes due to currency variation. Export and import prices can be set long in advance. The Airbus consortium, to name one example, which produces passenger planes from parts made all over Europe, will no longer have to worry that the price of its German parts has gone up while the price of its French parts has gone down due to currency speculation. That makes it much easier for Airbus to think longer term when it develops new planes and prices them for the market. It also gives Airbus an advantage over Boeing, which must deal with suppliers from around the world, each with different currencies. Those megabyte currencies fluctuate in price against the dollar on a second-by-second basis.

In the global economy, fixed exchange rates are simply better. They do away with price fluctuations caused by speculative shifts in the value of the dollar. That takes away some of the jarring uncertainty that has hurt American investment. In fact, fixed exchange rates would cause the speculative currency market to wither away. That would put the $800 billion that changes hands every day in the financial economy at the service of the real economy. That shift would produce jobs that generally pay more than jobs in the service sector.

It is time to abandon that volatile dollar, along with its wild ups and downs, and rethink our currency. We must make the dollar stable. Why not link it to the European currencies of today or the single European currency of 1997? Why not, just as easily, link the dollar to a market basket of goods—oil, gold, silver, grain, the new European currency, the Japanese yen, and so on, so that it will become a stable currency that does not vary over time? Setting a fixed and absolute value for the dollar would bring a measure of stability back into the world.

To create a fixed-rate dollar, we could use as an anchor a dozen or so commodities that individually fluctuate in price but that overall remain relatively stable. If there were a stable dollar, then British Airways, Japan Airways, and Lufthansa would know in advance—and possibly for years to come—the price of American spare parts for their engines and planes. China's power authority would know the price for years to come of General Electric's locomotives and its power-generation equipment. And the big American multinationals would know the value of the intermediate goods they buy from around the world. In fact, it is completely absurd to have a globally linked economy where companies manufacturing on a global basis are wired together with currencies that shift in value minute by minute.

Along with the dollar, interest rates must be stabilized if investment is to return to the high rates that were common in the past and that are now prevalent in Japan. To do that, the Federal Reserve and the Treasury must be forced by Congress to commit themselves to stabilizing interest rates.

Few policymakers realize it, but interest rates represent the threshold of return. Set rates at 10 percent, and every other investment must return 10 percent plus a risk premium for it to be attractive to an investor. But if the Federal Reserve sets its short-term rates—the funds rate and the discount rate—at no more than 2 or 3 percent and keeps them there for the long term, the entire rate structure of the country will eventually come down—with many positive benefits.

If the prime rate hovers at 4 percent to 5 percent for a decade, investment will flow into those parts of the economy that pay consistent but not necessarily spectacular returns, like manfacturing. Manufacturing is still the cornerstone of the economy, directly employing 20 percent of the workforce. Another 20 percent or so of the nation's workforce is employed indirectly in that sector by working for service businesses—shipping companies, engineering firms, consulting firms, insurance companies, design firms, and others—that do business almost exclusively with the nation's manufacturers. Increase investment in manufacturing, and productivity in that sector will increase. That will pull up wages, the nation's standard of living, and its overall buying power. If interest rates were at no more than 5 percent, productivity would grow far more rapidly than it does today. And if passbook rates were 3 percent to 4 percent over the long run, even the weakest banks would return to profitability.

There would be an added bonus as well. Since about half the mortgages today are at variable rates, dropping interest rates to 5 percent or so would put money in people's pockets. The drop in interest rates that occurred in 1991–92—about 2.5 percent for mortgages—is estimated to have put $20 billion to $50 billion in the pockets of consumers by cutting their monthly mortgage payments. Consumers then used that money to pay off some of their credit card debt, economists say. Another 2.5 percent to 3 percent drop would do the same. It would give the economy a significant boost.

But it would do more. It would also take a tremendous burden off the backs of the average family. Currently, nearly 20 percent of the average family's income goes to pay its installment debts— everything from auto loans to credit cards. Another 22 percent of that income goes to pay the mortgage or rent. That means that nearly half of each family's income is spent as soon as the paychecks come in. But since that 42 percent of income is fixed to interest rates, permanently lower rates would ease the burden quite substantially. If rates were in the range of 4 percent or so—mortgages and credit cards—a calculation shows that instead of 42 percent, only 35 percent or so of the average family's income would be committed to debt repayment.

That would ease the pain of everyday life substantially. And since financial woes are one of the top three causes of divorce, their absence might also do a great deal for domestic tranquillity.

If interest rates are low, stocks will be more attractive—for the right reasons. They will entice investors who want slightly higher returns than the standard 4 percent passbook rate in exchange for a little more risk. Those investors will be seeking investments that pay out consistently over the long term. They will be less likely to press management to buy back stock just to drive up prices. And if people invest in stocks for the long term, they will drive up the market slowly and keep it there. That will give companies access to capital.

But cutting stock market volatility is also necessary to put America's sick economy on the mend. To get rid of some of the volatility in the markets, there must be fewer opportunities for arbitrage. That can happen if rules are harmonized across markets, including identical margin requirements in the stock, futures, and option markets and identical clearing arrangements in each of those markets. If it costs no more to invest in stocks than in futures contracts, then the incentives for investing in one product over another will more closely match the real reason why those products were invented. The market will be less speculative.

To put a damper on volatility, Lawrence H. Summers proposed a stock transfer tax as one solution. The idea of such a tax is to cut down on rampant trading and create incentives for holding investments longer. Such a tax would add an extra cost to investing, creating incentives to hold stocks longer since an investor would not have any profit until there was appreciation above the cost of the stock, commissions for its purchase, and payments to the government. Since stocks would be taxed each time they were traded, it would generate revenue for the government and dampen what Summers thinks are markets that are too efficient.

There are precedents for these taxes, and they do appear to work. The highest taxes—about .25 percent on each transaction—are in the countries where investors are the most patient: Sweden, Japan, Germany, and Switzerland. In those countries individuals have higher tax rates than institutions to discourage speculation by small-time investors. A tax of .5 percent on each transaction, as Summers has proposed, is not likely to keep people out of the market, but it will make them consider their purchases more carefully and wait longer before they sell.

Such a tax probably would dampen the degree of speculation that has overtaken the markets. But it is, at best, a partial solution because it is also likely to stop investors from taking a fling on investing in new issues of young companies. New stock issues are where the markets work best—getting money to the companies that need it in order to expand. If a tax on investment were to stop the flow of funds into those companies, it would do real damage to the economy.

A tax on stock investment might also force companies to increase their outlays to the shareholders to offset the punitive aspect of the tax. If that were to occur, the tax might create less long-term investment rather than more since an increased share of profits would be diverted to the shareholder to offset the effect of the tax.

In a global market where stock can be bought and sold anywhere, trading would move to the country or market where the costs are lowest. If Luxembourg has no tax, the Luxembourg stock exchange may take business away from New York.

Whether or not a tax on stock transactions is implemented, international markets must be brought into line. That is a task Washington must initiate. Since you can sit at your terminal and trade stocks, bonds, money, or futures products anywhere in the world, there must be equivalent market regulations around the world. If rules were harmonized, money would flow to the country where the deals were best for all the right reasons.

And then there is trade. Certainly a fixed exchange rate environment would go a long way toward helping America's exporters. But it is not enough. America cannot go on forever maintaining a $40 billion to $100 billion or more annual trade deficit with the rest of the world, watching its domestic industries succumb to competition from abroad. And yet America cannot simply protect its industries in a wholesale fashion.

Congress must look at the trade picture and realize that if an industry is protected—autos, computers, steel—it must be required to deliver a quid pro quo. If automobiles are protected for a few years from competition from Japan, consumers will suffer with higher prices and possibly products that are of poor quality. Washington must therefore demand that each protected industry invest at the same rate as its foreign competition. If Japan's automakers invest 15 percent of their sales in new plants, equipment, research, and development, America's automakers must do the same or lose their protection.

Why should America tolerate what happened in the steel industry when United States Steel (now USX) bought Marathon Oil, with profits that came from operating in a protected market with factories United States Steel refused to upgrade? Those factories, which are still in operation, are technologically obsolete. There can be no protection for an industry without such a quid pro quo. But if industries were forced to operate under that quid prod quo arrangement, they would soon regain competitiveness.

America needs more than a few circuit breakers to prosper in the electronic economy. To begin growing again at rates that are consistent with those in Japan and Germany, America must recreate an environment of stability, one in which the long-term investor is rewarded; an environment in which it is rational— not reckless—to be a long-term investor.

Though it has done more than its share of damage in the past, Washington must act to counteract the damaging volatility created by speed-of-light electronics, a weightless dollar, and a host of interconnected markets. The global market must be returned to its original role of delivering capital to businesses that need it to grow. The financial economy must no longer dominate the real economy.

We need policymakers who understand that, for more than a decade, America has languished and its industrial base has withered away as an out-of-control financial economy swallowed resources and shifted the focus to ever shorter gains. We need policymakers who realize that while America has been caught in stasis, Europe and Japan have grown and even surpassed it.

The market has many, but not all, of the answers. It is time for our policymakers to temper their faith in the market with an assessment of what we have received in return. They must realize that today's short-term mentality is a response to volatility. Our policymakers must reexamine the successes of the European nations and Japan and recognize that, in the world's fastest-growing and most successful countries, the invisible hand of the market has always had a measure of help from the very visible hands of government. We Americans deserve no less.

INDEX

DATE DUE

GAYLORD

PRINTED IN U.S.A.